CW01563792

NATIONAL IDENTITIES AT THE CROSSROADS

NATIONAL IDENTITIES AT THE CROSSROADS

LITERATURE, STAGE AND VISUAL MEDIA IN THE IBERIAN PENINSULA

EDITED BY XABIER PAYÁ
AND LAURA SÁEZ

Francis
Boutle
Publishers

National Identities at the Crossroads:
Literature, Stage and Visual Media in the Iberian Peninsula

First published by
Francis Boutle Publishers
272 Alexandra Park Road
London N22 7BG
Tel/Fax: (020) 8889 7744
Email: info@francisboutle.co.uk
www.francisboutle.co.uk

Editors © Xabier Payá and Laura Sáez 2018
Contributors © 2018

All rights reserved.
No part of this book may be reproduced, stored
in a retrieval system, or transmitted, in any form
or by any means, electronic, mechanical
photocopying or otherwise without the prior
permission of the publishers.

ISBN 978 1 9999037 5 6

 XUNTA DE GALICIA

Acknowledgements

The editors of this volume would like to thank the Faculty of Medieval and Modern Languages at the University of Oxford for having hosted and generously contributed to the organisation of the XV Forum for Iberian Studies. We would also like to express our most sincere gratitude to the Etxepare Euskal Institutua, the Secretaría Xeral de Política Lingüística of the Xunta de Galicia and the Institut Ramón Llul, without whose help this book would not be possible. We are indebted to Dr. María Donapetry for her generous help and support during the organisation of the Forum. We would like to thank all those who kindly gave their time to make this book possible: Josep Soler and Ana Marques dos Santos from the organising committee, Marina Massaguer, Diego Pardo and Phoebe Oliver from the selection committee, as well as to the team of peer reviewers for their insightful comments. Of course, we are also grateful to the team of proof-readers who improved the quality of each article: Alison Coxon, Matthew Hillborn, Danny Rees, Sarah Burne James, Phoebe Oliver and Simon Whitaker. We would also like to thank Amir Netter for his IT support not only during the forum, but also any time we needed him during this long process. Finally, we are also grateful to Antía Pereira, Silvia Xicola and Kirsty Hooper, who enthusiastically engaged in this project and offered us their collaboration and invaluable input throughout.

Contents

Part III. National Identities, television and stage

Introduction

This book is the result of a long process that took over three years to become reality. It started with the organisation of the XV Forum for Iberian Studies, which took place in the Taylor Institution, at Oxford University on the 20-22nd June, 2012. This event is a Forum that has been organised by the peninsular lectores of the Faculty of Medieval and Modern Languages of Oxford University every two years since 1996. The XV Forum for Iberian Studies was, however, of an exceptional nature, since for the first time in its history, the organising committee was joined by the Basque and Galician lectores from the University of Birmingham. This provided – for the first and only time – a perspective on the issues tackled during the forum drawn from the entire Iberian Peninsula. After the celebration of the forum, the organising committee decided that the perspectives on identity exposed during the conference deserved to be reflected in a written work that could show at least some of the many approaches to the difficult concept of identity. It was then that we were offered this opportunity by the publisher Francis Boutle, and thus, the process of editing started. Given the vast amount of material produced at the forum, the selection process was long and tough. After the selection and peer reviewing processes, we came up with fifteen articles that provide an insightful view of the varied concepts of identity in the Iberian Peninsula today.

We decided to structure this book in three parts, according to the artistic medium discussed. Thus we organised the articles around three main disciplines: literature, cinema, and television and stage. This is intended as a practical division, since the complex concept of identity is in constant debate across all three parts. This volume shows that the limits between the "us" and the "other" are in constant flux and constantly questioned both from contemporary and historical points of view.

From a contemporary point of view, the articles in this volume question the nature of identity from different cultural constructions, such as territory (Zabalondo, Dasca); and current migratory movements, both external (Ramon), and internal (Dasca). It also tackles the construction of identity through language, linguistic behaviours and current linguistic policies (Pérez, Fernández, Lindsay et al.). From a historical point of view this work addresses the weight of the past in the formation of national identities: the role of dictatorships and censorship (Sande, Alves-Mendes), and their social and political consequences, such as migration (Olaziregi), immigration (Fernández) and the construction of gender (Gabantxo).

As a whole, this work aims to express the vast complexity and richness of the concept of identity in the Iberian Peninsula. For us it was very important to convey the idea of the Iberian Peninsula, not as a coherent unit formed by two uniform countries, but as a unique territory where many different national identities coexist in their struggle to maintain their differences, at a time when they inevitably must incorporate new aspects to these identities. This volume demonstrates that the struggle for identity is not new; identities are and have historically been questioned. This imposition and questioning of identity occurs both from the nation-state (Spain, Portugal) towards its component parts (whatever they are considered to be: historical territories, nations or regions), and within these components towards immigrants or new social and political situations.

Xabier Payá and Laura Sáez, editors.

Prologue

The nation as a *text* has had an impact on a number of works, particularly in literature, to the extent of transforming them into icons. This has often lead the impact of the concept to be viewed as hypertactic or even incidental to other forms of expression, such as the audiovisual.

In fact, if there are nations which are excluded from the official version of history, it is no surprise that it takes longer for certain types of production – those mediated by technical requirements and collective modes of exhibition – to reach the public sphere and to be recognized as an expressive and symbolic part of the community.

Perhaps this is why concepts such as those expressed in the title of this conference, *National Identities at the Crossroads*, are still enigmatic, and – like the beads of a rosary – still resound with an outer meaning that always seems to hide another, deeper meaning: a place that is in the process of formation. Because it is true that within the texts found in this volume there dwells a certain desire for adventure through uncertain landscapes, for a seductive pointlessness or, in other words, for enjoyment. And for the trace of something illuminating along the way, like the genealogy of the different ways of depicting and differentiating Euskadi, or the representation of migration(s) and of exile, which is one of the most common *topoi* in the articles collected here. Or even the need to address the idea of difference, as in the case of the New Galician Cinema.

All displacements of peoples and migrations, as they say, 'free' or forced, always involve gains and losses. Indeed, to take the paradox one step further, the finding of significant form and voice for this sense of 'loss' and the ways memory intervenes to give it shape, are some of the most powerful sources of contemporary creative cultural expression. The terms creativity and innovation may soften or disguise the degree to which, in cultural collision of this kind, questions of identity, recognition and power are always 'in play'.

Stuart Hall, "Foreword", in Cultural Expression, *Creativity and Innovation*, 2010[1]

Stuart Hall, cited above – the tireless promoter of Cultural Studies, the author whose slogan *go on theorising* taught us not to fear the unregulated, the most interstitial; the subversive teacher who chronicled identities in formation, the role of diasporas or the criticism of the great narrative of the nation-state in the context of contemporary politics where culture and communication become structural vectors – left us very recently. Nevertheless, in the rucksack of his generous heritage remains the consciousness of knowing ourselves as "situated" subjects. Today, we find ourselves in a unique position: on a transitional stage where our view of the national identities is configured by Iberian Studies. And those national identities are currently undergoing a process of re-institutionalization, and the creation of a new "speech act" to communicate with the conventional Nation-States.

Perhaps these preliminary reflections require a couple of further remarks.

The first takes into account the contrast between National Cinema Studies – which emerged in the sixties within the broader frameworks of "auteur politics" and the nation-state (except, for example, in cases such as Quebec) – and the transformations and variations that followed, leading to the emergence of dilemmatic concepts and to proposals such as that of Stephen Crofts. It is to him we owe the new typology of the *regional or national cinemas whose culture and /or language take their distance from the nation-states which enclose them*[2] and dialectic positions that open the door for diversity as a territory, as empowerment of "National Cinema", that artefact which emerges in specific historical circumstances and which develops different roles according to its relations with the State.

In addition, we must note the analogy established by Mette Hjort between "small cinema/minor cinema", which stems from Deleuze and Guattari's analysis of Kafka's works.[3] This analogy serves us well when connected with the idea of subverting dominant language and culture from within; the concept *minor* leads us to acknowledge "the existence of regimes of cultural power and [...] the need for strategic resourcefulness on the part of those who are unfavourably situated within the cultural landscape in question, be it a national context or a more properly global one".[4]

The second remark is concerned with the type of cinema that is projected by the adjective "national": works made for a model audience, for a viewer who, rather than considering him/herself to have been born a citizen, views him/herself as a more than a simple result, as an actor with the right to intervene in the definition of a new kind of citizenship (even without papers). This also applies in the field of culture, in cinema (even with the most alternative cinema) in which this viewer's own self is depicted, filling the void left by the false embrace of the institutional mode of Representation.

Marie-Jose Mondzain has said repeatedly that an image is not taken, it is produced and it awaits those who produce it and those who view it to construct a meaningful way of viewing it. And it is in that urge to deny death – in the specific place where the personal is both political and collective – where a thousand proposals, a thousand visions emerge.

The thought-provoking research that can be read in the following pages deals with trans-disciplinary and intercultural scenarios as representative of distinction and of the possibility of the exchange of knowledge and assets. As for myself, by way of a signature, I am proud to say that my own field is the cinema of small European nations made in their own languages.

Margarita Ledo Andión
Universidade de Santiago de Compostela

Notes

1 The cultures and globalization series 3 *Cultural Expression, Creativity & Innovation* (2010). Anheier, H. And Raj Isar, Y. (Eds.) London: Sage.

2 Crofts, Stephen (2006) "Reconceptualising National Cinema/s" in *Theorising National Cinema* (Valentina Vitali and Paul Willemen, (Eds.) London: BFI-Palgrave Macmillan.

3 Deleuze, Gilles & Guattari, Félix (1975), Kafka, *Pour une littérature mineur* Paris: Les Éditions de Minuit.

4 Hjort, Mette (2005) *Small Nation, Global Cinema* Minneapolis: University of Minnesota Press.

PART I

NATIONAL IDENTITIES
IN LITERATURE

Basque literature and its territories[1]

Bernardo Atxaga

P laces that have never been entirely uninhabited and whose soil is
as likely to contain a flint axe as a plastic bottle-top, a gas mask
from the 1914-18 war, an iron sword, the tooth of a mouse or the
shards of a water pitcher … these ancient places, inhabited for
thousands of generations, usually have many names. This is certainly the
case with the place represented on certain old maps by an elegantly
dressed lady, namely, Europe. It happens as well with the country that
corresponds, on that same lady's clothes, to her belt and which is
called… well, what exactly is it called? The words written on the belt
refer to "The Kingdom of Navarra", and that, of course, was one of the
names given to the territory until the reign of Catalina de Foix, who died
in 1517, but before that it had been *Vasconia, Bizkaia, Euskal Herria* and
other things too.

Wilhelm von Humboldt, one of the founders of the University of
Berlin and, like his geographer brother, Alexander von Humboldt, one
of the foremost intellectuals of his day, wrote a book entitled *The
Basques: Notes on a Journey through the Basque Country in the Spring of
1801*, and in the first lines of his introduction he says:

> Hidden among mountains, on either side of the western Pyrenees, live
> a people who, over many centuries, have preserved their original
> language and, in large part, their old way of life and their customs […]
> they are the Basques or *biscaynos*.

At this point, Humboldt feels obliged to add a footnote acknowledg-
ing the first difficulty one encounters when discussing the subject:

> When trying to find a name that can apply to the whole Basque nation,
> we are faced by a bewildering situation in which we search in vain for
> a term acceptable to the Spanish, French and Germans. The French

have no general term. They say *biscayens* when they speak of those on
the Spanish side and *basques* when they speak of those on the French
side, and, if necessary, resort to the old name, *cantabres*. The Spanish
restrict the use of Vizcaya to the province of that name and when
referring to the rest of the country use the term: *las provincias vascongadas* and for the language, *el bascuence*. The inhabitants refer to
themselves ac-cording to the names of the provinces: *vizcaínos,
guipuzcoanos, al-aveses*. Thus this unfortunate people have lost even
the unity of a name.

A translation of these *Notes* was published in the *Revista Internacional de Estudios Vascos* in 1923 and was translated by Telesforo de
Aranzadi, a scientist who, in the early part of the twentieth century, held
various university chairs, among them that of Descriptive Botany and,
later, of Anthropology, both at the University of Barcelona. He was a
first cousin of Miguel de Unamuno, from whom, presumably, he commissioned the translation of an earlier, shorter text by Humboldt
entitled *Sketches* from a *Journey through Bizcaya*. Unamuno also had
problems with names. In the introduction to his translation he writes:

> Humboldt writes 'journey through Bizcaya', but in doing so he makes
> an all too frequent mistake, referring to the whole Basque country as
> Bizcaya and all Basques as Bizcayans, even though, during his journey,
> he does not even set foot in Bizcaya itself. I have corrected this error in
> my translation.

Prior to Humboldt, it was even harder to find terms that were "accept-
able to the Spanish, French and Germans" and which could be applied to
"the whole Basque nation". Take *Vasconia* for example. This was the
name given by the Romans to the territory of the *vascones* and which
gained a certain popularity thanks to Navarro Villoslada and his novel
Amaya, or the Basques of the Eighth Century and, in the 1960s and 70s, to
a book written with revolutionary intent, calling for an armed struggle
and claiming a Basque territory five times larger than that shown on any
map. The book was *Vasconia* or *New Vasconia* by Fernando Sarrailh de
Ihartza – the pen name of the writer and politician Federico Krutwig.
After a few years, the fame of both books fell away and *Vasconia* was
forgotten once and for all.

Another historical name was *Vascongadas*. During the dictatorship,
this is how politicians and journalists who supported the Franco regime
used to refer to the place, and the term is now as much of a taboo as

Vasconia. Almost equally taboo are *País vasco-navarro* or *País vasco-francés*. More neutral terms have flourished in their place: *País Vasco* and *Pays Basque*.

When the independence movement began at the end of the nineteenth century, another name emerged, invented by Sabino Arana: *Euzkadi*. However, this did not last either. Some seventy years later, after the birth of ETA, *Euzkadi* with a "z" became *Euskadi* with an "s" and, paradoxically, that is now the official name, enforced by the law. Nevertheless, when Basque speakers talk about the "whole nation", the name they choose is *Euskal Herria*. This was, until recently, a stable, cultural term, but has lately taken on intense political connotations, with links to the independence movement, and, in time, it may well join the ranks of those other polemical names.

One could write a history of countries through their various changes of names, and it is clear that the number and mutability of those names is an indication of a turbulent past, full of social tensions and conflicts, but it is also a sign of life, because the only territories that haven't changed their names are those that contain no flint axes or plastic bottle-tops or shards of water pitchers: that is to say, the deserts, and only the most deserted part of those deserts.

The list of names could also serve as a description of what is there on the surface, above all those things that are buried. If one place can legitimately be called *Euskal Herria*, *País Vasco* and *Pays Basque*, this means that three languages are, or have been, spoken there. If that place is also known by invented names such as *Euzkadi* or *Euskadi*, we can be sure that these emerged out of a particular political manifesto and under pressure from contrary ideological forces. And if we add that a writer like Wilhelm von Humboldt used the word "hidden" to describe the Basque people – which, all poetic intentions aside, basically means "small" – we already have an inkling of the kind of territory available to books written in the Basque language: a small, heterogeneous territory, steeped in ideology and surrounded by two other very large territories – France and Spain.

In the first chapter of his book, *The Basques*,[2] the historian and medievalist Roger Collins writes:

> For few other peoples in the world, and surely no other in Europe, can the scholarly study of their origins and earliest history be a matter of such direct and contemporary importance, linked at not many removes to the political debate and even terrorism, as is the case with the Basques.

And later he adds:

> ...the present state of Basque nationalist arguments and the counter-thrusts of its centralizing opponents are such that few statements relating to the people, their history and their language can be treated as being politically neutral.

If this applies to everything, if even Neolithic flint axes and Medieval iron swords can take on political meaning, if a political slant can be given to the fact that the Basque language may or may not have been the original language of the whole Iberian peninsula, thus allowing Unamuno himself to say that "we are Basques, and being Basque makes us Spaniards twice over", what, then, is to be said of more overtly political phenomena, such as literature? Think only of the role literature played in Spain under the dictatorship, in the guise of "The Formation of the National Spirit", or think of our schoolbooks in French, in which, fortunately for us, we were encouraged to improve our French by reading examples from *la gloire littéraire*, or the way in which, in every country, so-called national literature forms part of the school curriculum.

As I said: "a small, heterogeneous territory, steeped in ideology and surrounded by two other very large territories – France and Spain". This, then, is the primary territory available to Basque literature. The question is: How does that territory impinge on what is fundamental to literature, the very basis of every writer-reader relationship, namely words, the words, for example, in the classic work Guero by Axular, which carry us from the first line *"Egun batez, konpainia on batean, euskaldunik baizen etzen lekuan nengoela"* ("One day, while in congenial company, in a place where we all spoke Basque") to the last *Eta halatan, mundu hunetako itsaso hunen tormenta guztiak iraganik, azken-finean salbamenduko portura salborik elduko zarela* ("And thus, having passed through all the world's tempests, you will reach the harbour unscathed").

The first problem faced by any author writing in Basque – given the characteristics of that "primary territory" – is doubt, other people's doubts, usually formulated in the question: "Why write in a language that very few people can understand instead of writing in one of the other languages that occupy a central place in the linguistic world? Why choose a territory no bigger than an asteroid, rather than Spanish or French, which are the equivalent of Jupiter or Neptune in the great linguistic scheme of things?"

The question is often accompanied by a feeling of suspicion about the language itself. A whole century has passed since Miguel de Unamuno's famous lecture on the literary and scientific non-viability of the Basque language and in which he proffered the oft-repeated view: "[...] languages inevitably die, that is the law of life, and we should not mourn the disappearance of a language's body, because it is far better that its soul should survive. The clothes it wears have simply become outmoded." However frequently quoted, that view, even at the time, at the beginning of the twentieth century, was already old, not to say old hat. The proof of this is that our first Basque author, Bernard Etxepare, tackled this question in his popular *Kontrapas*: "*Bertze jendek uste zuten ezin eskriba zaiteien, orai dute forogatu enganatu zirela*" ("A lot of people thought that it was impossible to write in Basque, but now they can see they were wrong"). The proof can be found, too, in Axular's prologue to his book *Guero*, published in 1643: "*Baldin egin balitz euskaraz...*" ("If as many books had been written in Basque as in Latin, French or in other languages, it would be as rich and full as them..."). To give a third example, we need look no further than the translations published by Juan Antonio Moguel in 1802, in a book entitled: *Versiones Bascongadas de varias arengas, y oraciones selectas de los mejores Autores latinos* [Basque translations of selected speeches and orations by the best Latin authors]. In the prologue, Moguel states:

> The Wise Prussian [meaning Humboldt, whom he knew] wishes to demonstrate that the Basque language is eloquent, pure and fecund. At his request and urging, I have made versions of selected speeches and orations by Q. Curcius, Livy, Tacitus, Sallust as well as translating Cicero's preambles to his two orations against Catiline, all of which are works of extreme elegance. As an example of a simpler elegance, I have translated two Latin Anecdotes: the one by Cicero about Dionysius of Syracuse and his obsequious courtier Damocles, and the other by Livy about the attempted betrayal of the Faliscan schoolteacher.

In any case, the question: "Why write in a language that very few people can understand, instead of writing in one of the other languages that occupy a central place in the linguistic world?" is completely meaningless, and if it is true that the word "absurd" comes from the Latin *surdus*, meaning "deaf", then the question is, quite simply, the absurd question of someone who can't or won't hear. A lot of plastic bottletops have been buried since the days of Etxepare, Axular, Moguel and Unamuno, and a lot of books have been published in Basque and continue to be published at the rate of about a thousand a year, with editions which, in general, sell more than a thousand copies; and these books, one assumes, do not always end up as dust or buried in the earth along with the plastic bottle-tops; but even if that were the so, the question is still absurd: what does it matter if an author chooses to write in a minority language – an asteroid located a hundred light years from the main planets – when there is a machine, a space rocket, capable of crossing outer space in a matter of months. The name of that machine? Well, sometimes it's *Translatio*, at others *Traductio* and in its gentlest form *Tradutrice*.

The chances of being translated are all the greater given that the vast majority of authors writing in asteroid languages know at least one planet language, and so can begin the task themselves. In that sense, it's entirely false to see us as subject to a single language. We are subject to two languages and whether we use them or not when we create literature depends on the circumstances. But the possibility is a real one. We exist in two linguistic and literary systems at the same time, and the rocket – *Translatio, Traductio, Tradutrice* – is always close by and can sometimes even be found in our own house. It might be useful to recall, at this point, that two of the books shortlisted for the 2012 Independent Foreign Fiction Prize came from "small" languages.

According to a Mallorcan proverb: "*mil mosques maten un burru*", "a thousand flies can kill a donkey". This is perhaps the only danger that faces the Basque writer when bombarded with other people's doubts about the size etc. of our "primary territory", although, in general, the flies are never that numerous and their bullying never goes beyond being a nuisance. Besides, it has no effect on that purely literary territory: the text and the words.

To return to what Wilhelm von Humboldt wrote at the beginning of his book *Notes on a Journey through the Basque Country in the Spring of 1801*:

> When trying to find a name that can apply to the whole Basque nation, we are faced by a bewildering situation in which we search in vain for a term acceptable to the Spanish, French and Germans.

Humboldt's comment is accompanied by a further note from his translator, Telesforo de Aranzadi, in which he explains that he hasn't followed the Prussian author literally in the matter of the names he mentions, because he considers them antiquated, and fears that their use might confuse and embarrass the reader.

Aranzadi adds:

> Please do not think, however, that I have taken any further liberties with my translation. For example, Humboldt uses the word 'nation', and the only change I have made is to change the 't' to a 'c' – *nación*.

Miguel de Unamuno makes the same comment when, in the prologue to his translation of *Sketches from a Journey through Bizcaya*, he states: "[Humboldt] calls the Basques a *nation*, a word I have preserved."

The translations of Humboldt's books were published in 1923, twenty years after the death of Sabino Arana Goiri and almost thirty after the founding of the Partido Nacionalista Vasco [Basque Nationalist Party]. After *Vasconia*, *País Vasco*, *Pays Basque* etc., many people used the word *Euzkadi* to refer to the territory occupied by the "Basque nation". Different winds blew across that land with its buried flint axes but not, as yet, any plastic bottle-tops; I don't know if these were the fourteen winds that appear in a traditional Catalan story, of which "*sept eran bons i sept eran dolents*" – "seven were good and seven were bad" – but there were a lot of them, and they were all in competition with each other, many of them blowing in different directions, and all with contrary views on the Basque language and culture. Those winds haven't stopped blowing since and they continue to blow now.

The question is: How does the nature of the primary territory affect the other purely literary territory?

I will return to this point and to the question I have just asked but, before I do, I must make a detour, because the answer involves something that you cannot find buried in the earth along with the flint axes, swords, gas masks, mouse teeth and the shards of a water pitcher, because it is ungraspable, metaphysical, spiritual, it has to do with what we call "the human soul", something that influences everything, in art and literature, in politics and in life. I could be referring to that ungraspable and very influential thing called Fear, but no, what I have in mind is Value, the quality Antonio Machado was referring to when he said: *todo necio confunde valor y precio* – "only fools confuse value and price".

In order to visualise this, we need think only of ancient maps, for example, the Mapamundi to be found among the illustrations in the eighth-century *Commentary on the Apocalypse* by St Beatus of Liébana. It is considered to be one of the prime cartographic works of the Early Middle Ages and, according to Wikipedia, its function was not to represent the world but to "provide enlightenment to the original diaspora of the apostles". Regardless of its creator's intentions, however, what we notice nowadays is the transposition of places, countries and continents. It's hardly surprising that America is nowhere to be seen or that Asia is relegated to a tiny corner of the map, but what is surprising is the prominence given to Biblical sites, which are right in the middle. Jerusalem is the centre of centres, and Bethlehem is close by.

Our surprise immediately subsides when we realise that the map is, above all, a representation in keeping with the prestige and value given to those places by its creator(s) and that what determines the position of Jerusalem is the Biblical story spread by the followers of a religion that started as a sect, but which, by the eighth century, had spread throughout much of Europe. Logically enough, the places given pre-eminence are those that bore witness to the birth and life of Jesus.

Put another way, the story picks one city out from among all the other homogeneous, anonymous ones and places it in the very centre of the map; then it is the turn of an organisation or power to intervene and spread the story and, in a way, justify that city's position on the map and give it some kind of temporal reality.

Cartographers no longer make maps of the world that so clearly reflect the value placed on certain cities, but if they did, I'm sure that certain cities and nations, such as New York or the United States, would occupy a vast amount of space, far greater than on any ordinary map; Latvia, for its part, would take up even less space than usual. This means that, as regards value, Bernard Shaw's comment about elephants and fleas does not apply; he said that elephants in drawings tend to be smaller than they are in reality, while the opposite is true of fleas. However, when it comes to value, large things get larger and small things get smaller.

And what about Euskal Herria, the Basque Country? Would it appear on such a map? Not on the mapamundi drawn up by St Beatus of Liébana, nor on the maps that were made in the centuries that followed. In fact, prior to the nineteenth century, it didn't appear on any maps at all. Up until then, Euskal Herria had no story to give it value. Its language and traditions were invisible to the surrounding territories. The Basques who continued the work of Etxepare, Axular or Larramendi[3] in trying to put the Basque language and nation on the map found that all their efforts were in vain. Their story was not like the one that had placed Jerusalem at the centre of the world; it wasn't a powerful story, but the work of private individuals, who lacked any political institutions to give their words real, social, official existence, for example, by teaching *euskera* in schools.

On the other hand, the story that did have power during the eighteenth century despised the very thing that those same Basque intellectuals deemed most important. Some sixty years after Larramendi published his Basque grammar, the Marquis de Condorcet, an enlightened intellectual, presented a report on Public Education to the National Assembly of France, explaining what and how French children and young people should be studying. There is not a single mention of the Basque language. Condorcet called for universal education, but, of course, he excluded from the curriculum something which, in his eyes, was without value and was, therefore, invisible to him: the language, culture and way of life of the Basques.

The reasoning of these enlightened intellectuals and politicians was, as one would expect, sound and well-intentioned. The so-called "Rapport Barère"[4] said among other things: "Federalism and superstition speak Breton; emigration and hatred of the Republic speak German; counter-revolution speaks Italian; and fanaticism speaks Basque. Let us smash these instruments of prejudice and error." Bertrand Barère himself says in the report that the Basques are dominated by counter-revolutionary priests, who use their language to fanaticise the Basques and turn them away from Reason and from the values of the Republic.

Barère states:

> Leaving citizens in ignorance of the national language [French] is tantamount to betraying the nation, to letting the clear-flowing stream of the Enlightenment be poisoned and obstructed, and abandoning all the advantages of the printing press, because every printer is a public instructor in the language and the law.

There was no personal animus behind the attitude of these enlightened men – not at least in the case of Bertrand Barère, who praised the Basque language as a language and claimed to admire the patriotic attitude of the Basques – nor was his point of view entirely misplaced, because the subjection of the Basque-speaking populace – *euskaldun* – to the priests was something that had been noted by Basques and non-Basques alike. However, it still constituted a humiliation, assuming, as it did, an acceptance of the natural superiority of French as a language and, therefore, the superiority of French-speakers. It applied to the Basques, the Bretons, the Italians and the Germans, all of whom were, from the point of view of intellectuals like Bertrand Barère, the lowest of the low, whose countries had as yet remained untouched by the Enlightenment.

With a story like that, there was no possible way forward. Neither money nor languages can survive outside the law. They become, at best, museum fodder. However, everything changed with the arrival of a new story, a new vision of the world, as powerful as that of the French Enlightenment. It emerged in Germany and was called Romanticism.

In his book *The Crooked Timber of Humanity*, Isaiah Berlin writes that Germany felt it had been relegated to a corner of Europe, as if it had never achieved anything great – with no Golden Age, no geniuses like Shakespeare or Cervantes, with no artists to bear comparison with Leonardo, Michelangelo et al., and that this feeling of inferiority only grew in the face of the Great France of the seventeenth and eighteenth centuries where, along with hundreds of other intellectuals and artists, there were giants such as Rousseau, Diderot, D'Alembert, Voltaire and Napoleon. Berlin writes:

> The sense of relative backwardness, of being the object of patronage or scorn to the French with their overweening sense of national and cultural superiority, created a sense of collective humiliation, later to turn into indignation and hostility that sprang from wounded pride. [...] The humiliated and defeated Germans responded, like the bent

twig of the poet Schiller's theory, by lashing back and refusing to accept their alleged inferiority. [...] This mood rose to fever pitch during the national resistance to Napoleon, and was indeed the original exemplar of the reaction of many a backward, exploited, or at any rate patronised society, which, resentful of the apparent inferiority of its status, reacted by turning to real or imaginary triumphs and glories in its past, or enviable attributes of its own national or cultural character.

This was the origin of Romanticism, the explosion of something buried not in the earth but in men's minds, although it should be said that Germany's passionate resistance to Napoleon required no greater motivation than that provided by Napoleon and France itself with their policy of military expansionism, which, although associated with the ideals of the Enlightenment, brought with it no light, only corpses, millions of them. However, what emerged was a new story and new maps of what was now considered valuable. Languages like Basque and Europe's small, "hidden" nations were about to be recognised.

In his *Treatise on the Origin of Languages*, Johann Gottfried Herder asked: "Why is European civilisation so advanced and so brilliant?" And he answered: "Above all because of the abundance of peoples and ideals, its temperate climate and the relations it has with other peoples".

When evaluating nations and their populations, Johann Herder took into account their language and what that language had transmitted to us, often through the oral tradition, in the form of stories and songs. He saw language as an indicator of human life and believed that the particular spirit of different peoples and races – what he called the *Volkgeist* – is to be found in the syntax and the particular – *sui generis* – phonetics of their languages.

The Enlightenment aspired to cultural equality by dint of transforming different individuals and countries into "ideal" subjects, enlightened by reason and imbued with republican values. Herder, however, had no faith in such a vision nor in any other such homogenising visions, including Christianity, whose aim was to evangelise, that is, to subject all peoples to the same pattern, the same map. And Herder practised what he preached. Like the Romantics who came after him, he was an ardent traveller, eager to learn about the many societies, cultures and languages of Europe and the world.

Needless to say, educated Basques were happy to embrace the

Romantic story. On the one hand, the special nature of *euskara* – a Pre-Indoeuropean language, a rare exception in the linguistic system – fitted that new sensibility perfectly (Engrazio de Aranzadi even wrote: "As any superior mind can see from the extraordinary verbal structure of our language… Basque civilisation in prehistoric times must have been remarkable"; on the other hand, there was still the humiliation of not appearing on any map and speaking a language which, while an exception, was accused by its detractors of being "primitive", "coarse", "uncultivated", or else the language of fanaticism, opposed to the language of Reason.

After Wilhelm von Humboldt had travelled to the Basque Country and written his *Notes*, many Basque intellectuals enthusiastically signed up to that story. It wasn't just what the Romantics were saying in general – "languages that may seem small and rudimentary provide important raw material for other more refined and complex cultures" – it was what Wilhelm von Humboldt said specifically about the Basque language: "It is one of the most perfectly formed of languages, surprising in its vigour, the structure of its words, its brevity and boldness of expression". In this he was in complete agreement with his friend and companion in the Basque Country, Pedro Astarloa, the author of *Apologia for the Basque Language*, published in 1803.

We have now reached the beginning of the twentieth century. A hundred years have passed since the publication of Humboldt's *Notes*, and another hundred or so since Pablo Pedro Astarloa's *Apologia*. Under their influence, Sabino Arana, who has just founded the Basque Nationalist Party, considers *euskera*, the language, to be the nation's identifying mark, its main differentiating characteristic, a language different from all others, a language – and here is the nub of the matter – that should be even more different: it should be a language that does not say *eliza* (church), which comes from the Latin *eclesia*, but *txadona*; that does not say *tren* or *telefono*, but *bultzia* and *urrutizkina* respectively. Sabino Arana creates and promotes not exactly a neo-language, but a neo-lexicon and a neo-onomastics. "Pedro" will become "Kepa"; "Enrique" will become "Endika"; "Maria" will become "Miren" and so on. Also, as I mentioned, the country will be called "Euzkadi". In other words, Sabino Arana is a purist as regards the language. He is, in the strict sense of the word, an idealist. To his way of thinking, the Basque language should be as it ought to be and not as it actually is according to history and tradition.

To go back to Axular's *Guero*. The first line reads: *Egun batez,* **konpainia** *on batean, euskaldunik baizen etzen lekuan*. And the last: *Eta halatan, mundu hunetako itsaso hunen* **tormenta** *guztiak iraganik, azken-finean salbamenduko portura salborik elduko zarela*. Each of these sentences contains a word that Sabino Arana and the early-twentieth-century purists would have found unacceptable. In the first, *konpainia* (*lagundia* in the neo-lexicon), and in the second, *tormenta* (for which the purists found a good popular equivalent: *ekaitza*). Nor would they have accepted – their followers certainly didn't – the Latinate syntax of which Axular was so fond and which he found extremely useful as a writer.

And so – after Humboldt, Astarloa, Arana and the others – the first consequence of that change in the ideological territory for writers of Basque and for the texts they wrote was a positive one, because it placed them on the map and gave them a social identity; on the other hand, their purism had a negative effect, since it meant a rupture with tradition, with the texts we now refer to as "Basque classics".

People often say that purism does not create any problems for languages such as German, with its many millions of German-speakers, because the neologism quickly becomes accepted as the norm. The same could have been the case with the Basque Country, as shown by the spread of onomastic inventions – from Euzkadi or Euskadi to Kepa and Miren and so on – but it was not to be. Not entirely. As we all know, 1939 saw the end of the Spanish Civil War and the triumph of Fascism, and from that moment on, for nearly forty years, almost until the end of the Franco dictatorship, the previous map was destroyed. The Basque language and its literature were violently suppressed. The territory in which Basque writers could move became a highly dangerous place.

It is a well-worn story, and I will add just one significant example, by quoting from a diary kept by José de Arteche, a writer – and a good one too – who had fought on the side of General Franco in the war, but who could find no peace or comfort in the new situation. It appears in his book, *A Basque in Post-Civil War Spain*, published in 1977, and refers to his diary entry of 14 June 1952, thirteen years after the end of the war.

> I have received a letter informing me of the censors' decision regarding my article 'Basque poets of the Eucharist', which I wrote for the Eucharistic Congress in Barcelona. Permission denied. They will not authorise the article because of a few brief lines in Basque (with their corresponding Spanish translation) with which I chose to illustrate my article. A tiny measure of Basque – half a dozen verses – caused an article on the Eucharist to be considered subversive.

At the beginning of this talk, I spoke of the territory that books written in Basque have at their disposal, saying that it was small (750,000 speakers), heterogeneous (it lives alongside Spanish and French), steeped in ideology and surrounded by other very large linguistic territories (French and Spanish). I could also add that it was a territory beloved by some (the Basques in general and Basque-speakers in particular) and loathed by others (in particular by the fascists); a territory which, from the 1960s on – once we had recovered from Romanticism and created *euskera batua*, standard literary Basque – began to acquire a certain gravitas and allowed for the existence of writers and books.

In an article by Kike Amonarriz in issue 2355 of the magazine *Argia*, I read that data from the so-called Calvet Language Barometer have just been published, the aim of the barometer being to measure the strength and importance of the world's various languages based on eleven factors, among them, "the number of books translated into a particular language" or "the number of books translated from that language". In 2012, English was top of the list, Spanish second, French third, Mandarin Chinese tenth, and *euskera* or Basque…fifty-first. This fact, which will surprise many, is a good example of how Basque has developed in recent years. The territory it covers grows ever more robust. The quality of our books depends solely on our inspiration as writers and on the demands of our readers.

Notes

1 Translation by Margaret Jull Costa.
2 Oxford: Blackwell; 2nd edition, 1994, pp. 1 & 3.
3 The author of the first grammar of the Basque language, *El imposible vencido* (*The Impossible Achieved*), published in 1729.
4 The Report on languages from the Committee for Public Health, published in 1794, two years after Condorcet's report on education.

The emigrant as symptom – the representation of the American emigration in Basque literature[1]

Mari Jose Olaziregi

Je est un autre (Rimbaud)

In *Strangers to Ourselves* (1991), Julia Kristeva assumed that the foreigner lives within us: "he is the hidden face of our identity, the space that wrecks our abode, the time in which understanding and affinity founder. By recognizing him within ourselves, we are spared detesting him in himself. A symptom that precisely turns "we" into a problem" (Kristeva 1991: 1). He represents a sign of the difficulties faced when sharing our lives with others and a symptom of the limits of the Nation. Both psychological and political aspects are reflected within the literary work that depicts stories of alienation and self-discovery of those foreigners, those migrants who wander in no man's land. In essence, "the foreigner's face forces us to display the secret manner in which we face the world" (Kristeva 1991: 3–4).

This "secret manner" can be analyzed through various representations of the migrant subjects in creative works of literature, and thus the purpose of this paper will be to examine, following the contributions of postcolonial criticism to the study of the subaltern/colonized/dominated Other, the representation of America and Basque immigrants in Basque literature. These immigrants become symptoms of the ideological struggle that displacement provokes for these diasporic people, for their host communities, and for the communities they left behind. Questions concerning the kind of individual and collective identity depicted within the analyzed literary works will be crucial in this paper. I will consider the characteristics of that identity, and, for example, whether it includes the foreign Other (i.e. America) or not.

How does the new homeland permeate the emigrant or the exiled Self? Different experiences of the diaspora will be discussed by means of comparing the narratives of first-hand historical experiences with the experience of the postmemory generation, which is not first-hand (as defined by Marianne Hirsch: 2008).

In my analysis, I will assume that Otherness includes doubleness, both identity and difference, so that every Other – every "different than" and "excluded by" – is dialectically created and includes the values and meaning of the colonizing/dominating culture, even as it rejects its power to define (cf. John Lye, 1997-8). Furthermore, the analysis of those representations will show the ways in which Basque literary works have depicted the alienation and dislocation of Basque migrants, as well as the motivations and consequences that those modes of representation have had in the construction of Basque identity.

However, before proceeding to analyze representations of the Basque emigrant and of America in Basque literature, I should perhaps specify that although I refer here to one of the Basque literatures (Lasagabaster: 2005), namely that written in the Basque language, this representation, these stories of immigration and *saudade* or *herrimina* ("*herri*" (country) + "*mina*" (pain)) also exist in the literatures written by Basque emigrants or their descendants in other languages. In this sense, I think it useful to incorporate into Basque studies the theoretical approach that José F. Colmeiro defends regarding Galician cultural studies, a postcolonial interdisciplinary method (Colmeiro 2009: 214). As Colmeiro points out: "This approach implies decentring language and Galician literary production as the privileged institutional channels of cultural identity, while still recognizing their crucial importance for Galician cultural identity (…)". (Colmeiro: 214). Such a concept entails the study and analysis of a nation that is also outside the territorial limits of the Basque Nation. It is an approach that will doubtless have to evaluate and reflect upon the effect that the diaspora provokes on current Basque cultural identity, an identity that would include the transcultural migratory experiences of many Basques. Ultimately, it would hint at a cultural production in which, paraphrasing and adapting to the Basque case what Colmeiro suggests in regard to Galician cultural studies, the periphery is reimagined as central and Basque identity as global (Colmeiro 2009: 213).

The work of the first Basque writer to whom I will refer is a prime example of the literary representation of the Old World Basque identity. Mirim Isasi went into exile in the United States after the Spanish Civil War and published works such as *Basque Girl* (1940) and *White Stars of Freedom: A Basque Shepherd Boy Becomes an American* (1942), the latter written jointly with Melcena Burns Denny and aimed at children. These are some of the few texts that represented Basques within the corpus of American literature prior to 1950. Clearly autobiographical, *Basque Girl* narrates the yearning of the author herself for the Basque Country; a country that, following the essentialist traditional Basque nationalism of Sabino Arana, is described as Catholic, Basque-speaking, and possessing a noble past. As regards *White Stars of Freedom*, the novel relates the process Narbik goes through to become an American citizen. All roads lead to America: being Basque is, in *White Stars*, a prelude to but consistent with being and becoming an American (Sands-O'Connor 2011:18). The life quest of Narbik, a young boy exiled in the United States during the Spanish Civil War, exemplifies a process of changing citizenship that implies renouncing part of oneself (cf. the melting pot notion).

Both works are examples of exclusive identity representations, insofar as they formulate, in the final analysis, two identities (Basque and American) that are mutually exclusive in the figure of the Basque emigrant. It was not until the publication of Robert Laxalt's novel *Sweet Promised Land* (1957, University of Nevada Press) that the Basque identity question was not necessarily linked to a coveted land (the Basque Country) or assimilated into the new American landscape but, instead, came to occupy a third "in-between" space (cf. Bhabha, 1994), an intermediate space that made it both hybrid and permeable. As William Douglass has stated, *Sweet Promised Land* is a novel about Basque emigration, but I would add that it is also a novel of the experience of the postmemory Basque generation. The alienation and estrangement that Dominique, the Basque sheep-herder protagonist of Laxalt's novel, faces on the return journey to his native land is similar to that which he experiences in the mountains of Nevada (*"My father was a sheepherder and his home was the hills"*). One could say that this novel served to dignify the image of Basque emigrants, giving them visibility and making them representative of a whole series of works set in the American West that have used the Basque sheep-herder as a literary archetype. "I can't go back. It ain't my country any more. I've lived too much in America ever to go back" (176), says Dominique to his son Robert, once he has to accept that the promised land, at least for him, is in Nevada and not in Zuberoa, his birthplace.

The novel dignified the image of Basque immigrants, according them a clear presence, and this image subsequently served as the basis for a whole series of works set in the American West that have used the figure of the Basque sheep-herder as a literary archetype. Laxalt's subsequent novels, *The Basque Hotel* (1989), nominated for the Pulitzer Prize (Río 2000), *Child of the Holy Ghost* (1992), *The Governor's Mansion* (1994), and *Time of the Rabies* (2000), also give a privileged position to the figure of the Basque sheep-herder. Yet, as David Río (2000) points out, despite being sheep-herder literature this is not at all pastoral, given that the sheep-herders in question are not portrayed in an idyllic or bucolic fashion. Instead, these are often realist stories centered on the difficulties of adapting to a hostile physical environment. Meanwhile, one should mention other Basque-American authors such as Frank Bergon, in his historic novel *Shoshone Mike* (1989), and Martin Etchart, in his debut novel *The Good Oak* (2005), as continuing this tradition of recreating the figure of the Basque sheep-herder in the United States. In any event, the texts mentioned, along with novels like *Deep Blue Memory* (1993) by Monique Laxalt Urza, offer representations of the Basque emigrant that are far removed from those nostalgic and essentialist depictions that former works, such as those written in English by writers like Isasi, had suggested in the 1940s.

Representations in literature written in Basque language

In what follows, I will refer to literature written in the Basque language. As we will see, the vast majority of these works were written by authors who did not emigrate to America, and who endorsed the negative representation that the continent and Basque emigration had received in Basque literature for many years, especially since the late nineteenth century. What is surprising, though, is that a number of the texts composed by writers who had themselves experienced exile, such as Irazusta, maintained this negative representation and depicted a protagonist (a Basque emigrant or exile) for whom the American land and reality was almost invisible as a result of the pathological nostalgia that he suffered.

References to America appeared very early in the classical literature written in the Basque language, thanks to the testimonies of missionaries and Basque sailors of canonical Basque-language texts from the seventeenth century. Their preponderance meant that America would finally come to represent a sort of *otherness* in the Basque literature of the eighteenth century at the same time that the emphatic term "erbeste" (exile, banishment), which is composed of the words "herri" (town, country) and "beste" (other), came to replace less emphatic words with the same meaning (for example "atzerri"). The academic Pierre Lhande examined supposed Basque atavisms to find the underlying causes for such abundant Basque emigration (cf. *L'Émigration basque*, 1910), but the reasons for the exodus must be sought in socioeconomic factors. For example, the growing industrialization in the Basque Country throughout the nineteenth century and the resulting transition from an agricultural and livestock-raising society to an industrialized one may have provoked the emigration. Other reasons include demographic pressure, war (the Carlist Wars, the thousands of French Basques who fought in the First World War), and mandatory military service, as well as the hereditary system in place in Basque villages, the *mayorazgo* or *fideicommis*, a legal system of bequest whereby all property is inherited by one son (or daughter if there is no son to inherit). In the light of this, it is understandable that the waves of emigrants were vast, especially as the century wore on. South America became the first destination for Basque emigrants, but after 1850, with the so-called gold rush in California, the migratory flow edged upward to the North American West. There, once the gold mines ran out, Basques turned to the work they were mostly called on to do in North America: sheep-herding.

It was during the first decades of the twentieth century that a new type of character entered into Basque literature. The *amerikanua* or *indianua* was the Basque emigrant who returned as a wealthy man (or not) from his American venture. The representation is usually negative, and clearly conditioned by the allusion to an eternal return to the motherland – in this case to the Basque Country. That is the case of the novel *Jayoterri maitia* (1910, *Beloved Homeland*) by Jose Manuel Etxeita, in which a group of herders living in the idyllic valley of Ardibaso are obliged to emigrate to America because of the difficult economic situation in the valley. The scarcity of descriptions about the American land and its inhabitants seeks to underline the central concern of the novel: the longing and nostalgia for the motherland until the main characters go back to their beloved birthplace as wealthy *indianuak*.

In each of these narratives written by authors who did not themselves emigrate, America is viewed as the place where Basque emigrants ran the risk of losing their faith, as occurred in the case of the protagonist of the novel *Ardi galdua* (1918, *The Lost Sheep*) by R.M. de Azkue, where vice, especially involving women, is a predominant theme (see J.M. Hiribarren in his *Montevideoko berriak* (1853, *News from Montevideo*). It was a place that was definitely good for the body but not for the soul, as the journalist Hiriart Urruty was to proclaim in 1905. One of the books "adopted" by the Basque youth of the nineteenth century was Antero Apaolaza's *Patxiko Txerren* (1890), which also contributed to spreading the negative image of the emigrant to America, an image that underlined dishonesty and an excessive eagerness for money. Another author, Ebaristo Bustintza, "Kirikiño", whose books *Abarrak* (1918, *Branches*) and *Bigarren Abarrak* (1930, *More Branches*) were very popular with both adults and young people, and went through various reissues up until 1980, did not hesitate to beseech the reader in *Bigarren Abarrak not* to go to America, and even argued that it was equally possible to make money in the Basque Country.

One could say that the Basque nationalism of Sabino Arana penetrated literary production in Basque and kept doing so until the mid-twentieth century. Even the news from the 400,000 Basque emigrants who were already in the American continent in the first third of the twentieth century was filtered through the prism of this ideology (Alvarez & Tapiz 1996). The church in the Basque Country also aligned itself with nationalism in its rejection of emigration. The pastorals against emigration written by the bishops of Pamplona, Bayonne and Vitoria-Gasteiz in 1852, 1855 and 1867 respectively are a good example of this tendency (Alvarez: 1999).

The form of Basque identity depicted in the aforementioned narratives and mostly written by Basques who did not emigrate themselves was what I would term, following a sociological analysis akin to that of

Gabriel Gatti (2007), a strong form of identity. In other words, an identity based on a name (the Basque last name), territory (Basque Country) and heritage (Basque history). If we add to those characteristics the typical racist comments about the native inhabitants of the migrants' destination countries (South Americans are described as lazy, for example), we can conclude that the representation of the American "other" is highly conditioned by the pathological melancholy that these migrants feel at having lost their motherland.

That melancholy is widely present in other kinds of cultural production, such as the testimonies and stories that were published in publications like *California'ko Eskual-Herria* (1893-1897), and *Eskualduna* (1847-1944). Nevertheless, these latter publications also included truthful and heartbreaking accounts about the travels, difficulties, and happy endings of the thousands of Basques that emigrated to the American West. Some of them have been compiled by Asun Garikano in her stunning *Far Westeko Euskal Herria* (2009, *Far West, Basque Homeland*). Many of these testimonies are histories of shepherds who had to make the difficult decision to emigrate to America, as pioneers in a savage countryside, but for whom caring for herds of thousands of head of cattle was a dream of freedom and adventure. Others were adventurers who had heard wild tales of the gold mines of the Far West and were seduced by the idea of getting rich. These are stories filled with characters that are not nameless and faceless pioneers and adventurers; stories written in peripheral genres such as the *bertsolaritza* (improvised rhymed verses) in which the Other (America) is much more visible than in the texts written by the aforesaid canonical Basque writers (Azkue, Kirikiño). As well as a means of communication, *bertsolaritza* presents us with an intriguing depiction of the inner sentiments of the Basque emigrants. In other words, we are faced with a cultural production that allows completion of the representation of Basque immigration to America.

Stories of Exiles

Just as occurred in other Iberian Peninsula literatures, the Spanish Civil War (1936-1939) had a devastating effect on Basque literary production. It was in exile that literature written in Basque found the impetus for its revitalization, both in publishers such as Ekin, founded in 1942 in

Buenos Aires, and in journals such as *Euzko Gogoa* (1950-1955/ 1956-1959), established in Gautemala by Jokin Zaitegi, which moved to Biarritz where it continued active publication. It is in fact Ekin which published the first postwar novels, *Joanixio* (1946) and *Bizia garratza da* (1950, *Life is Hard*) by Jon Andoni Irazusta (1881-1952). Although both take place against a backdrop of Civil War Spain, neither of them deals in depth with the drama of political exile for thousands of Basques. The first of these novels, *Joanixio*, describes the life of a person obliged to emigrate to Argentina for economic reasons but who desired to return to the Basque Country, his idealized fatherland. In the second work, two protagonists flee the European political convulsions, emigrating to Colombia – never to return again – following personal odysseys full of dramatic episodes that also affect their fiancées.

The work of Martin Ugalde deserves its place among the milestones of Basque literature for its treatment of the alienation and upheaval of political repression and exile experienced by many Basques. The literary trajectory of the author is commensurate with a biography marked by the three upheavals he himself experienced in his own lifetime. Noteworthy among Ugalde's novels is *Itzulera baten istorioa* (1989, *Story of a Return*), which was awarded the Mirande Prize in 1990. It narrates, in a clearly autobiographical tone, the history of a Basque family in exile and the impossibility of their return to the Basque Country. This story, which centers on the hybrid identity of the narrator, the daughter of exiled parents, was the first example within Basque writing of a narrative which dealt with the dislocation and alienation suffered by the exiles. The novel speaks of an impossible return, and that impossibility is reflected in the distance and the rupture between father and daughter. Exile marks a breach between them, a division of identity that is highlighted by the identification the protagonist establishes with the Creole Venezuelan servant Rosa Chacón, a character whose physical and psychological description reveals the necessity of the novel to make the Creole Other "visible," that other that is symptomatic of the otherness the protagonist-narrator of the novel also inhabits. As Ugalde himself observed, in terms of his own identity (Torrealdai 1998: 123), two homelands inhabit the protagonist.

Both Ugalde's novel and the translation into Basque of Laxalt's *Sweet Promised Land* were published in the late 1980s, just at a time when the

Basque literary system had, for the first time in its history, administrative support in the form of the co-official status for Euskara, the mandatory use of the language in education, and grants to help publish in Basque. The arrival of democracy in Spain in 1975, despite not provoking a drastic change in the Basque literary paradigms of the time, made possible the objective conditions necessary for the establishment of the Basque literary system, at least on the Spanish Basque side (Olaziregi 2013: 159–162). It was Bernardo Atxaga's novel *Soinujolearen semea* (2003, Pamiela, trans: *The Accordionist's Son*), which marked a true renovation in the representation of America and the Basque emigrant. Translated into fourteen languages and winner of, among others, the Mondello and Grinzane Cavour Prizes in 2008, the novel is, as I have stated on previous occasions (Olaziregi 2005; 2011), the text that closes the cycle dedicated to Obaba in Atxaga's career and, without doubt, is one of his most significant works.

In *Soinujolearen semea*, America is compared to a heavenly desired place where Basque political exiles can begin a new life. It is a place where David, from the vantage point of his Californian ranch, recounts those memories in which he tackles his childhood in Obaba, and experiences a painful awakening following his discovery of the serious events that took place during the Spanish Civil War and the postwar era.

This is a ranch whose original owner, Henry Johnson (p. 2), as well as his wife Mary Ann, were part of the Mariposa family, a family of Miwuk Native Americans. Atxaga pays homage to this legacy with marks that render the reader's interpretive role implicit in the text, marks which nevertheless do not superimpose the real echo of the name Stoneham. In effect, the illusion of a Californian utopia is broken by the link established, from the outset, with the Spanish Civil War. Stoneham Fields, near Southampton in the United Kingdom, was the destination for 4,000 Basque children who fled the civil war on May 21, 1937 aboard the ship "Habana." As we observe, America, the New World, far from being the longed-for Arcadia that had inspired travellers and artists from the Renaissance to the present day (cf. Kafka's *Amerika*), becomes in *The Accordionist's Son* the destination of politically motivated Basque self-exile.

As we have seen, then, Basque narrative has undergone a dramatic transformation, from affirming, in texts written in English or Basque by writers such as the diasporic Isasi or Irazusta, or Azkue and Kirikiño, a type of essentialist and nationalist individual and collective identity by means of excluding the foreign Other, to representing a type of hybrid identity that is already present in English language novels by Laxalt, and Basque language novels by Ugalde and Atxaga, in which the emigrant or exiled Self is permeated by that space that becomes its new home. While Laxalt represents the experience of the postmemory generation, the case of Atxaga is different from both Ugalde and Laxalt, as his representation is that of an author attempting to write the great Basque novel (in America) with *Soinujolearen semea*, and in this particular case literary influences are as important as historical memories. He exemplifies the figure of the writer in global times.

Note
1   This article is a part of the IT 806-13 project, funded by the Basque Government. Translated by Cameron J. Watson.

Works cited

Apaolaza, Antero. *Patxiko Txerren*. Donostia: Auspoa, 1962.

Alvarez Gila, Oscar. "Clero vasco y nacionalismo: del exilio al liderazgo de la emigración (1900-1940)". *Studi Emigrazioni* 133 (1999): 101-18.

Alvarez Gila, Oscar & Tapiz Fernández, José María. "Prensa nacionalista vasca y emigración a América (1900-1936)". *Anuario de Estudios americanos* 53.1 (1996): 233-260.

Atxaga, Bernardo. *Soinujolearen semea*. Iruñea: Pamiela, 2003. English: *The Accordionist's Son*, translated by Margaret Jull Costa. London: Vintage, 2008.

Azkue, Resurrección María. *Ardi galdua*. Donostia: Jesusen Lagundiaren Elaztegia, 1918.

Bhabha, Homi K. *The Location of Culture*. London: Routledge, 1994.

Bustintza, Ebaristo, "Kirikiño". Abarrak. Bilbao: Grijelmo, 1918.

– *Bigarrengoabarrak*. Bilbo: GEU, 1980.

Colmeiro, José. "Peripheral Visions, Global Positions: Remapping Galician Culture". *The Bulletin of Hispanic Studies* 83 (2009): 213:230.

Etxeita, José Manuel. *Jaioterri maitia*. Bilbo: Labayru, 1988.

Garikano, Asun. *Far Westeko Euskal Herria*. Iruñea: Pamiela, 2010.

Gatti, Gabriel. Identidades débiles. *Una propuesta teórica aplicada al estudio de la identidad en el País Vasco*. Madrid: CIS, 2007

Hiribarren, Juan Martin. "Montebideoko berriak"(1853). *Bertsolaritzaren historia II*. Ed. Patri Urkizu. Donostia: Etor, 1991.

Hirsch, Marianne. "The Generation of Postmemory." *Poetics Today* 29. 1 (2008): 103–128.

Isasi, Mirim. *Basque Girl*. Glendale, CA: Griffin-Patterson, 1940.

– *White Stars of Freedom: A Basque Shepherd Boy Becomes an American*. Chicago: Whitman &Cía, 1942.

Kristeva, Julia. *Strangers to Ourselves*. New York: Columbia University Press, 1991.

Lacapra, Dominick, *History in Transit: Experience, Identity, Critical Theory*. Ithaca: Cornell University Press, 2004.

Lasagabaster, Jesús María. *Las literaturas de los vascos*. Bilbao: Universidad de Deusto, 2005.

Laxalt, Robert. *Sweet Promised Land*. New York: Harper, 1957.

Lye, John, 1997, "Some Issues in Postcolonial Studies", http://www.brocku.ca/english/courses/4F70/postcol.php (date of access: 4-11-2013)

Olaziregi, Mari Jose. *Waking the Hedgehog. The Literary Universe of Bernardo Atxaga*. Reno: Center for Basque Studies, University of Nevada, Reno, 2005.

– , ed. *Basque Literary History*. Reno: Center for Basque Studies, University of Nevada, Reno, 2013.

Río, David. "Presencia de los vascos en la literatura norteamericana contemporánea", *Euskonews & Media* 91 (2000): 15–22.

Sands-O'Connor, Karen. "A Fervent Sermon: Multiculturalism in Children's Literature and Criticism." *El libro infantil y juvenil desde la diversidad cultural /Haur eta Gazte liburua kultura aniztasunean*. Eds. Mari Jose Olaziregi, Itziar Zubizarreta, and Izaro Arroita. Donostia: Erein, 2011.

Torrealdai. Juan Mari. *Martin Ugalde: Andoaindik HOndarribira Caracasetik barrena*. Donostia: Elkar, 1998.

Ugalde, Martin. *Itzulera baten istorioa*. Donostia: Elkar, 1989.

Basque identity, Otherness and narcissitic enjoyment in *Rossetti's Obsession* by Ramon Saizarbitoria

Ur Apalategi

ossettiren obsesioa (*Rossetti's Obsession*) is a short novel by Ramon Saizarbitoria, written in Basque language (or Euskara) and published in 2000 in the collection of novellas *Gorde nazazu lurpean* (*Keep me underground*). It is a first-person narrative of two successive and curiously linked love affairs. The narrator, Juan Martin, a Basque writer who has not been translated into Spanish, gets to know a Madrid lawyer who is keen on literature – Eugenia – whom he manages to seduce thanks to a short erotic text he sends her in the mail. They see each other and sleep together several times in a hotel near Chamartín station in Madrid. He was never really emotionally invested in their relationship, though, and it ends when the narrator falls madly in love with Victoria, a young woman of Basque origin but with a cosmopolitan profile whom he meets in London. Not knowing how he should go about seducing her, he eventually convinces himself that only the erotic text he had earlier written for Eugenia will provide him with the means to this end. But he does not remember the exact words of the said text, and he will not be content to reproduce it only approximately. The text becomes an object of fetish to him, to the point of giving it a magical value. So he sets about recovering the original text, leading him to invent a ploy to reconcile with Eugenia. His obsession for the erotic text is on a par with that of the pre-Raphaelite painter Dante Gabriel Rossetti, about whom he speaks regularly with Victoria. Indeed, the English painter is known for, among other things, having exhumed the corpse of his wife Elizabeth Siddal several years after her death in order to retrieve certain poems that he had given to her. Despite Victoria's warning – she continually tells him how pathetic Rossetti's behavior seems to her – the narrator will not be swayed and goes to Madrid for a final rendezvous with Eugenia at the hotel. The latter, who has guessed the self-interest of the invitation, waits for him in readiness, with the intention of taking vengeance on the man who rejected her. This she does in a surprising way – which, through an unfortunate turn of events, ruins the narrator's chances with Victoria. Having placed the rolled-up piece of paper inside her vagina, she invites the narrator to "come and find it," and, seeing it, the narrator runs away. She follows him down the corridor of the hotel, calling him a "wretch", and it is then that Victoria, who happens to be in the hotel, bumps into the narrator and sees the scene.

Pierre Bourdieu's approach (1992) seems to us to be the most profitable, for a text whose major concern seems to be a redefinition of the situation of the Basque language writer in a globalized context. Furthermore, Bourdieusian analysis has the advantage of emphasizing the importance of the process through which European literary fields become autonomous in the historical process of their development. However, Basque literature of the beginning of the twenty-first century finds itself at a historical stage of its development, in which the question of autonomy again becomes paradoxically central. Indeed, after having been painfully removed from the suffocating grip of nationalism in the 1980s, Basque literature seems from that moment on to be threatened by a heteronomization of quite another kind: the one represented by the strength of the attraction of the Spanish literary field which is felt by the writers. This field has, since 1989, practiced a new policy of integration of works written in Basque (via translation and literary prizes or via promotion of the multlingual concept of iberian studies).

Having led the heroic stage of modernization of the Basque novel during the 70s, Ramon Saizarbitoria completely disappeared from the Basque literary scene for 19 long years. He reappeared on the Basque literary scene in 1995. The Basque literary life of the mid-1990s was no longer anything like the embryonic literary system of the 1970s. The most important event in Basque literary life that took place during Saizarbitoria's long silence was the international recognition of Bernardo Atxaga after he was awarded the Premio Nacional de Narrativa for his work *Obabakoak* in 1989. The prize was the first outside recognition of the literary value of a work written in Basque.

Thus, when Saizarbitoria began to publish his texts again in 1995, he found himself facing a literary system in which the indisputable central figure was Bernardo Atxaga, the only writer of Euskara who also had an international dimension. However, the figure of Atxaga had a particular characteristic: he only came to international recognition at the price of a preliminary denationalization of his work. Indeed, the translations of Atxaga's work (in English, in German, etc.) were not from the original Basque version but from the Spanish version. Furthermore, the Spanish version was not, as it happened, a translation, but a self-translation. In other words, Atxaga rewrote his Basque work in Spanish, technically becoming, de facto, a fully fledged Spanish author. The effect of this was to make the Basque literary field dependent on the Spanish literary field with regard to any potential access to work written in Basque on the international literary market. This means that the Basque literary field (until then, totally independent, although suffering from its invisibility on the international scene) was imperceptibly transformed into a sub-field of the Spanish literary field.

Faced with the incontrovertible paradigm represented by the Atxagan trajectory, Saizarbitoria would attempt, with his return, to construct an alternative figure of the Basque writer, one who does not denounce the project of reaching the international literary field but who means to do it neither at the price of submitting to the direct influence of the Spanish literary field, nor at the price of accepting the status of an exotic "Other." The difficulty of such a project is exposed through the romantic dilemma of the male protagonist of *Rossetti's Obsession*.

Let us now establish a list of the elements, which we will use to support a meta-literary reading of the text. The main character –Juan Martin– is a writer. He meets Eugenia on a trip to Aranjuez, during a literary meeting organized by the Ministry of Spanish Culture, in which he is supposed to represent Basque writers. Furthermore, Eugenia is an avid reader (of Spanish literature) and when she shows the narrator around her town – Madrid, which is one of the two literary capitals of the Spanish literary field (in competition with Barcelona) – she takes him only to places that are charged with literary symbolism. As a worthy representative of the Spanish literary field within the symbolic economy of the novel, Eugenia flaunts the wealth of Spanish literature to impress the Basque narrator and to attract him to her. But Juan Martin does not "believe" in (Spanish) literature and takes an amused look at Eugenia, fervent supporter of Spanish letters. And what about Victoria? Her symbolism is not as transparent as Eugenia's. We are told that she is of Basque origin but that Basque is not her maternal language. This polyglot learned Euskara late in life, and this at the Basque Center in Paris, as it is pointed out. We know also that she spent her adult life outside the Basque Country. For the last few years she has been settled in London, where, she explains to the narrator, "You can still feel like you're at the center of the world" (Saizarbitoria, 2006: 67). However, her profession – she is an art dealer – means she constantly has to move from one artistic capital to another, and this symbolically merges her with the polycentric structure of the postmodern global literary system. She is so far removed from national Basque stereotypes that the first time the narrator meets her he thinks she is English. To possess Victoria represents, then, for the Basque writer, an access to postmodern literary universality. Moreover, as someone of Basque origin, she becomes an ideal figure (and effectively an idealized one as well), because accessing her love does not engender a loss of identity in the narrator or a denationalization of his work. On the one hand she symbolizes the dream of a direct passage for literary works written in Basque to international literary recognition, that is to say without passing through the castrating medium of a greater language (in this case Spanish). On the other hand she symbolizes – due to her cosmopolitan character – the removal of the obligation of exoticness ordinarily imposed on authors of the literary Third World (Gabilondo, 2006).

The Saizarbitoria of the 1990s knows that he has strong chances of being translated and published by a major Spanish publishing house. But, despite being a potential candidate for an Atxagan trajectory, he remains conscious of the handicap stemming from his double choice not to self-translate and not to produce an exotic-archaic literature. The artistico-ethical dilemma of the Saizarbitorian character is thus perfectly encapsulated by the pairing of Eugenia and Victoria. On Eugenia's side, the enterprise of the universalization of his work seems more accessible, but at the price of accepting the status of an exotic, minority author; on Victoria's, it remains utopian, but the compensation is so very much more authentic. If, for Saizarbitoria, the genuine literary utopia, the authentic victory – Victoria – comes through conquering the literary field without the mediation of the Spanish literary authorities, reality inevitably takes him back to Eugenia, the representative of a Spanish literary field careful to integrate – or perhaps assimilate – the Basque writer, in exchange for an international literary status.

The story of the relationship between the narrator and Eugenia is highly enjoyable in more than one way for the Basque reader. Saizarbitoria actually gives the Basque public the realization of an unavowed fantasy through a symbolic reversal of the habitual tensions between the Spanish and Basque cultures. In his novella, Saizarbitoria makes the great Spanish literary system the Other of the modest Basque literary system. He manages this through a double movement. On the one hand he presents us with a Basque writer character who resists the enterprise of Eugenia's seduction which tries to make him exotic. The question, "¿Qué os pasa a los vascos?" – as recurrent as it is aggressive – must be seen as one which points out the willingness to reduce the Basque question to an essentialized identity (the Basques should be atavistically violent and primitive). On the other hand, Saizarbitoria presents us with a narrator who through his literary tastes – he is interested in the literature of the entire world as well as Basque literature, but manifestly uninterested in Spanish literature – makes Eugenia conscious of the regionalization of her Spanish literature on a globalized scale. This of course angers her, as well as leaving her perplexed. It pushes her to increase the exoticizing aggressiveness towards Juan Martin, making their relation a perfect vicious circle. When they first meet, she makes the first move: "O sea, que vascos" ("So you're Basque, then") (Saizarbitoa, 2002:21). The label is stuck to him, with that mixture of condescension and contempt particular to the dominant species. From the outset, the Basque writer is forced to adopt a defensive position in order to justify his presence around Madrid: "I had to admit that I was … a civilized Basque," he explains (*idem*), meaning he is not nationalist or at the very least nationalist but hostile to the armed struggle. This is the price to be paid for the potential right of entry into the Spanish literary system.

The cultural ethnocentrism of Eugenia indeed means she cannot possibly imagine being nourished by literary staples other than those reaped by her powerful Spanish literary system, especially if one comes from the Basque Country – that is, in her conception of things, from the periphery of the Spanish national field. She cannot imagine that a writer born in a peripheral literary field might first find sustenance in the production of his own field, and only then from the production of other fields (French, English, etc., and – why not? – other minor literary fields). A Basque writer who is ignorant of the current Spanish literary situation seems unthinkable to her.

No longer knowing how to get through his opacity, Eugenia ends up asking him (39): "Write something for me one of these days, will you?" Everything may be found in that indirect object pronoun, "for me". The gift is real – the narrator finds Eugenia's lips appetizing – but poisoned, because to write for somebody means just that: he must write for the Spanish readership (directly in Spanish), which would turn the narrator into a writer who is technically Spanish. Such, it seems, is the tax to be paid for "making love" to the Spanish literary field and for indulging in its symbolic riches and its economic ones.

As to him, he has only sex to offer and seems to rejoice – not without perversion – to see her confused by this. She sees him as "Other," as is shown by the question-leitmotif which she asks him each time she comes up against his emotional resistance – "What's wrong with you Basques?" – as though this resistance to her personal desire has to be the symptom of another resistance, much greater and more collective – in sum, political. And Juan Martin ends up taking on this otherness, making it his own and drawing from it a pleasure that is at once masochistic and narcissistic. For the confusion is shared by the two characters.

The Basque writer produces in Eugenia the same irritating and fascinating effect that femininity provokes in most men. For Eugenia the Basque man is a "dark continent": something incomprehensible, eluding all known logic, just like the nationalism of the Basque Country is still today (or was until recently, maybe), in the collective imagination of contemporary Spain (the one which is fuelled by the media), a "heart of darkness" inside Spain, an unknown territory, exotic and terrifying, populated by a people inclined (naturally) to violence. Why should the Basque writer cling to his modest Basque identity when she, Eugenia, is giving him the chance, through her love, to become part of the glorious Spanish identity? This is what she cannot understand. Eugenia is confused by the resistance of the Basque object, by his willingness to use himself as a subject. And what pleasure the writer derives from Eugenia's distress. He might even go as far as believing that he is different, that he is genuinely "other."

The narrator's pleasure is not sexual but specular (in other words, narcissistic): he enjoys feeling "other" in the "other-ing" eyes of the Madrid woman, at the risk of eventually convincing himself that he really is different. It is a narcissism of otherness, truly an onanist and regressive posture. The problem is that the narrator does not really want to heal his national neurosis. He accommodates it very well. Worse still, he rejoices in it, masochistically. He agrees to play the game proposed by Eugenia, degrading as it is, as she treats him as an exotic, essentialized Other, and not as a subject who is equal to herself. Faced with terrifying liberty, he prefers nationalist melancholy and the victimized enjoyment that goes with it. On the other hand, this effect of Otherness, and the masochistic-narcissistic enjoyment which goes with it, does not work with the Basque woman, Victoria – hence his disorientation in her regard. Victoria would be ready to consider him her equal, and it is precisely this which scares him. An amorous relationship with Victoria, by fulfilling his aspiration to the status of a hegemonic Basque subject (both decolonized and universalized), would deprive him of the enjoyment of his national neurosis.

What is it that ruins the relationship between Juan Martin and Victoria? The real obstacle is that he convinces himself that his "literary success" with Eugenia – the short erotic text which seems to have given him access to her bed – is the only weapon he has at his disposal to seduce Victoria. His cultural self-esteem is so low that only this mimetic scenario seems plausible to him; at no moment does he think that Victoria could quite simply fall in love with him, for him, for the person that he is, a Basque writer without international renown. Through the figure of the contemptible Juan Martin, Saizarbitoria tells us something about the condition of the writer working in a minority language. The true victory – Victoria, Love – cannot be obtained through contempt for oneself. The writer who has decided to work in a minority language must not believe that simply being desired by a more powerful literary system makes him universaly desirable – not, at least, if he wishes to maintain the love of his "natural" readership (the people who read in the language in which he has originally chosen to write). Not believing in himself and in his own language is therefore the moral fault for which Juan Martin makes himself guilty. The Basque writers of the 1990s, noting the huge exterior success earned by Atxaga thanks to his self-translations, are then inclined to believe that to write (or re-write) in Spanish gives them immediately – as if by magic – a literary quality that the Basque text would lack (essentially so).

Works cited

Apalategui, Ur, *Ramon Saizarbitoria. L'autre écrivain basque*, Paris, L'Harmattan, 2013, 246 p.

Bourdieu, Pierre, *Les Règles de l'art*, Paris, Seuil, 1992.

Casanova, Pascale, *La République mondiale des lettres*, Paris, Seuil, 1999.

Gabilondo, Joseba, *Nazioaren hondarrak. Euskal literatura garaikidearen historia postnazional baterako hastapenak* (*Remnants of the Nation: Prolegomena to a Postnational History of Contemporary Basque Literature*), Bilbao, UPV :EHU (University of the Basque Country Press, 2006; in Basque; coming soon in English translation), 121- 156.

Saizarbitoria, Ramon, *Rossetti's Obsession* (translation by Madalen Saizarbitoria), University of Nevada Press, Basque Studies Program/322, 2006, 189 p.

– *Gorde nazazu lurpean*, Donostia, Erein, 2000 (Guárdame bajo tierra, Madrid, Alfaguara, 2002).

Without exile, who am I? Metaphors of Basque exile and discursive traces of subalternity in the work of Martin Ugalde

Larraitz Ariznabarreta Garabieta

The terrain of Basque nationalist exile during General Franco's regime is yet to be decisively and analytically explored beyond the heaps of hagiographies and the abundant accounts of biographical memoirs written about different Basque nationalist authors. The work of these "admirable losers" (Sarasola, 1982) remains ostracized and the precise charting of their literary and cultural attainments remains incomplete despite the fact that the *generation of the catacombs* – intellectuals, writers, and activists in exile – are widely accredited by the general public as the custodians of the so-called *Basque nationalist code* and its constituents – mainly language and cultural identity – under the dark years of Franco's dictatorship.

But, certainly, the problem goes beyond merely ensuring the representation of individual authors. In the last decade, the Autonomous Basque Government has pursued an administrative policy of endorsing the republishing of literary works written during the forties and fifties. However, this practice does not quite manage to cast light on the ideological nature of a subordinate group of writers that was at the time characterized, among other traits, by a shared and strongly felt, "foundational aesthetic". That is to say, by the belief that the peripheral character of Basque culture and identity within Spain had historically been the result of Spanish centripetal and antidemocratic power.

This group are bound together by certain shared practices and characteristics: an explicitly defensive tone in the political discourse of all group members, a joint urge to problematize the "monolithic and intolerant truth of fascism" (Ugalde, 1976:49), a manifest desire to evade the marginalization stemming from the utter lack of access to political power and media control, and their engagement in the creation of an alternative and ideologically strategic media network. These common aims and practices indicate the ideological galvanizing of a group whose obvious concern was to dodge ostracism and endure through "*franquismo*" until such time as the legitimate government of the *Republic* was re-established.

Unless the social and discursive practice of "translocal" Basque nationalism under Franco's regime is analysed from this collective perspective, chances are that a significant revisiting of issues central to traditional Basque nationalism, such as the strategy through which the (re)construction, maintenance, and transmission of the subaltern collective identity was scaffolded in the nationalist "conflict-space", will remain undisclosed. Moreover, without such an analysis, a reformulation of concepts central to the Basque community – still in need of deep revision today – may well also go unexpressed.

A metaphor of Basque exile

The obvious lack of critical interest around the colossal work of the Basque writer, journalist and political activist Martin Ugalde (1921-2004) is representative of the aforementioned hermeneutic ostracism. Born in the Basque village of Andoain, Ugalde experienced the hardships of the Spanish Civil War as a child, and was at a very early age deported to Saint Jean Pied d'Port (Continental Basque Country – France) along with many other Basque children, who were offered instruction under the patronage of the Basque Government. After the supporters of the *Republic* lost the war, Ugalde returned to his hometown, and was soon to follow the rest of his family members who had fled fascist Spain. So, as a young man he left Spain a voluntary exile and headed for Venezuela, where he was re-united with his family.

Ugalde soon adapted to his "new homeland" – as the writer often referred to Venezuela – where he became a reputed journalist and short story writer, being awarded several prizes for his short literary pieces and obtaining general acclaim for his journalistic work. It could well be argued that Venezuela allowed Ugalde to become a whole individual by permitting him to cultivate those elements of his identity of which fascism had left him bereft. His sympathy for other socially and economically deprived human beings on an individual level, his conviction that democracy was a real possibility and his conception that no individual could wholly develop in a foreign political setting were made clear to the Basque writer during his years in Venezuela.

After forty years of exile in Venezuela, where Ugalde combined his work for the most important Venezuelan newspapers and magazines with contributions for undercover Basque nationalist publications, Ugalde decided to return to the Basque Country, conscientiously claiming that "if my country of origin were culturally and politically prosperous, if I had not felt the call of a politically and culturally lessened country, I would not have returned". Paradoxically, however, his culturally and politically committed return to his motherland did not do away with the feeling of estrangement which exiles carry. Ugalde eloquently delineated this feeling in an interview for the Spanish newspaper *El País* in 1977:

> Al llegar a España, tras veinte años de exilio en Venezuela, me encontré desarraigado en mi país. No puedo ni decir que soy vasco, ni escribir, ni decir lo que pienso. Todo el pueblo vasco estaba desarraigado… con las raíces al aire. Por ello me puse a escribir para aprender sobre mi país – siempre escribí para aprender–, para conocer su problema vasco y saberlo mostrar a los vascos.

Upon his return to the Basque Country in the 1960s, Ugalde was exiled from the mainstream of Basque and Spanish culture, and canonical literary circuits. In an excruciating experience, he was proscribed from access to central power and media outlets during his last days, when he was dispossessed of all his economic assets. This happened because he was the honorary president of *Egunkaria*, the only national newspaper written in Basque language which was closed down by Spanish authorities, due to allegations that it had an illegal association with ETA, the armed Basque separatist group – allegations of which he was later acquitted.

Throughout his eventful life Ugalde was a "recurrent exile", as Bernardo Atxaga astutely pointed out. Ugalde embodied the hardships endured by the coreligionists who shared his fate – and ideological creed – in exile and, ultimately, contributed in the flesh to unveiling some of the contradictions of the embryonic Spanish transition to democracy. Ugalde does not reach us as a metaphorical representation of Basque culture and the experience of exile from his homeland. Instead he stands, in the words of the Spanish intellectual José Luís Abellán (2002: 346), as a synecdochic symbol of this Basque exile and culture;

> Quiero referirme al valor simbólico de la figura de Martin Ugalde como intelectual vasco representativo de los valores universales encarnados en un pueblo que, a través de avatares múltiples y difíciles, ha sabido conservar una identidad cultural propia, sin que esa personalidad se hundiese en las simas de lo excluyente ni quedase tampoco absorbido por influencias avasalladoras.

Hence the semiotic analysis of Ugalde's work necessarily involves the study of a social problem that goes beyond his literary and journalistic texts as an object of investigation. The temporal and local contexts in which his work was produced, the testimonial and representative nature of his literary vocation, his political commitment – invariably anti-hegemonic and resistant – all provide evidence of such a claim.

A twofold identity exegisis

Martin Ugalde's contrapuntal oeuvre could well be defined as a twofold auto-referential exegesis through which the author attempts to reconstruct his maimed individual and collective identities. The author himself admitted this when in 1964 he conceded to a Venezuelan publication that his work responded to a "complex psychological process of adaptation and interpretation". Under this light, Ugalde's Venezuelan narratives abound in re-construals of individual identity, which convey an obvious longing for adaptation and personal development, and disclose strongly rooted Christian and humanistic values. Ugalde's Venezuelan fiction depicts a "world of accents" (Ugalde, 1958: 52) and it is concerned with the numerous adaptive techniques – linguistic, economic, social and psychological – which allow individuals to adjust to a new and hostile environment.

In his short stories and journalistic reports, the devastating consequences of "commercial voracity" (1963: 267) and "unconscientious progress" (1963: 266), pursued regardless of any human dimension, are denoted in the lyrical, yet blatant, description of the precarious living conditions in the slums of Caracas, areas plagued by substandard housing and inadequate infrastructure. The impossibility of offering medical assistance or education to the children of dispossessed families is narrated in stories like "El otro Amuay" (1963: 179) or "Del barro" (1964: 40). The ill health of workers is starkly portrayed in "¿Qué pasa con el clima en Caracas?" (1963: 252). The devastation of natural resources is severely censured in "¿Qué pasa con los parques nacionales?"(1963: 265) or "Nuestra vida comienza en los bosques" (1963: 259). Likewise, the increasing loss of original, national and idiosyncratic cultures and values is revealed in his reports: "El periódico de Clarines acaba de morir" (1963: 273) or "Cristo en Guayaco" (1963: 312).

To sum up, through the fictional illustration of the tremendous difficulties with which individuals must wrestle in trying to adapt to a new reality, Ugalde's Venezuelan fictional and journalistic works narrate the quotidian struggles of sizeable segments of the population, who had been left without points of reference on account of the "painful uprooting derived from the hypertrophic growth of Venezuelan cities and the vertigo of their changing (social) architectures" (Kohut 2003: 117). Indeed, all of the textual evidence analysed amounts to a rationalization of the author's urge to systematically expose and decry the suffering of "a community that depends on such an uncertain and socially untenable economy" (1963: 182). In that sense, it can be concluded that the Basque author's Venezuelan texts contribute to the power of a collective voice attempting to propose an alternative historic viewpoint regarding the consequences of the "miracle of oil" in Venezuela.

However, far from outlining revolutionary proposals or justifying ideological prejudices, the lesson Ugalde's Venezuelan fiction and its semiotic analysis seem to suggest is that the chances for collective social transformation are limited. The oxymoron that constitutes the title of his short story "El hombre se calló y dijo" (1957) sheds light on the constituents of a strong-rooted adaptive identity. It is an identity in which traditional Christian values such as charity, friendship, sympathy for others, family life and the value of work displace rebellion or insurrection as a means for social reform. Ugalde's Venezuelan texts exhibit a manifest lyrical yearning to deepen the core of universal and ethical human values; in brief the very ethical values that allowed the exiled writer himself to successfully adapt to a hostile environment and (re)construct his own individual identity.

Conversely, the author's work spinning around the axis of Basque culture – his Basque narratives – could well be regarded as a practical set of arguments, strategically devised with the clear objective of contributing to the reconstruction of the silenced Basque communitarian identity while problematizing imposed "colonial stigmatism and its iniquitous legacies" (Ugalde, 1980: 227). The writer identifies himself with a community with which he shares "a system of difficulties, a system of risks" (Ugalde, 1980: 47). The author's choice of semantic resources and lexicalization to describe "the other" – namely "fascist bigoted oppression and its pervasive mechanisms" – in his introduction to *El problema vasco y su profunda raíz político-cultural* (1980) are eloquent of this identification. Noun phrases such as "opresión cerril" (49); "burla cruel" (226); "imperialismo lingüístico" (241); "asimilación cultural" (239); "imposición por la fuerza" (21); "asedio despiadado" (47); "interpretación tendenciosa" (29); "violencia descarada" (223); "conjuración sistemática y permanente" (219) are assigned to "alien power".

Conversely, terms linked to the idiosyncrasy of Basque identity and its re-construal abound, in vocabulary from the semantic fields of defenselessness and resistance. To name but a few examples of the above mentioned range of rhetorical moves: "cultura huérfana y desatendida" (16); "alma mortificada" (210); "desprestigio" (158); "fatalidad" (158); "supeditación colonial" (228, 182); "pueblo al que se le niega hasta el nombre" (31); "angustia profunda de no poder vivir la esencia de una cultura"(31); "dificultad de ser vasco" (25); "nacionalidades sin abrigo institucional" (21); "esfuerzo descomunal" (17); "lucha desigual" (221); "dinámica revolucionaria" (22); "desafío cultural" (39); "pueblo enérgico, activo" (197).

The principle of positive self-representation and negative other-representation finds its expression at many other different levels of Ugalde's discourse: rhetorical devices such as contrast: "resistencia vasca frente al levantamiento franquista" (1980: 206); metaphor: ("isla cerrada sin accesos" (32); hyperbole: "salvajada genocida" (209); irony: "divina españolidad" and euphemism: "universalidad generosa" (53) are merely some of the resources displayed in the author's permanent discursive challenge to the orthodoxy of fascism and his attempt to subject it to an in-depth critique. Other discursive illustrations of the writer's strategic effort include the topic selection in the short stories compiled in *Iltzaileak* (1961) and *Tres Relatos Vascos* (1974), the defensive and pedagogical discursive essence of the only theatre play published by the author: *Ama Gaxo Dago* (1964) or the counter-argumentative nature of his long essay *Unamuno y el Vascuence* (1966). Likewise, most of the author's press articles share a similar trend towards a certain defensive strategic essentialism, which, not surprisingly, crops up in the texts of other Basque Nationalist authors in exile.

Discursive traces of subalternity

The recourse to discursive polarization and the recurrence of collective enunciators both illustrate the markedly political nature of Ugalde's Basque texts. These texts attempt to outline the logic of his own ideology as a corrective to "the enthronement of fascist rhetoric" (Ugalde 1962). However, Ugalde is no essentialist utopian nationalist and his discourse by no means discloses an ideology of nationalist fundamentalism. On the contrary, Ugalde is careful not to "radicalize his cause" and through the cultivation of a rational, logical – and even "ethical" (Beti 2002) – mode of discourse the author aims to "persuade rather than wage a war on our enemies" (Ugalde 1994-6-7). Hence, in asserting Basque identity, Ugalde shuns uncritically embracing any political or cultural essentialism – not even when referring to the idiosyncrasies of Basque culture for which he demands respect. Rather, he aims at the enlightenment of "our detractors" and "our own education".

> La mayoría de las diferencias entre los hombres, si son sinceras, dependen de su particular jerarquía de valores; todos no pensamos en el mismo orden de importancias y preferencias, afortunadamente, y todos tenemos el derecho y la obligación de defender nuestro punto de vista y, si podemos, de convencer a otros. Esta es la dinámica de la verdad. (Ugalde, 1965: 4).

In order to achieve these two discursive objectives Ugalde clearly demonstrates an awareness of "the intimate relationship between the degree of evaluativeness with which the text producer imbues his utterance, and the state of the receiver in terms of his preparedness to accept or reject the propositions put forward" (Hatim 1997: 48). This discursive awareness can be traced in the distinctive linguistic, rhetorical and grammatical resources put forth in different articles targeted at diverse communicational addressees. Articles written for "ideologically foraneous" publications – discursive fields dominated by "other voices" – were all written in Spanish, rather than in Basque, and are sustained by a number of idiosyncratic discursive strategies, brought into the discursive play in order to evade any marginalization of the author's ideology. Many of Ugalde's opinion articles written while in exile, often discursively scaffolded in the form of counter argument essays, were prompted by ideological opponents and were meant as discursive responses to an "offensive provocation" to which the Basque writer "could do nothing but react":

> Yo acepto gustoso la controversia, porque soy amigo del dialogo, que constituye la razón cimera de la democracia, y comprendo muy bien que muchos discrepen de mis puntos de vista, y, claro está, de mi actuación en tal o cual actividad literaria o de partido o de directiva, lo que podemos llamar vida pública. Así, sin dolor, trato de aceptar siempre la opinión adversa. Lo que me duele es que argumente maliciosamente o se recurra al premeditado cambio de conceptos o de palabras para tratar de defender una postura cualquiera. (Ugalde, 1958a).

Ugalde truly believes that the demand for political democracy is inseparable from a certain *ethos* on the personal level, and the journalist tries to refute his ideological opponents by applying "discursive politeness maxims" (Leech 1983:13). Accordingly, the author avoids resorting to sophisms, logical fallacies, arguments on *ad hominem* grounds, or libellous statements intended to discredit his opponent on a personal level. Instead, the author often opens his articles by exposing his ideological opponents' views and goes on to resort to dialogical rhetorical devices such as the use of direct speech to guarantee the polyphonic presence of opposing voices. Similarly, the author takes a tolerant stance in even the harshest of controversies by avoiding qualifying adjectives or the enunciation of opinions that could be injurious to his opponents.

Significantly, Ugalde's ideological opponents did not always afford him equally amiable treatment. The long controversy (April-July 1958) held between Ugalde and the Spanish poet Antonio Aparicio, also an exile in Venezuela, and at the time a colleague of Ugalde's in *El Nacional*, reveals an obviously uneven distribution of social power between the nationalist author and the Spanish republican poet. Whereas Ugalde takes it upon himself to observe maxims of textual courtesy, Aparicio's texts abound with abuse at a personal level, referring to Ugalde as a "pretentious hack" ("gacetillero con pretensions que lo fía todo a la bombarda verbal") whose articles "deserve no response" ("porque una respuesta hay que, también, merecerla"). Aparicio's discourse includes several strategies aimed at impoliteness such as claiming an uneven relationship between the two journalists in terms of erudition ("mi contradictor revela un desconocimiento total", "se abraza al latiguillo politico"), the avoidance of any lenient treatment towards Ugalde in order to reduce ideological friction; and Aparicio's obvious desire to maintain his ideological terrain by presenting a dichotomy between the universality of his opinions and the ethnocentrism allegedly sustained by the Basque journalist.

In short, the discourse strategies to which Ugalde resorts clearly reveal an attempt to surmount a segregated power structure and avoid the marginalization of the author's ideology. The textual resources employed disclose an urge to be approved of at an individual level and a desire to transcend a defensive identity. On the contrary, the litany of insults which Aparicio aims at Ugalde and his ideology triggers the implicature – made explicit at the end of one of the articles – that Basque nationalism is a reactionary and fundamentalist dogma that leaves no room for a rational analysis of any issue. The implication is that the pleading of separatist values hinders the democratization of fascist Spain ("el divisionismo criminal que es el causante de sostener y perpetuar la tiranía").

Still, no matter how harsh the dispute, Ugalde makes unremitting efforts to deny the offensive scope of his collective ideology and claims that "even though Basque nationalists are often accused of elitism or ethnocentrism, our position and our group dynamics all entail a defensive sign against a radically unjust historical ostracism" (Ugalde, 1985:25). Thus, as the heteronomous nature of his discourse, the sustained resorts to endogenous polyphony and his recourse to discursive polarization make clear, Ugalde thinks his collective identity in relation to the margins established between the groups that are in contact with his own community and are perceived by the writer as "aggressive forces" towards the emancipated construal of Ugalde's own social and cultural identity.

It is prevailingly within discourse, and in particular within narrative, that we find the answers to many questions about the construction of personal and collective identities. In the case of displaced authors such as Martin Ugalde the bare need for an explicit discursive exegesis accounts for the yearning to survive, to adapt, to rethink oneself; while, at the same time, it necessarily implies a problematic rethinking of one's collective identity. Parallel to the exiled writer's effort to combat the denial of individual and collective identity cast upon him by fascism, Ugalde's literary and journalistic narrative is also an ideological proposition that positions him in different settings, in relation to different powers. In that light, whereas in the writer's Venezuelan narratives one should pay special attention to the discourse traces that account for a perennial urge to adapt to his new homeland, his Basque narratives convey a strong practical and defensively combatant signature. Ugalde perceives reality, understands reality, from different angles and in differing perspectives; and yet his urge for democracy and reform informs his literary and journalistic narrative from beginning to end. Through his work Ugalde shows an acute awareness of the close link between collective emancipation on the political sphere and the free exercise of human rights on the individual level. The author takes it upon himself to sustain a democratic stance that "will fight the totalitarian inhibitions which destroy the mechanisms of moral rebellion" and which, in turn, do away with individual and collective responsibility.

> Los poderes coercitivos que ejercen los regímenes totalitarios (...) destruyen en el hombre el sentido de responsabilidad individual y de grupo, amansándolo y predisponiéndolo para cualquier clase de sumisión moral, social y política de signo totalitario. (Ugalde, 2003:84)

In this sense, and by contrast with what has been argued by some of his critics, Ugalde's discourse does not unveil a hyphenated, conflicted, plural or hybrid identity. The close and detailed analysis of his narrative provides a clear view of a multifaceted yet solid identity and ideology. Hence, Ugalde's discursive synthesis rejects the frequently established antithesis of collectivism versus individualism. In other words, Ugalde's anti-hegemonic discourse – his Venezuelan and Basque texts alike – represent a practical effort to demonstrate the real possibility of a synthesis between universalism and nationalism through dialogue concerning diversity, ethics, and political reform.

Works cited

Abellán, José Luís. (2002). "La recuperación de la memoria del exilio." *Encuentros con Martín Ugalde*. (341-347).San Sebastian. Saturrarán.

Atxaga, Bernardo. (2001, 6 November). *Diario Vasco* [San Sebastian]: 68.

Angulo, Javier. (1977, 28 January). "Los dramas que viví y el desarraigo que me han enriquecido." *El País* [Madrid]: 56.

Aparicio, Antonio. (1958a, 1April). "Ruralidad y nacionalidad." *El Nacional* [Caracas]: 6.

– (1958b, 28 April). "Unamuno también dijo esto." *El Nacional* [Caracas]: 6.

Beti, Iñaki and Larraitz Ariznabarreta. (2002). "La escritura ética de Martin Ugalde." *Encuentros con Martín Ugalde*. (19-53). Apaolaza (et al) (coord). San Sebastián. Saturraran.

Gurruchaga, Ander. (1985). *El Código Nacionalista Vasco durante el Franquismo*. Barcelona. Anthropos.

Hatim, Basil. (1997). *Communication Across Cultures*. Cornwall. University of Exeter Press.

Ugalde, Martin. (1957). *Un real de Sueño sobre un andamio*. Caracas. Cromotip.

–(1958a, January-February). "Respuesta a una declaración de Matxari". *Eusko Gaztedi*. [Caracas]: 4.

– (1958b, 22 April). "Unamuno también dijo esto". *El Nacional* . [Caracas]: 6.

– (1958c, 2 June). "Contra la Razón de la Fuerza". *El Nacional* [Caracas]: 4.

– (1961). *Iltzaileak*. Caracas.Cromotip.

– (1962). "El analfabetismo de los vascos." *Euzko Deya México*: 18-20.

– (1963). *Cuando los Peces Mueren de Sed. Mérida*. Universidad de los Andes.

– (1964a). *Ama Gaxo Dago*. Caracas. Cromotip.

– (1964b). *Las Manos Grandes de la Niebla*. Caracas. Cromotip.

– (1965, September). "La importancia del euskera". *Tierra Vasca* [Buenos Aires]: 4.

– (1966). *Unamuno y el Vascuence*. Buenos Aires. Editorial Ekin.

– (1974). *Tres Relatos Vascos*. San Sebastián. Txertoa.

– (1980). *El Problema Vasco y su profunda raíz político cultural*. San Sebastian. Confederación española de cajas de ahorros.

– (1985). *Euskal Herria (1936-1984): Errealitate eta Egitasmo*. San Sebastian. Lan Kide Aurrezkia.

– (1994, June 7th). "Demokratikoki lortu ahal dena." *Egunkaria*: 2.

– (2003). *Idazlan Politikoak. Andoain*. Joan Mari Torrealdai (ed.).

Kohut, Karl. (2003). *Literatura Venezolana Hoy*. Caracas. Fondo Editorial de Humanidades y Educación. Universidad Central de Venezuela.

Leech, Geoffrey. (1982). *Principles of Pragmatics*. Singapore. Longman.

Sarasola. (1982). *Historia social de la literatura vasca*. Madrid. Akal.

Confused Otherness. A reading of the *L'atzar i les ombres* (1997-2005) trilogy by Julià de Jòdar[1]

María Dasca

The phenomenon of immigration is partly a socio-political construct related to exile, migratory movements, integration policies and the acceptance and management of differences, and is also a subject of growing interest within literary creation, especially in societies whose origins have been influenced by this phenomenon. Some elements of a reflection upon immigration (such as the questioning of identity or a hybridising of influences) have allowed contemporary literature to employ it as a thematic pretext in writing in which polyphony is promoted.

At the same time, it is worth remembering that writing, and especially the type of literature that takes space, identity, language and immigration as its central themes, may be seen as a place where one can feel like an outsider. That is why writing that deals with the phenomenon of migration has been considered *migrant writing*, where a hybrid code is used (between the native and foreign languages, in a space known as *in-betweenness*). By referring to past events, this has implied a rewriting of history from a different viewpoint. The use of a polyphonic discourse has also made us question the existence of a hegemonic discourse, supported by the principles of authority that legitimate it. But how can this problem be applied to a scenario such as Catalan post-war literature (1939-1975), in which Catalan culture was the subordinate in a single official culture: that imposed by the Franco regime? How has the subject of migration been represented in Catalan narrative in recent years? Has there been migrant writing?

In contemporary Catalan literature the phenomenon of immigration has been rarely dealt with. Despite the fact that contemporary Catalan society is well-known for having experienced migratory flows, it was not until the 1980s that authors such as Maria Barbal made the phenomenon not only an object of fiction but also a subject of discussion within the discourse. Before that, although immigration was the subject of numerous articles and appeared in some works of fiction, it did not manage to gain a voice in the literature written in Catalan.[2] One of the triggers of the representation of the reality of migration was the 1964 publication of *Els altres Catalans* (*The Other Catalans*) by Francesc Candel, a book that exposed Catalan society in direct testimony to the lifestyle of the immigrants who arrived during the 1950s from the centre and south of the peninsula. Currently, the migratory phenomenon interests playwrights such as Sergi Belbel, Carles Batlle and Victòria Szpunberg, especially in relation to the so-called *poetics of subtraction*.[3]

In narrative works, authors such as Julià de Jòdar have used the topic of immigration not only as an object but also as the subject of a process of signification. Furthermore, in his work, immigration may be interpreted from the viewpoint of the establishment of a socio-symbolic pact between the native and immigrant communities. The objective of this study is to analyse the way in which this Murcian author approaches the phenomenon of immigration in the trilogy *L'atzar i les ombres* (Fate and Shadows), made up of *L'àngel de la segona mort* (1997) (Angel of the Second Death), *El trànsit de les fades* (2001) (The Fairies' Journey) and *El metall impur* (2006) (Impure Metal).[4]

Through three choral novels, centred on the *xarnego*[5] character Gabriel Caballero, a broad picture is built up of the lifestyles of the immigrant community that settled in the Gorg neighbourhood of Badalona (a Catalan city close to Barcelona) before the Civil War. Situated between the streets of Cervantes and Guifré (two clearly allegorical names representing close contact between the newcomers and the local people) and in the area around the mouth of the River Besòs (where there are factories such as La Catalana, gypsy neighbourhoods such as La Mina and farmland such as Camp de la Bota), the story, which takes place during the 1950s and 1960s, talks of a space that is symbolically associated with the frontier. It is a liminal territory, the result of negotiations between several orders of cultural values, in which the voice of the other (identified with Gabriel or disseminated in the other characters that appear on Jòdar's ample stage) is confused with that of the host community.

The place where the character of Gabriel Caballero evolves can be related to the dynamics of the negotiation of cultural differences, in the sense that, according to Homi K. Bhabha, difference does not imply opposition but rather a legal process and cultural interpretation:

> The aim of cultural difference is to rearticulate the sum of knowledge from the perspective of the signifying position of the minority that resists totalization. […] The subject of the discourse of cultural difference is dialogical or transferential in the style of psychoanalysis. It is constituted through the locus of the Other which suggests both that the object of identification is ambivalent, and, more significantly, that the agency of identification is never pure or holistic but always constituted in a process of substitution, displacement or projection. (Bhabha, 1994: 162)

My reading of the trilogy, based on a consideration of the discourse of cultural difference introduced in *L' atzar i les ombres* (1997-2005), is constructed through the assumption of the other. Setting out from this premise, the study will focus on the following interdependent aspects: 1. the construction of a double alterity (identification with the immigrant and the local); 2. the production of a hybrid discourse both in terms of registers and text modes, not to be dissociated from the distorting role of memory, and 3. the creation of a liminal space that unmistakeably appeals to specific historical and geographical coordinates: Badalona in the 1950s and 1960s, in the move from economic autarchy to the politics of *desarrollismo* (*developmentism*).

The construction of a double alterity

Conceived of as an *amplification* of the unpublished novel *La pira dels dies* (1982), the trilogy represents the unfolding of digressive prose articulated in an ennobling and emphatic tone used to create a moral view of the world. Avoiding a dichotomist stance, the work implies the deconstruction of cultural clichés –"Ja som carn de tòpic" states the anarchist Gregori Salicrú in *L'àngel…* (p. 269). On a formal level it includes great linguistic variety and combines complex text types (narrative passages, parts of letters, songs, poetic monologues, soliloquies and conversations).[6]

An equivocal voice that manipulates the past and which we identify as being that of the "noi que va prendre el relleu a l'Eulògia", or Gabriel Caballero, modulates the narration. In doing so there follows an ontological investigation – the entire narration can be understood as a *Bildungsroman* – in which the character gives a voice to "la pobra gent, sense [...] ni pàtria ni llar" (*L'àngel...*, p. 376). The efforts of the main character-narrator are a result of the desire "de fixar amb paraules allò que només podia expressar amb l'alfabet dels muts" (*El trànsit...*, p. 25). His voice is therefore receptive to the voices in the community in which he lives. The representation of the other is conditioned by this ambiguous positioning of the voice, which adopts three different forms: 1) a plural which involves the reader, 2) a third figure identifiable with the external narrator, and 3) a third figure that carries the thoughts of Gabriel's character.

Gabriel therefore becomes a deposit for memory and voices, in which his condition of "foraster" (for reasons of birth or blood) remains latent. The first novel, *L'àngel de la segona mort*, focuses on the generation of Gabriel's parents, Boni Caballero and Angustias Pacheco, who settled in Gorg in the 1910s. It goes on to tell the story of what happened in 1956, the year when Gabriel's best friend, Àngel Cucharicas, died. At the centre of the story is a grocer's shop called El Rancho Grande, owned by Angustias and Boni, which acts as a meeting point for the whole eclectic community. In Gorg the locals (Font, the baker, Father Bonaventura and Gregori Salicrú, the anarchist prophet) mix with the Caballero and Pacheco families and other newcomers such as La Maña, the prostitute, and Cayetano, the police officer, but such relationships are not lacking in conflict.

Despite sharing the same physical space (on the outskirts of Badalona), the outsiders and the locals establish a range of symbolic frontiers throughout the novel that are above all economic (only immigrants from Andalusia, Murcia and Extremadura go to El Rancho Grande), linguistic and social. Concerning this last aspect, right from the start the narrative voice ironically refers to the desire of the "nouvinguts" to better themselves (*L'àngel...*, p. 32).

Characters such as Don Bonaventura and Quimet Font express their concern about the arrival of a contingent that knows neither the Catholic roots of the host land nor the wise, "pactist" tradition of the country.[7] The sense of being an object of disdain is also evident.[8] With the exception of Salicrú, who accepts the neighbourhood "sense distinció d'orígens ni de classe" (p. 245), the mistrust between the two communities is expressed through prejudices, the victims of which are the outsiders, and through mutual exclusion which, despite daily contact, is manifested in the feeling of belonging or cultural identification ("[no] eren dels meus", p. 101).

El trànsit…, set a year later, in 1957, talks of a second death. In this case it is a double death that affects the father of the main character and also Lilà, the girl who works in El Rancho Grande, who provides the erotic force of the novel. It also coincides with the time of the Stabilisation Plan, the Scientific Organisation of Work (p. 141) and the arrival of the Opus Dei in the Franco government (p. 149). The story is polarised between two worlds (the factory and the theatre), and combines them through the creation of two characters (Assumpta and Santiago Messeguer) who are the symbiosis of it.[9] Both embody an industrial middle class of ambiguous morality, with the privileges of belonging to the ruling class, and who, despite defending a cultural Catalan tradition, make use of a repertoire of social drama in Spanish when they approach the periphery (Jacinto Benavente, especially, and Antonio Buero Vallejo).

In a setting that is critical of the way in which the Catalans have treated the outsiders,[10] Gabriel seeks a kind of social betterment by mixing with the girls from the centre of the neighbourhood,[11] even though he knows this will mean rejection by some of the others.[12] This temptation, as explained in *El metall…*, ends in failure because of the lack of acceptance by the host community:

> [U]na ciutat crescuda sense control, amenaçada per onades d'estranys sense cultura i llengua estranya; un nucli tancat de gent que mirava de reüll els nouvinguts i els imposava unes regles d'accés que molts pocs podien complir (*El metall…*, p. 244).

The third volume of the trilogy, *El metall impur*, set in 1962, focuses on Gabriel going into the foundry at the mouth of the River Besòs, and the character's awareness of and identification with the working class at a time when it was subject to fierce repression. The deaths around which the story revolves affect two of the foundry workers, and the motive is revenge. Gabriel is 18 and is torn between two erotic poles: a Catalan girl from the city centre with an enigmatic fishtail plait, and Torva, a skinny gypsy girl (*El metall...*, pp. 237 and 251) who offers him a fascinating and, at the same time, repulsive erotic experience next to the sea. Both experiences imply, in terms of the subject that interests us, contact with a controversial otherness, either because it can be identified with the hegemonic class (the former) or because it is the subject of a kind of marginalisation that is greater than that which affects the character (the latter).[13]

The past of the working class, with Catalans mixing with people from Aragon (p. 56), Extremadura (p. 57), Madrid, Andalusia and Castile (p. 182), Asturian miners (p. 114) and Galician sailors (p. 121), is in contrast with the current situation[14] of a character who is external to the events: Sr. Lotari, who investigates (and dismisses) the veracity of what is said in Gabriel's manuscript. The documentary counterpoint that this character brings also includes the introduction of long monologues in Spanish.

In the same way that the trilogy, which concedes nothing as far as moral relativism is concerned, directly criticises the repressive systems under Franco (that have a double effect on the working class, which is the victim of both its class and social circumstances), Jòdar also expresses sharp criticism of the hermetic exclusion that exists in both communities:

> Però tampoc els xarnegos agraïts tenien al cap una visió pròpia; tampoc ells no podien pensar un espai diferent, perquè les fàbriques de voramar els havien *contingut* i, un cop obsoletes, n'eren expulsats, jubilats, oblidats; tampoc ells ni els seus fills ni els fills dels seus fills no farien res per conservar l'única llar que havia donat sentit a la història col·lectiva (*El metall...*, pp. 336-337)

Consequently, this division imposes delimitation in the uses of the tribal language, a delimitation that involves a strong feeling of belonging (*my people* is commonly used in the text), and one that Gabriel manages to subvert thanks to culture.

A hybrid discourse

Throughout the stories, Jòdar uses a wide range of linguistic and textual resources that cause problems for the hegemonic code imposed by Franco's Spain. As Homi K. Bhabha states when referring to the migratory movements within a national culture, "such cultural movements disperse the homogeneous, visual time of the horizontal society" (Bhabha, 1994: 141). In Jòdar's writing there is a double questioning because it involves both the construction of a hybrid, reiterative discourse, merged with the host culture, a culture that is subordinate to that imposed by the dictatorial regime, and also because despite carrying a code that identifies with the hegemonic language, it creates marginal spaces with respect to the official spaces. It is significant, then, that the author's choice of references is mixed with cultural symbols that identify both communities.[15]

Given that the story, as it appears in *El metall...*, is written by Gabriel himself, it is possible to conceive of the writing as a territory that opens up a reflection on space, identity, language and immigration. "[E]squerrà contrariat" (p. 311), Gabriel's writing is motivated by a sense of guilt[16] that forces him to consider his own origins and those of his community.[17] The result of that process is migrant writing, a complex code that gives way to a re-reading of history in the form of fiction. In the story, the principles of verisimilitude that have to be maintained are explicitly questioned (especially through the figure of Sr. Lotari), while the fact that it contains plural voices creates problems when identifying authorship.

All of the resources used by Jòdar are employed to create a story which, right from the start, is marked by convention. That is why he distinguishes between a high cultural register (used in most of the narration and the dialogues) and a more colloquial register (in the inclusion of extracts from operettas and erotic poems, etc.) The result is ostentatiously fictitious in that the narrator raises the tone of some of the characters to the extent that their artificiality becomes obvious. The main character seems to be aware of these presuppositions (most clearly in *El metall...* where more ideological text types are included):[18]

> Amb el rerefons de la llengua oficial imposada pels vencedors de la guerra, la parla d'ell reflectia la ruda exigència de qui vol amagar les empremtes de la grolleria salaç, la xerrameca buida, la cridòria fàcil. (*El metall...*, p. 242)

Also, it should be noted that highly oneiric passages are added to the narrative, especially in the epilogues of the first two parts of the trilogy, which revise decisive aspects of it. Through the prism of Gabriel's enchanted outlook (and memory), some of the characters (such as Lliris and Torva) are presented as epiphanic revelations that, like Li Chang (*El metall…*, p. 381), the Chinese magician of Badalona, transform the situation as it is told. That is why Gabriel is often associated with muteness (a "mudesa" seen as a "mostra de coratge contra el soroll del món", *El metall…*, p. 31); in his voice there is a desire to immerse himself in the language of the worker community (*El metall…*, p. 62), the origin of which is very diverse (*El metall…*, p. 85).[19] It is therefore about giving a voice to (and dignifying) the *xarnegos continguts* who do not have their own means of expression (*El metall…*, 336). This is the final lesson in his quest: the condition that allows him to set himself up as "I" in the plural,[20] in the face of an official rhetoric that is clearly projected and full of euphemisms.[21]

In the same way as contemporary "repetition fiction" (Balló, Pérez 2005), the trilogy is arranged as a narration-in-series that unfolds in a double temporal logic: it renders itself to an everyday sense of time that makes it possible to meet a series of characters, and it also represents a progressive expansion of the world it refers to, thus complicating the plots by introducing mythological paradigms. The novels operate from metaliterary parameters, partially concealed by the ways in which the characters are designated.[22]

These two representations can be related to the distinction between pedagogical and performative time that Bhabha talks of. The first (which is unique to the production of the nation as narration) is "continuist, accumulative" and results in a process of sedimentation; the second is a "repetitious, recursive strategy" and involves the loss of identity in the significative process of cultural identification (Bhabha 1995: 145-146). This second representation of time, iterative and metonymical (Bhabha 1995: 155), is what we find in Jòdar's trilogy.

A liminal space

As we have seen, the material used in the composition of *L'atzar i les ombres* is of a hybrid nature. As stated in *El metall…*, the story traces a geographical map situated in the "dictadura més sagnant que ha conegut el país" (p. 15); a "[t]erreny d'al·luvió de varietats regionals espanyoles i terra obrera de prometença, la població autòctona, que a tot estirar deu constituir-ne la tercera part" (pp. 15-16). This is a place which, according to *L'àngel...*, is situated between the hills, the sea and the main roads.[23] There are cultivated fields, with workshops, small businesses and factories,[24] and related to Eulògia's spoken tales, this is a socially important space, marked by the impact (and bombings) of the Civil War, and one that would be destroyed at the end of the 20th century.

Jòdar's fictional space coincides with what Homi K. Bhabha calls a "third space" or interstice; in other words, a dynamic territory prone to hybridism.[25] It is a liminal space where the local people and the new-comers negotiate cultural differences. In interstices, according to Bhabha, there is a projection of the symbolic value of the space onto the migrant identity, which functions by contamination or contiguity. In *L'atzar i les ombres*, that relationship can be seen in the interrelationship of cultural references that form Gabriel's cultural sedimentation.

El metall... takes place outside Gorg, at the foundry, in a "retícula suburbana sense asfalt ni clavegueres" (p. 17). There is a progressive abstraction of the landscape,[26] which becomes oneiric[27] or internal as a result of the assumption of the disappearance of some physical construc-tions that form part of the human geography. It is almost certainly for that reason that the last part of the trilogy adds visual testimonies (photos) to the story and expresses a clear objection to the way in which most recent governments have assigned the industrial and social past of the Gorg neighbourhood to oblivion. As Jòdar has repeatedly criticised, if the story is now an elegy it is so because a physical, historical and cultural legacy has recently been wiped clean.[28]

An alluvial work, *L'atzar i les ombres* constitutes "un món *altre*, amb lleis i reglaments que havien d'impossibilitar qualsevol arbitrarietat dels grans amb els menuts" (*El metall...*, p. 359). Through hybrid discourse, both effective and affective, it allows a liminal space to be formed and, duly reinvented from the present time, to counteract the hegemonic and homogenizing power of Francoism and to denounce certain recent urban planning policies (such as the Universal Forum of Cultures in 2004), which are oriented towards the destruction of certain places of memory.

The languages spoken there are "[l]lengües que traïen mots primige-nis per tornar al passat pels ponts definitivament trencats del present." (*El trànsit...*, p. 391) and they are the invention of individual memories that give rise to the collective memory. This is constructed from the present and in recovering the events (and texts) of the past it is influenced by a contemporary ideology. Above all, it involves a voluntary affiliation[29] to memory that is in constant motion.

At present, the literary reconstruction of a specific social past, proposed from the recognition of cultural difference and also from the assignment of a plural tradition, implies a perspicacious awareness. This awareness is inferred from a narrative intention that allows living dialogue to be established with the past and questions cultural and historical premises to place the migratory phenomenon at the centre. It invalidates the possible senses of triumph and conquest, inherent in the process, through the creation of a liminal space, and places the emphasis on its justification through art. In the end Gabriel dies, but his existence transcends his death through the written manuscript of a story that, in turn, stimulates a new reality. That is why Jòdar channels a work of fictional recovery, implying complex fabulation both in terms of the use of registers and the references (alluded to or implicit) and representations of time (iterative and recursive). It is also the reason why, in doing so, he poses one of the most significant questions in modern Catalan society: that of establishing a plural identity, which makes contemporary narrative more complex and interesting.

Notes

1 This work has been carried out within the framework of the TRILCAT consolidated research group of the Pompeu Fabra University.

2 See Julià Guillamon, "La novel·la catalana de la immigració", *L'Avenç*, 298 (January 2005), pp. 46-49, which talks of the articles by Josep M. de Sagarra and Carles Soldevila in *Mirador*; and the work of Xavier Benguerel, Josep M. Espinàs, Francesc Candel, Jordi Sarsanedas and Lluís Ferran de Pol. Some recent novels that have dealt with the subject of immigration are *Geníssers* (by Xavier Díez), *Aiguafang* (by Joan Lluís Lluís), *Retrat de la nova immigració africana* (by Toni Sala) and *Els castellans* (by Jordi Puntí), among others. Internationally, the success of *L'últim patriarca* (2008), by Najat El Hachmi, which focuses on Moroccan immigration, should be highlighted. We have excluded authors writing in Spanish from this study (such as Manolo Vázquez Montalbán and Juan Marsé).

3 This is the name by which a series of works with an ambiguous tone are known (also called relative dramas), centred on the topic of incommunication and which hide the dramatic conflict. They mainly make use of monologue to show the intrasubjectivity by which the characters see themselves related. This is a topic, in fact, which connects with the effect of *alienation*, inherent in the migratory experience. That is why these playwrights seek a theatrical language that will allow

them to create situations where the spectators' perception and experience of the world are questioned (Batlle 1999 and 2006).

4 The editions were published by Quaderns Crema (the first two books) and Edicions Proa (the third, which won the 2005 Sant Jordi prize). The quotations referred to in the study come from these three editions.

5 *Xarnego* is a pejorative word used in Catalonia to refer to the immigrant arriving from a non-Catalan and Spanish-spoken territory.

6 In this sense Jòdar's work pays homage to an eclectic, undiscriminating tradition that includes references to "Els pastorets" (*El metall...*, p. 72), "L'emigrant" (*L'àngel...*, p. 230; *El metall...*, p. 73), parodies of military anthems (*El metall...*, p. 141) and some of the resources specific to Espriu's literature (in the part that refers to education under Franco, *El metall...*, p. 272).

7 See the position of Don Bonaventura: "quan van créixer les fàbriques químiques vora mar i els amos van necessitar més braços, la primera onada de nouvinguts va canviar de dalt a baix les nostres vides, pobres i desarrelats com eren, desconeixedors de la nostra llengua i dels nostres costums, presa fàcil de l'ateisme racionalista i de la subversió social." (*L'àngel...*, pp. 215-216).

8 See the thoughts of Patro: "¿Saps, tu, què representa patir el menyspreu d'una gent estranya, que envaeix la fortalesa bastida per generacions d'avantpassats, una horda tan segura d'ella mateixa, en la seva orgullosa ignorància, que no pot adonar-se dels mals que infligeix a qui ha volgut romandre fidel a la seva terra?" (*L'àngel...*, p. 242).

9 Too weak to handle change, Santiago Messeguer, Don Tiago, the big boss of the factory, shows his weakness in defending a capacity for integration that he is unable to take on in practice (*El trànsit...*, pp. 147-151).

10 "'Els catalans ens han xuclat la sang als andalusos i, a sobre, ens miren de dalt a baix', deia la Cati." (*El trànsit...*, p. 138).

11 "[Gabriel] [v]olia lluir-se, anar ben elegant entre les nenes del centre de la Vila; ell, un xarnego de Guifré i Cervantes; jo no entenia, diu l'Adelina, per què s'amoïnava tant, si se li veia d'una hora lluny, que no era un Niubó, ni un Cuixart, ni un Borràs: ara penso que no se sabia a ell mateix." (*El trànsit...*, p. 284). The boy's attempt will come to nothing, however, when he is seen as a "castallufo" by the city centre community (*El trànsit...*, p. 287).

12 "Calia demostrar de què era capaç un xicot de Guifré i Cervantes. Enlairant-se als ulls de la Madrona redimia la culpa d'haver de negar els seus per tal d'enlairar-los a través d'ell." (*El metall...*, p. 242).

13 Much more so than in previous books, the presence of gypsies grows in *El metall...*, often in the form of a threat (p. 34). They represent an otherness with no discourse and, at the same time, are inferior to the immigrant community. They are alluded to in graffiti (p. 126), a painting by Picasso (p. 321), the use of Caló (p. 353) and in the present (p. 404).

14 Now, in the 21st century there is a new migratory situation: the "moros y negros" (Muslims – most of them Maghrebis – and sub-Saharans, *El metall...*, p. 261) and the Orientals (*El metall...*, p. 407).

15 As an example see the "tangos i boleros empiocats" (*L'àngel...*, p. 27) and the Andalusian copla or films (*L'àngel...*, pp. 25-26).

16 "Potser la culpa de qui va tornar sa i estalvi del front. La culpa de qui va poder sobreviure a la repressió brutal." (*El metall...*, p. 172).

17 He introduces himself as "un xicotet de la perifèria a la recerca de mèrits per

aconseguir el vistiplau de la gent assenyada, un estrany que, indefens davant d'allò negat de la pròpia història, es veu obligat a utilitzar recursos impostats, malbaratadors del caràcter." (*El metall*…, p. 242).

18   See the Marxist criticism of the system: *El metall*…, pp. 342-343.

19   It is interesting to see the positioning adopted by the immigrants and the locals in relation to the use of Catalan ("subordinate" to the official language). Carlos (Jordina's theatre friend) doesn't want to learn Catalan because he thinks it is the language of country folk (*El trànsit*…, p. 396); however, Camàndules Cucala uses Catalan to mark class differences (*El metall*…, p. 103).

20   Regarding the use of the plural, see for example, *El trànsit*…, p. 313. Assuming a collective voice, Gabriel seems to answer the question of the old manager "¿y la gente como nosotros?, ¿quién hablará de lo que hemos vivido y está desapareciendo ante nuestros propios ojos?" (*El metall*…, p. 365).

21   See for example: "no hay accidentes, sino fallos de prevención" (*El metall*…, p. 297).

22   The name Gabriel, for example, comes from the biblical angel – the bible is a recurrent reference when legitimating the exploitation of the workers in *El metall*…, pp. 51 and 268–; Lothario, in Quijote, etc.; there are also allusions to the errant Jew (*El metall*…, p. 80), Diogenes (*El metall*…, p. 213), Dionysus the madman (*El metall*…, pp. 99-102) and Aqueront (*El metall*…, p. 148). Other elements with archetypal resonances are the vainly prophetic voice of Hèctor Salgueiro (*El metall*…, p. 368) and Angustias's dreams of horses (*L'àngel*…, p. 30) – both anticipating tragic events.

23   "[E]ntre la fosca dels plàtans de Guifré, més enllà de les Vint Cases i fins al carrer de Tortosa, límit del món civilitzat amb els camps de blat de moro de can Clos." (*El trànsit*…, p. 312).

24   "Barri guanyat als aiguamolls, voltat de camps de remolatxa, blat de moro i alfals que s'estenien com un mantell de capes de colors" (*L'àngel*…, p. 20). Some of the distinguishing elements of this landscape are: the silk factory and the chemical industry, the tileworks, the brothel, the allotments, the auto repair shop and bicycle workshop and the cinema. (*L'àngel*…, pp. 22-26).

25   "It is that Third Space, through unrepresentable in itself, which constitutes the discursive conditions of enunciation that ensure that the meaning and symbols of culture have no primordial unity or fixity; that even the same signs can be appropriated, translated, rehistoricized and read new" (Bhabha 1995: 37).

26   This is a new, more open and abstract space: "Des del pont de tren, el panorama fluvial desprenia aquella qualitat de la naturalesa quan es fa peresosa i l'activitat humana s'hi acobla sense miraments." (*El metall*…, p. 196); "no s'havia pogut sostreure a la sensació que la foscor i el silenci donaven forma a l'espai del seu trajecte gràcies, precisament, a la indefinició de les masses, dels volums i de les línies" (*El metall*…, p. 208).

27   Interior landscape, made of dreams: "sense experiència onírica prèvia, no hi ha experiència estètica del paisatge." (*El metall*…, p. 67) "[Gabriel] a la vegada actor i espectador enmig del barri adormit" (*El metall*…, p. 40).

28   Cf. Julià De Jòdar: "La qüestió rellevant és demanar les raons per les quals les ciutats cuiten a desembarassar-se olímpicament dels espais on la vida popular havia arrelat fins a crear un paisatge, històricament i culturalment significatiu." (Jòdar 2011: 107).

29   We use the term in the same sense as Edward Said (1983).

Works cited

Balló, Jordi; Pérez, Xavier. *Jo ja he estat aquí*. Barcelona: Editorial Empúries, 2005.

Batlle, Carles. "Drama català contemporani: entre el desert i la terra promesa". In: Francesc Foguet, Pep Martorell (coord.). *L'escena del futur. Memòria de les arts escèniques als Països Catalans* (1975-2005). Vilanova i la Geltrú: El Cep i la Nansa, Col·lecció Argumenta, 2006, pp. 75-102.

– "Escriure l'escena, escriure per a l'escena". In: Glòria Bordons, Jaume Subirana (ed.). *Literatura catalana contemporània*. Barcelona: UOC, 1999, pp. 392-397.

Bhabha, Homi K. *The Location of Culture*. London/New York: Routledge, 1994.

Jòdar, Julià de. *El metall impur*. Barcelona: Edicions Proa, 2005.

– *El trànsit de les fades: segona part de la trilogia "L'atzar i les ombres"*. Barcelona: Quaderns Crema, 2001.

– *L'àngel de la segona mort: primera part de la trilogia "L'atzar i les ombres"*. Barcelona: Quaderns Crema, 1997.

_ Juliana, Enric. "Oblit". In: *Radiacions*. Barcelona: Edicions Proa, 2011.

Said, Edward. "Introduction: Secular Criticism". *The World, the Text and the Critic*. Cambridge: Harvard UP, 1983, pp. 1-30.

Portraits of contemporary Portugal in the narrative fiction of recent decades. Critical readings of the novels *O Meu nome é Legião* by Lobo Antunes and *Myra* by Mª Velho da Costa

Micaela Ramon

The problem of identity and identity as a problem are ever-present topics in various European literatures, and the Portuguese case is no exception. Despite its precocious opening-up to the world as a result of the specific circumstances of its history, Portugal has traditionally been a country with a strong, cohesive and stable national identity. However, with the establishment of democracy and full integration in Europe, Portugal has been involved in a process of profound identity change. The influx of immigrant communities was a determining factor in constructing the urban cosmopolitanism that we see today and in the consequent adjustment of its traditional social features.

Within the scope of more recent literature, this different reality is aesthetically reflected in the introduction of narrative fiction (in prose) to new contents, new themes, new protagonists and new geographic areas through which it is possible to reformulate the problem of national identity/identities and parallel issues.

Therefore, this article will draw a brief picture of the profound changes – political, economic and social – to which Portugal has been subject in the last four decades, and will reflect on the way(s) in which this new reality has been translated in the narrative fiction produced within the same time period, taking as examples the novels *O Meu Nome é Legião* by António Lobo Antunes, and Myra by *Maria* Velho da Costa.

New configurations of the post-revolutionary Portugal

Since the military coup of "25 April" in 1974, which put an end to over four decades of dictatorship, and as the advent of democracy overturned an isolation stigma, embodied in the myth of "proudly alone" (keeping the country in dissonance regarding the remaining Western partners), Portugal, a small state on the periphery of Europe, has undergone profound changes that have led to substantial adjustment in terms of its national makeup. These changes were determined by the loss of overseas colonial possessions and the consequent influx of vast and successive waves of immigrants from the former colonies that no longer sought the former metropolis of the Empire. Equally relevant was Portugal's accession in 1986 to the European Economic Community (EEC), after which the traditional concept of borders gradually dissipated before the creation of an ample circulating space of people and goods with a view to a potential federalisation of Europe.

Thus, since the last quarter of the twentieth century, the perception of Portugal as a poor and retrograde country, essentially of rural and Catholic origin and inhabited by people with an awareness of their secular identity based around a historically unitary language and culture, has gradually given way to a less stable form. The presence of immigrant communities has affected the traditional matrix by providing Portuguese society with the urban cosmopolitanism we see today.

In fact, Portugal has copied many other European countries in which, despite the specific idiosyncrasies of each, the old continent as a whole has been targeted by the diaspora of migratory waves that have converted it into a "colourful continent with all the mutations, adjustments, conciliations and shocks that [result] from that" (Eco, 2007: 278). In recent decades, particularly since the end of the Cold War and notably the fall of the Berlin Wall, Western Europe has absorbed immigration flows mainly originating from Maghreb, Africa in general, Asia and South America, but also from countries of the former Soviet bloc.

In just a few years, Portugal has also undergone major change, moving from a country of emigrants to a host country of foreign groups. However, this trend is changing as a result of the economic downturn since the onset of the global financial crisis. The immigrant population currently stands at around 400,000. Among the foreigners with legal residence in Portugal, those from Portuguese-speaking countries stand out, with Cape Verdeans and Brazilians forming the largest contingents. Alongside these, immigrants from Eastern European countries (especially from Ukraine) and China are also prominent. Most of them came to improve their economic situation and have marginal jobs the Portuguese reject either entirely or partially.

The new setup sketched very briefly above has imposed a set of political, legal, religious, social and even emotional problems that have questioned "the theory of 'white Christian Europe' (…) consolidated by traditions and customs bequeathed by history" (Vitorino, 2006), a theory which today, more than ever, seems inadequate with regard to the new situation.

The emergence of new paradigms for the Portuguese narrative fiction
The relevance of the problems cited above is inevitably reflected in the sphere of literary creation since, as argued by the literary critic Miguel Real in the monograph entitled *O Romance Português Contemporâneo. 1950-2010*,[1] by Caminho, the recent history of the Portuguese novel "is embryonically related to significant events in the history of contemporary Portugal" (Real, 2012: 18). Miguel Real reviews the last sixty years of literary production in Portugal, highlighting the "very strong homology" verified "between the evolution of the novel (…) and the evolution of society as a whole" (Real, 2012:17-18), and summarises such homology as follows:

> Indeed Portuguese society transitioned from an authoritarian regime of rigid social and imposing order (the 'Estado Novo' of Oliveira Salazar), corresponding to, in the consciousness of the author, a strict obedience to classical literary precepts of realistic art, to a slow deconstruction of social Salazarist institutions (agony of the Empire, Colonial War, the creation of new parties and clandestine political organisations, social and student protest, illegal emigration of nearly one million Portuguese, denial of the classical structure of the family, women's liberation movements…), aesthetically corresponding to the emergence of the deconstruction of the novel's classical categories (…). Finally, following the restoration of the social order of post-25 April 1974, and the consolidation of the democratic and liberal political system with the integration of Portugal in the European Community, the realistic vision of the novel returns, (…), thus giving birth to a new realism, the perspective, fragmentary and cosmopolitan realism of ludic nature specific to the Portuguese cosmopolitan society of today (Real, 2012: 18).

Thus, within the context of post-revolution Portuguese literature, there are several authors whose thematic fictional universe provides the contours of a new way of "being Portuguese", one whose human base is being rapidly and continuously transformed. Such a transformation is reflected in the switch from portraying a reality focused on social, psychological and historical characteristics that sought to evoke the essence of an almost parochial "portugality", to the novel of the last decades of the twentieth century and the beginning of the twenty-first century that contrasts a cosmopolitan, predominantly urban milieu exploring themes of a universalising character and reconstructing multidimensional geographical areas in which characters marked by racial, religious, cultural and linguistic heterogeneity move freely.

O Meu Nome é Legião and *Myra,* two case studies

Fictional narratives of two of the most respected contemporary Portuguese authors have been selected for analysis, the novels *O Meu Nome é Legião*[2] by António Lobo Antunes (ALA), published in 2007 by Dom Quixote, and *Myra* by Maria Velho da Costa (MVC), published by Assírio & Alvim a year later.

ALA is perhaps the living Portuguese author from the post-25 April generation enjoying the most national and international recognition. His oeuvre, initiated in 1979 with the publication of two autobiographically-inclined novels entitled *Memória de Elefante*[3] and *Os Cus de Judas,*[4] is comprised of 26 published works, including both novels and chronicles. MVC published her debut work, *O Lugar Comum,*[5] when the Salazarist period was in full swing (1966), maintaining since then a more or less regular literary activity which has led to more than a dozen novels, chronicles, essays, translations and cinematographic, television and theatrical collaborations.

O Meu Nome é Legião

In *O Meu Nome é Legião*[6] it is clear from the opening paragraphs of the first chapter that the theme addressed is the representation of the urban violence commonplace in contemporary societies, led by gangs of young people from peripheral areas of big cities who practise violence with an absolutely startling ruthlessness and gratuity.

The story develops after an initial alleged police report written by an

agent at the end of his career who is deeply disillusioned with the institution to which he belongs. This report reconstitutes, step by step, the
progress of criminal activities (mainly robberies and violent assaults, but
also rapes and all kinds of physical assaults perpetrated with or without
the use of firearms) conducted by a group of delinquents, some of whom
just out of childhood. Among the felons there is the "so-called Capitão,
sixteen years of age and mestizo, Miúdo, twelve and mestizo, Ruço,
nineteen and white, and the so-called Galã, fourteen and mestizo (…)
the so-called Guerrilheiro, seventeen and mestizo, Cão, fifteen and
mestizo, the so-called Gordo, eighteen and black, and the so-called
Hiena, thirteen and mestizo" (MNL, p.14). In its heterogeneity, this
group is an effective representation of the ethnic complexion that
currently constitutes the woven Portuguese social fabric, an amalgama-
tion of individuals of various skin colours but united by the same
feelings of mutual disruption and conflict and a reality to which they are
not adapted and against which they react violently.

The setting in which such characters appear is designated the "Bairro
1º de Maio", a fictitious name where very real spaces are recognisable; in
this case, the degraded suburbs of Lisbon, which functions as a metonym
for the Portuguese society. The wanderings of these young people allow
us to meander through several areas of the big metropolitan area of the
capital, from dormitory cities such as Almada to traditional and "chic"
areas such as the small town of Sintra. Through descriptions of these two
areas, the reader is confronted with a map of the city where the stark
contrasts that keep significant groups living in different worlds,
separated by a social gap that seems insurmountable, are laid bare.

The racial prejudice and discrimination based on aprioristic value
judgements emerge as major factors to justify such heterogeneity and
the contrasts so detrimental to social cohesion and harmony. Besides
being, as already stated, the detailed police report of the acts performed
by a group of criminal youths, MNL is also (or mainly) the story of how
the facts are perceived by each of the voices entrusted with the narration
of the story. It is also in the subjectivity of those voices that ways of
thinking are revealed that lay bare traces of the traditional way of distinguishing the Portuguese identity. This is how the police officer, the
initial narrator of the story, introduces the theme of racism, voicing
xenophobic concerns so often shared by the ordinary citizen: "[It should

be noted] the importance of the so-called Ruço being the only Caucasian (white race in technical language) and all his companions being semi-Africans and one black, and therefore more prone to spontaneous violence and cruelty which leads the signatory, outside the present report, to freely question the fairness of the national immigration policy" (MNL, p.14). These observations, attributed to the discourse of the authority figure, are based on a stereotypical way of thinking that dates back to the colonial period in which, according to one of the most respected Portuguese researchers of the phenomenon, Maria Manuela Baptista, "the black population [was] generally seen in the newspapers of the [colonial] time as strange, bizarre, barbaric, exotic and extravagant" (Baptista, 2006:30).

This same viewpoint is taken up again from a new perspective, this time giving voice to those who are victims of discrimination and prejudice. In fact, the report of the police officer is complemented by several testimonies of those who somehow relate to the gang of criminal suspects, and a prime example of this is the story of "Hiena's sister". From her testimony three themes are extracted that, in their own way, reveal the status of minorities in contemporary Portugal. The first of these themes is concerned again with the latent racism that leads the police officers conducting the interrogation to treat the witness with contempt, deducing her guilt in the case from the fact that she is mestizo,[7] and also manifesting other covertly discriminatory behaviour.[8]

A second theme relates to the great need for social integration revealed by ethnic minorities as they attempt to escape socio-racial determinism and rise to less disadvantaged strata of the social hierarchy. In the case of the character whose story we are considering, this results in the abandonment of the district of origin ("I left the district at the age of sixteen not because I was made pregnant by a white, don't insist on that, but due to a job in Lisbon and I don't remember anything else", MNL, p.187), in the adoption of the living standards of the members of the dominant super-stratum ("Despite not becoming white I don't rot in this place (…) and due to my efforts I'm a married woman, I have a decent job, I live in a place with white people with two bedrooms, a balcony with glazing, good neighbours", MNL, pp. 190-191), and in the inter-racial coupling whose advantages obliterate any weakness of the white partner ("Do you really want to marry him?/and I, shrunken behind the branch (…) ashamed of myself and him, seventy-eight years old and the mouth moving before being able to construct a sentence and continuing to move after the finished sentence", MNL, p. 197).

Finally, a third theme connects to the professional status of immigrants, condemned to occupy the jobs that natives despise and doomed to a fate of pain and misery: "don't bother me with my brother, who I left open-mouthed in the cradle, resolved in swallowing the world, (…) and today he has grown, I don't care in what he occupies himself, I assume he is in the construction works waiting for a girder to detach from the crane and empty the sleeve as the fate of the poor is to lose bits until nothing is left unless hunger and the (…) extended hand/Could you spare a few coins", MNL, p. 193.

Using techniques that are typical of his style (such as the proliferation of voices and narrative discontinuity), and making sure to focus on the themes that are dear to him (childhood, life, death, lack of love, lack of communication), ALA finds the purpose of this novel in the reality of these degraded districts in the outskirts of the capital, fuelled by waves of immigrants, especially Africans, who have been establishing themselves in them, thereby constructing a painful picture of today's Portugal.

Myra

Myra is a narrative of twenty-five chapters that tells the story of the eponymous young Russian immigrant as she flees through the landscapes of a contemporary Portugal in the company of a fighting dog, Rambo, who she befriended after finding him wounded and bruised. The duo, deprived of life, will embark upon an aimless journey while trying to find their place in the world. Along the way, both show an extraordinary survival instinct, manifested in the assumption of different identities forged in relation to the needs imposed by their circumstances.

We can consider the narrative as unfolding in two parts. In the first, narrated at a faster pace, there are reports of several meetings "on the road" between the protagonist, her dog and several characters representing the social types of modern, blended and cosmopolitan societies. Myra and Rambo come across the trucker Kleber who leads them to the house of the painter Mafalda in the Alentejo; with an orthodox cleric that transports a woman about to give birth and dying of AIDS in his truck; with Alonso, a crippled sailor; and with a wide range of other minor characters. All these meetings prepare the reader for the description of the encounter with Orlando, a "dark-skinned boy", Cape Verdean, all dressed in white and driving a car which is also white, an encounter around which the entire second, slower and more reflective part of the novel rotates. With this boy, Myra will live a short romantic idyll, interrupted by a violent scene of carjacking that precipitates movement into the underworld of violent crime again.

The multiplicity of the characters that populate the novel makes it possible to portray a complex society in all its contradictions; on the other hand, the way the main character continually reinvents herself in contact with these characters also shows her desire to construct an identity that is in direct confrontation with the other human beings and other cultures. This purpose is also highlighted by the main spaces the two protagonists inhabit. From the escape from an unhomely house shared with a whole Russian family on the outskirts of Lisbon, the journey will be marked by three other distinct spaces, all learning sites for the character. The first of these is the "Casa Grande" of the painter Mafalda, an eccentric, cultured and narcissistic Portuguese that introduces Myra into the world of knowledge and art, despite wanting to turn her into her own exotic ornament. Next comes the "Casa Branca", a house which she shares with Orlando, the rich, exquisite Cape Verdean mulatto, marked by the consequences of a brutal act of racism that leaves him genitally mutilated but from whom Myra learns love.[9] Finally, Myra will encounter the house of the procuress Adalgisa, situated somewhere in Oporto, where she learns that "bad people dominate", a discovery that leads her to put an end to her life, leaping into the abyss in the company of her faithful Rambo whom she cannot do without.

In a straightforward, quick, agile and almost cinematic style, MVC creates a story in which the problematic social adaptation of diverse identity groups culminates in a senseless and inescapable violence. Going beyond the mere reporting of an immigrant story in search of her place in the host society, the author describes experiences of cultural confrontation in a composite and fragmented society where the provincial quietness of previous times gives rise to the senseless violence of a new urban world marked by non-adaptation.

In conclusion, it should be stressed that the readings of the novels by

ALA and MVC have aimed to emphasise how both authors highlight a facet of a rapidly changing Portugal. Namely, they stress that the nation is involved in a process of integrating multicultural and multiethnic elements that test its capacity for acceptance and assimilation of difference, a process that is not always successful. The readings intended to demonstrate how these recently published fictional narratives sketch the outlines of the new features of an old nation that is being renewed through the reception and integration, often imperfectly, of new aspects which, with their own idiosyncrasies, are after all based on the new identity of a country that reinvents itself, and of which the new literature becomes the privileged spokesperson.

Notes

1 Translation: *The Contemporary Portuguese Novel. 1950-2010.*
2 Translation: "My name is Legion".
3 Translation: "Elephant Memory".
4 English version: "The Land at the End of the World".
5 Translation: "The Commonplace".
6 Henceforth, MNL.
7 Attention to the misunderstanding and regret that the character repeats by way of chorus against the disregard of which she is the target: "I don't understand your question or what you want me to say, I'm not a shameless unfortunate on the street corners for money or for vice and I little understand why they treat me this way as I don't look like them in misery, in clothes, modes, I'm a married woman, I have a husband, a son to raise and a serious job, if you don't believe me, ask my neighbours and everyone will tell you I have a serious job" (MNL, p.187) and "and that is what I say, disregard, scorn, for madam and for you as the unfortunates of the street corners" (MNL, p. 210).
8 Take as an example the reference to the attitude of the witness' doctor: "One afternoon I found the doctor saying in a low voice/Isn't the smell of your wife disgusting?/and I understood the reason for examining his palm after greeting me, the patients would refuse him/You have black hands" (MNL, pp. 196-197).
9 Note that, although the characterisation of this mulatto character substantially differs from that made by ALA in relation to characters with the same racial traits, this does not preclude this character from being marked by the stigma of racism, embodied in the violence associated to castration, which can be understood as one of the most radical forms of extermination of a race.

Works cited

Antunes, António Lobo (2007), *O Meu Nome é Legião*, Lisbon: Dom Quixote.

Costa, Mª Velho da (2008), *Myra*, Lisbon: Assírio & Alvim.

Baptista, Maria Manuela (2006), «A lusofonia não é um jardim ou Da necessidade de "perder o medo às realidades e aos mosquitos» in *Comunicação e Lusofonia. Para uma abordagem crítica da cultura e dos media* (org. Moisés Martins, Helena Sousa, Rosa Cabecinhas), Porto: Campo das Letra, pp. 23-44.

Eco, Umberto (2007), *A Passo de Caranguejo. Guerras Quentes e Populismo Mediático*, Lisbon: Difel.

Lourenço, Eduardo (1999), *A Nau de Ícaro, seguido de Imagem e Miragem da Lusofonia*, Lisboa: Gradiva.

Real, Miguel (2012), *O Romance Português Contemporâneo. 1950-2010*, Lisbon: Caminho.

Santos, Boaventura (2001), "Entre Próspero e Caliban: Colonialismo, pós-colonialismo e interidentidade" in *Entre Ser e Estar – Raízes, percursos e discursos da identidade, org. Mª Irene Ramalho*, Porto: Afrontamento, pp. 23-85.

Vitorino, A, *Diário de Notícias*, 21/4/2006, online ed.

PART II

NATIONAL IDENTITIES IN CINEMA

In Search of the *Novo Cinema Galego* (New Galician Cinema) – history, narration(s), identity and models of representation

José Manuel Sande

Faced with a small and not particularly robust corpus – as is the case in Galician cinema history – any analysis attempt inevitably involves the examination of a series of examples and iconic moments. Undoubtedly, this outline culminates in the positive changes that have occurred in recent years, such as the awakening of young Galician creators who share a clear creative impulse, underpinned by production techniques that, despite their heterogeneous nature, are understood as independent, peripheral or alternative, resisting the prototypical methods of production and distribution.

The review of traditional structures (regarded as dependent, as opposed to independent) and the analysis of some of the most notable examples – amongst which we can do no more than highlight isolated heterodoxies or distinctive signs – reveals three moments that could hint towards a hypothetical splendour, immersed in the palpable hopefulness of our current period of vitality, a virtual space which, until now, has witnessed little continuity of progress. The work of Carlos Velo in the 1920s and 1930s, contains examples of correspondence cinema (cine de correspondencia), and a civic republican documentary tradition of considerable maturity. There was a (by no means unexpected) revival of old affirmations of identity during the period of the Spanish transition to democracy, which gave rise to a stream of works of fiction, in some cases of a strongly literary and socio-political nature. This same period paves the way in the 1980s for professional training and the development of new narrative and aesthetic forms. It is a moment of splendour for video art, which culminates in the appearance of the public television channel (TVG) and the first governmental grants, as well as the recognition of the audiovisual sector as a strategic one. All this facilitates an examination of key issues, both aesthetic and sociocultural. These issues, broadly speaking, include: identity; the relations between cinema and other artistic spheres; language use; and combination of forms – to give just some idea of the wealth of current offerings. Despite its limitations, this framework deserves, as an epilogue to this introduction, the approach to a selection of some of the most relevant filmic texts.

The narration of any historical journey takes us back to the origins; in this case, the beginnings of cinema in Galicia were no different from those of other communities. Cinema competes for the viewer's attention against popular forms of leisure and entertainment, rooted in the traditions of the late 19th century (variety shows, fairground amusements, operettas and *género chico*...). In this initial period, characterised by no more than local adaptations of the Lumière model – documentaries and social events in these early years, a key figure is José Sellier, originally from the Lumiere brothers' native Lyon, who is based in A Coruña from 1886. The Lumière technology is brought to Galicia in 1897 by company representatives Marques and Azevedo – both originally from Portugal –, who travel through some of the region's major cities and villages (Pontevedra, Vigo, Tui, A Coruña, Ferrol and Lugo). When they arrive in A Coruña in May, they find that Sellier has recently bought a camera identical to their own. With this camera Sellier would film a series of titles, which were premiered in the city, including *Orzán, oleaje* and *Fábrica de Gas. Entierro del General Sánchez Bregua* is the oldest film recorded in the history of Spanish cinema. Despite the loss of the film itself, it can be dated precisely to June 20th, 1897. These and other films by Sellier exactly follow the Lumière model, as do films made in many other locations. They are attempts to reach local viewers by d°epicting the fundamental components of the socioeconomic structure of urban life in A Coruña at the turn of the century. Other examples include: *San Jorge, salida de misa* and *Matadero, salida de operarios, Descarga de Carbón*.

In this period, the work of exhibitors and operators throughout Spain who attempt to enrich their film programs with local footage plays a key role. The oldest surviving Galician works of this kind are: *Botadura del acorazado Alfonso XIII* (1913) and the film of the *Ano Santo en Compostela* (1915), made by Portuguese company Invicta Films. Under such circumstances, it is unsurprising that the scarce production that is happening in Galicia during the period is confined to the two most populated cities: Vigo, where the most notable figure is José Gil (1870-1937), originally from Pontevedra; and A Coruña. Nor is it surprising that production is almost entirely limited to documentaries and reports. Gil filmed one of the exceptions, *Miss Ledya* (1916), a short film in 35 mm., sponsored by the ladies of Pontevedra's high bourgeoisie. It is the first known example of a Galician fictional film and it was restored by CGAI/Filmoteca de Galicia in 1996. Notably, it features Alfonso Castelao ¬– a key figure of Galician nationalism – as a protestant pastor. The film itself is highly primitive, with a delirious narrative, lacking in dynamism, and little knowledge of the use of framing. The film was commissioned by the Child Protection Board, surprisingly prompted by the attack in Sarajevo that lead to the First World War. From today's perspective, this film is the prototypical example of combination of good intentions and lack of expertise that will characterise so many of the ventures in Galician cinema history.

During this period of consolidation of the young cinema industry, are several major events took place. José Gil founded the first Galician production company, Galicia Films, promoting the *Noticiario de Galicia* (News of Galicia) and continuing to focus on documentary, education and tourism. This time is also when the omnipotent exhibitor Isaac Fraga appears on scene. There are several feature films with Galician settings: *La Casa de la Troya* (1925) by Alejandro Perez and Manuel Noriega Lugín; *La vírgen del cristal* (1925), by Saturno and Manuel Lois Piñeiro; *Carmiña, flor de Galicia* (1926) by Rino Lupo; and *Maruxa* (1923), by the French Henry Vorfins, but produced by the company Celta Films, with Galician funding. The decade ends with the first Galician fiction feature film, *A traxedia de Xirobio* (1930) directed by José Signo, a frustrating and very amateur adaptation of a story by Castelao.

As a result of the strong flow of emigration in this period of the 20th century, the first true innovation in cinema history in Galicia arises: correspondence cinema. This is an epistolary practice that uses images as a complement to the written word, produced outside the industry framework. It is therefore a phenomenon that arises from a specific requirement of Galician society. It deals with Galicia and America, incorporating in the colonies of immigrants in different countries. This cinematic form is not novel in its manners, but it is in its gestures and intentionality. Again, we face the filming of social and cultural events and everyday life still images. José Gil, director of *Nuestras fiestas de allá*; and *Galicia Buenos Aires* and *Elixio González*, author of *As imaxes de Castelao*, will become the key figures in a sort of sub-genre whose narratives and visual possibilities are characterised by anonymity and amateurism, well integrated clichéd forms that sharpen the exercise of interaction. The form persisted (as a popular media) even as late as the 50s with films such as *Tierra de nuestros mayores* (1959), by Manuel Arís; *La Coruña al día* (1955) by Amando de Hermida; and *Así es Galicia* (1956) by the Docampo brothers.

The documentary genre, at the time of the first pieces of correspondence cinema, has another moment of creative glory in our story. Besides the news bulletins of the 20s and 30s; the figure of Antonio Román (*El hombre y el carro*) – who is later to become a renowned post-war director –, and José Suárez with his film *Mariñeiros*, which has been lost, we also find the noteworthy figure of Carlos Velo (Cartelle, Ourense, 1909 – México, 1988. Settled in one of the most successful socio-cultural and artistic veins of the Second Spanish Republic, Velo – together with Fernando Gutiérrez Mantilla –, directs a number of important documentary titles: *La ciudad y el campo* (1934), *Felipe II y el Escorial* (1935), and *Castillos de Castilla* (1936). Their partnership is dissolved in 1936 with *Galicia*, an ethnographic panegyric tinged with socio-political criticism, a mythical piece that opened the way for representation of the Galician people (until 2011, only seven minutes worth of footage were preserved, an amount later extended with additional footage from a coil found in the Russian State Film Fund). This film was selected by Luis Buñuel for the Spanish Pavilion at the Paris International Exhibition in 1937, and it received an award.

Exiled after the Spanish Civil War, Velo continued his work in Mexico, where he was recognised as a pioneer of documentary film practice in Spain and directed titles such as *Torero* (1955) and *Pedro Páramo* (1966). Meanwhile, Mantilla, a former critic at Union Radio, left the profession after producing militant works during the civil war. Both directed documentary shorts that were inspired by the model of significant, didactic non-fiction, commisioned by official institutions (or members of the private sector) in order to promote the desired regeneration in all areas suggested by the educational programs of the country's new public administration. The short films by Velo and Mantilla are made in the style of an exposé, and are planned with patience, rigour and remarkable skill.

Velo's work is notable for the elaborate purification of the components, austerity, strength and search for formal styling, the beauty and poetic meaning of the images, the narrative concision and clarity, thanks to which the author conveys the vision of a human, industrial and laboral universe that takes on metaphorical nuances. An admiration for Flaherty combines with the tracking of filmic experiences contemporary to those of Mantilla and Velo, such as the works of the British school led by Grierson, the experiences of Joris Ivens and Paul Strand, and the whole series of revolutionary Soviet proposals (Vertov).

Despite the fact that the introduction of sound and the proclamation of the Republic in Spain happened at the same time meaning a boom not only for exhibition but also for the popular success of cinema, there will be very few footprints or tapes from this period. One of the most interesting is the creation in the midst of the civil war in A Coruña of the magazine *Radio y Cinema*. The economic decline during the post-war period led to an absolute centralization of the film industry. Cities, especially A Coruña, an emblematic place of the summer holidays of the dictator and his family, began to feature in many docummentaries of the NO-DO (*Noticiarios y Documentales Cinematográficos*), a propaganda agency which had impeccable professionals, created in late 1942 and which – in the case of A Coruña –, generated an average of 6 pieces of news yearly between 1943 and 1950.

A short film, *El andamio*, directed by Rogelio Amigo and produced by the Docampo brothers between 1957 and 1958 achieved fame in the amateur film circles, by referring to the Spanish Civil War itself with extraordinarily audacious and skilful narrative. At this time the cinema clubs and amateur productions are almost the only noticeable activity, apart from certain state-sponsored efforts, except for specific shootings from state institutions. The figures of José Ernesto Díaz-Noriega, and

Cayetano Luca de Tena will have an effect on new generations of creators. Ramón Saiz de la Hoya deserves to be named here. He was an operator at the NO-DO, and the only cameraman allowed by Franco to make close-ups. He filmed, outside of NO-DO, several agile elaborate and propagandistic documentaries made under institutional orders: *Petroliber* (1964), the opening of the oil refinery; the paradigmatic *La Coruña, ciudad en la que nadie es forastero* (1965), an order by the municipal government; *Galicia hoy* (1969) and *Accesos a La Coruña* (1971).

In the 70s – a moment of vindication, combative dissidence, hopes and expectations, experimentalism and a desire to break with the past – specific groups arise (Imaxe, Enroba, Lupa) and professionals (such as Castelo, Gato, Villaverde, López Piñeiro), with interesting short films (the first ones in 35mm.). at this time we can feel the recovery of very specific tones, identities and narratives, which, together with a certain militant cinema (such as that of Varela Veiga and Soler) allows us to envision the seed of something greater. The negative experience of *Malapata* (1980) annuls part of the euphoria. The decade of the 80s will be marked by video creations (Reixa, Caeiro or Ignacio Pardo), the advent of the regional television channel (1985) and the legislative decisions derived from the new state structure (the first funding lines from the Galician Ministry of Culture are from 1984), all of which will lead to the culmination year of 1989. In this moment it took place the coexistence of three feature films in 35mm: *Urxa, Sempre Xonxa* and *Continental*. The support of public administration and the birth of training schools and colleges lead to a new state of affairs. On a relatively stable basis, since 1993 the names of Xabier Bermúdez (author of two of the most outstanding films, *León y Olvido* and *Rafael*), Xavier Villaverde, Héctor Carré, Carlos Amil, Ángel de la Cruz, Raúl Veiga, Ignacio Vilar, Jorge Coira or Patricia Ferreira develop a type of filmmaking that strives to compete – despite some disadvantages and in most of the cases with budget restrictions – in an industrial sector. Despite all this, the period 1997/2002 includes 27 feature films. A weak past, formed between inexistence and frailty, and the dependence on larger structures (the Spanish film industry, itself precarious), outlines a time when progress and democratization lead to changes, global changes and new agents that will be known as the *Novo Cine Galego*. This term first arises as a wake-up call, a strategy to find talents and to assess skills rather than an exercise of confrontation or a generational war.

The set of features or confluence of factors shared by this troop of peripheral individuals, with freedom as a common link, will define innovative ways and some of the most remarkable successes. If the differences with past practices range from funding to production modes and narratives, there is also a change in their attitudes, since a broad freedom of mind facilitates their independence. People of their time in the most appropriate way, training (eclecticism, the importance of visual culture, among other cultures), contacts, progress, interaction, culture, sensitivity, a natural approach to the eternal conflict with the language or accessibility, allow easy synergies. A formal, rather than thematic, iconoclasm, serves the hybridization of genres and formats common to the most demanding contemporary cinema, the one that allows the advance in film language: recycling, creative documentary, forms of cinema-rehearsal, diaries and autobiographical explorations, video creation, more experimental aspects.

With the best expectations, in the last 15 years, sometimes from the diaspora or in search of old genealogical trees, we can find the names of, among others, Alberte Pagán, pioneer in his radical proposals, the biopolitical animations of Peque Varela (her short film *1977* was shown in Sundance 2008), Oliver Laxe, Eloy Enciso, Xurxo Chirro, Lois Patiño, Jaione Camborda, Víctor Hugo Seoane, Marcos Nine, the fruitful fiction visitor Ángel Santos, Lara Bacelo, David Castro Sopeña, Pela del Álamo, Ramiro Ledo, Xan Gómez Viñas, Pablo Cayuela, Diana Toucedo, Iván Castiñeiras, Eloy Domínguez or the duet WeAReQQ (Usue Arrieta and Vicente Vázquez). Other previous names such as Sandra Sánchez, DSK or Alfonso Zarauza, added to the presence in documentaries of Margarita Ledo, cause a flow of valuable variety.

The grants schemes from the Galician Audiovisual Agency during the period 2005/2009; new own and vital festivals understood as meeting points and dissemination activities (such as Filminho, Mostra de Ciencia e Cine, Play-Doc, (S8) Mostra de Cinema Periférico, Mostra Cineuropa..); the need for dissemination, distribution, exhibition and the internationalization in specific circuits that took place after the Director's Fortnight in Cannes and later premiere of *Todos vós sodes capitáns* (2010), by Oliver Laxe, point towards some of the symbolic and defining elements of this change of paradigm.

The breakdown of the Institutional Model of Representation brings avant-garde and non-fiction films to the fore. Banned resources at the time of shaping and creating the filmic text have appera frequently in this works: dead times; dissociations; silences; fragmentation; rhymes and visual associations; the management of spaces in action; the structural use of sound (sometimes reaching up to the radical separation of image and text); ellipse; counterpoints; new framings; abandoned or *in medias res* characters; temporal discontinuities (puzzle, collage); juxtapositions; relevance of the absence of stress, the off-screen, figurative configurations, disconnection of items that could or could not be threaded to the narrative; the tonic and atonic, lack of logical connection (sensory world, dream world, etc.), the movements and the mixture of components or visible changes of shots. In other words, breaking up with the historical model of the invisible transparency. The destruction or combination of genres and the growth of so often paradoxical relationships between avant-garde and non-fiction subvert the order of the narrative, the story, of the everyday logic of the viewer, thus discovering endless possibilities ignored hitherto. The art of researching this genre will be able to overwhelm the show-system.

Let's now examine some of the most relevant examples of the aforementioned *Novo Cinema Galego*.

Todos vós sodes capitáns (2010)

The first feature film by Oliver Laxe, *Todos vós sodes capitáns* was selected for the Director's Fortnight at the Cannes International Film Festival in 2010. It would be the only film made by a Spanish director and with Spanish capital that year in the contest, and it finally won the prestigious critics' award, FIPRESCI. The film was one of the big filmic surprises that year. It was finally premiered in Galicia, and nowadays the author is preparing another project situated in Tangiers, *As Mimosas*. It should be noted that Laxe (Paris, 1982) had already left footsteps of his talent in previous pieces of work, several hints of a personal cinema that offered the perspective of an author of unusual talent, rigorous discourse and vast knowledge. A traveller in search of authenticity which situated him as more than a promising young man, but de facto, a heterodox explorer, progressively more mature and wise, from whom it was only possible to expect nothing but the best.

Two experiments, *Las chimeneas deciden escapar* (2006) and *Suena la trompeta, ahora veo otra cara* (2007) are neceesary to explore in understanding this title. *Las chimeneas deciden escapar* (2006) allowed us to glimpse the playful aspect of his creative condition. Well thought, any experiment is not more than an intrinsic part of the notion of a game, an element, which, united to the concept of learning, becomes a key in the construction of a project such as *Todos vós sodes capitáns*. In those initial works, the ability to keep a certain hermetism was not an obstacle in order to create. In the first example (co-directed with Enrique Aguilar) a notable (counter)symphony of a city where the anthropocentric fluctuated as a subtle garland that allows a narrative about pain and empty spaces; and in the second example, to establish an approach to an initiatory Arab world where the dissolution of images, faces and references constituted a contestation of the overwhelming relativism of any colonial look, always impure.

The works of Oliver Laxe grow in simplicity while the multiplication of the evocative and the crescendo of the poetic ductility led him towards a determined essentialism, a complex and enriching purification. *París#1* (2008), a project initially titled as *As copas dos árbores tremen sobre os restos dun incendio*, allows us to show the frankness of his perspective. The initial situation, a group of friends (among which we distinguish Vicente Vázquez and Usue Arrieta – WeareQQ – an excellent duo of collaborators for Laxe), who share a filmic experience in Galicia, transforms into a travel story, a notebook full of sketches and looks, an exciting route (close to the best universes frequented by people such as Esteva or Jordá), which stages an intense exploration around the visión of traditions and ethnography, as well as of their own mechanisms of filmic construction.

That simplicity and celebratory nature of life itself mixing an amalgam of these features hatches in *Todos vós sodes capitáns*. Laxe presents and articulates one experience, the *real* film workshop he shared with poor children in Tangiers, while threatening with the destruction (overcoming) of any category. Fiction and non-fiction die as expressions derived from our limits and the intimate and the collective converge to show us the austere silences, itineraries and heartbeats of film history, of our story and that of the protagonist children.

In a conversation with the director, I heard a clairvoyant sentence from Oliver: "Love does not end, it simply mutates. It is freedom of sight". In its constant impregnation of this spirit of liberation, the film rhymes, links and runs through the sources of its legacy, the trends and important names in the History of cinema, at the same time it tries to get rid of them and tries to help to write its own future. Kiarostami, Pasolini, Tarkovski, Cassavetes, Bresson, Vigo and many of the great pioneers ennoble this work of *revelation*. And in this crossing of sensations that links heritage and future, tradition and modernity, Laxe traces a delicate story full of wrinkles, a genius and libertarian plateau, a lover of the *carpe diem* as necessarily irregular that even reminds us to the great Jonas Mekas in his cancellation or destruction of the convention of the frame.

However, there are several relevant aspects regarding the reception of the film and the figure of Laxe himself. First, *Todos vós sodes capitáns* seems to reinvent or, rather, reorient and add the previous cinema of the author. At the same time, the embryo idea comes back to us with the constant resonance (and almost compulsory in any relevant film nowadays) of a radical rethinking of the very own concept of cinema (the film itself contains many films, one of them the result of the filming of the young participants in the singular film workshop that sets the idea of the whole project), and the concepts associated to the idea of vision, avoiding the sophisticated and vacuous meta-narration. Secondly, the film avoids or subverts several concepts of contemporary cinema with which some critics are still obsessed, constantly crashing against them: the permanent suspicion that arises around the first narrative person (the subject Oliver Laxe) and, therefore, over every attempt of (self)representation; the standardization of prefabricated images or, simplifying, how curious it is after so many years speaking about exotic cinemas, to keep observing the overwhelming anchorage in limited models though cultural stereotypes – in this case a humanistic conception of a certain Arab cinema –, with obvious outbursts and/or signs of life, which are not validated in a more exhaustive analysis. The confusion that any change of tone causes in an open piece of work, that leads to an arbitrary need for structure which splits the film in two distinct segments for some critics: a narrative one, and the other, (about the last 15 minutes of footage, moments of joyful roaming of the protagonists), disperse and supposedly contemplative.

Javier Rebollo remembered with his usual perspicacity how the film applies the pedagogical premises of the Alain Bergala from *L'hypotèse cinéma. Petit traité de transmission du cinéma à l'école et ailleurs*. First of all, we face the figure of the educator, the one who conveys knowledge. Film and pedagogy, image and relay or transfer, everything well exemplified in two crucial sequences. Oliver, a risky protagonist, becomes a despotic director and is expelled from the process by the own children; later on, he requests the help of his friend Shakib on a balcony. The film inevitably changes the transmitter of knowledge and he is pushed to the erratic and beautiful climax. Secondly, the link with the pure and primitive proposed by the work of Laxe situates us on the antipodes of academic learning and of any hint of traditional subjects. As in the Jean Vigo from the child revolt in *Zéro de coinduite*, underlies a parallel tension between the narrative proposal and the own devices or formal procedures skilfully intertwined for the achievement of a common goal: the crumbling of the canonical and moth-eaten, of any servitude to the norms as a plethoric symptom of the free work, without prejudices, fresh, open, an opera prima distant from models, only anchored to the need for creative expression.

I cannot help to approppriate other evocative words about the film that do not belong to me. Carlos Muguiro writes in a letter to Martin Pawley that he has a "feeling of watching the outbreak of something (not sure what, but beautiful) that leads me to Pasolini: from them (Pasolini and other teachers) I learned that it is good to unlearn (not to forget, but to unlearn) in order to do something honest", a film about "how to teach to make films which, after the 'orthodox' learning, leads its protagonists to forget everything and run wild, to forget everything and simply shoot a tree. A beautiful story about going back to the wild, of going back, of healing or liberation…"

Vikingland (2011)

Vikingland is the creation of Xurxo Chirro (A Guarda, 1973), one of the most active (in different ways), personal and influential Galician cultural agents and artists. Chirro or Xurxo González, is backed by a theoretical and managerial work, by an influence and protean institutional cultural animator. He is an expert in the work of Manoel de Oliveira; he is also the programmer and creator of the original festival Filminho; a thinking mind and activator of the regional and state grant schemes for film creation and promotion, togheter with Manolo González, in institutions attached to the Xunta de Galicia and the own ICAA. He is a person able to overcome the boundaries of conformism and the assumption of the *status quo*.

Chirro develops this tasks along with his own audiovisual production, self-managed designs and models of creation. With *Vikingland* he found a suitable place for the world premiere: it appeared in 2011 in the 21st edition of the Festival of Documentary Cinema in Marseille (FID), one of the most important specialized world events. Marseille remains as an emblematic place for the non-fiction world, an event that has awarded essential filmmakers in its bulky history, figures of the relevance of Frederick Wiseman, Patricio Guzmán, Eduardo Coutinho, Péter Forgács, Jia Zhang Ke, Wang Bing or Raya Martin.

Perfectly detecting the creative trends in the contemporary best non-fiction, it is relevant to fix our attention in such as a singular and well interwoven piece of work such as *Vikingland*. This film, "idea and manipulation" by Xurxo Chirro, comes from an alien accumulated material, product of the personal recordings of the sailor Luis Lomba, "O Haia", a traveling companion of Chirro's father, recorded in Denmark and Germany between October 1993 and March 1994.

A modern immersion and a definitive questioning of the (supposed) own audiovisual aesthetic delay, an ebullient title filled with humour (*retranca*, a very personal perspective and hardly understood by the obsessed with pretentious humour), Vikingland, a more than free transposition of Melville's *Moby Dick*, embeds a narrative structure broken down into 11 chapters: Crew, Luis, Cold, Christmas, Vikingland, Work, Passages, Deck, Ice, Whiteness and Epilogue, allows Chirro to link with the best tradition of re-editing, finding a new meaning to the (amazing) images and craftily blended diary, letter, essay and appropriation, while articulating a fresh speech on the condition of the eye, the effect of (self)representation and the consequences of the meta-narrative.

Placed on a balanced narrative device (moving towards a healthy abstraction as it moves forward), the colossal demiurge that is "O Haia", a charismatic thief of looks, obtains anthological moments (as the karaoke zapping in the cabin, or Christmas eve dinner), and an impression of authenticity and poetry not exempt of a reflection that avoids hyperbolic theoretical frameworks in order to reach a multidimensional enjoyment.

The work of Chirro becomes a good example of the universal through the particular. Preceded by notable (and consistent) pieces, all of them located in his area of origin, *A Guarda*, he starts with *Os señores do vento* (2008), a witty exploration of the ramifications of contemporary art, in this case, Land Art, and reconsideration of the segregation of popular art forms. He continues with contemplative *13 pozas* (2009), a tribute to James Benning with the addition of an unexpected playful and humoristic dimension, and *36/75* (2009), in a time of the review of historical memory, a "reflection on the difficulty of remembering, of the problems of History, of the meanings of the spaces, the fragility of memory, the documentary nature and the will to forget by a part of society that cohabits, without wanting to take much notice, in scenarios that witnessed barbarism", a terrifying look towards the origin of the images and the sources of the numbness of sensitivity, a chronicle of a raw and (still) deeply immature society. In *Cellular movie* (2010) an abstract prelude of the operation of the found footage of *Vikingland*, Chirro records the task of recycling on very different sources, in this case, scientific images. The last and stimulating stop is the film *Une histoire seule* (2014).

In the worlds of the practice and analysis of creation, in which two of the most severe handicaps, submission and lack of humour, are constantly manifested, it is very appreciated that in *Vikingland*, both its tone and subversive desire, as manifested in the credits, with the *institutional support* of an institution, the Galician Audiovisual Agency, and the presence of the Casa das Atochas (a social radical space, epicentre of various socio-cultural and political movements). Both istitutions revealing examples (or attempts to) of the existence of alternative models of intervention, such as a humorous vein, far from the arbitrators of *indie* fashion and good taste, and therefore pouring postmodernity well married even with trends, records and speeches around the cultural identities that seemed to be (falsely) overcome.

Canedo (2011)

A piece of work by the duo WeAreQQ (Usue Arrieta and Vicente Vázquez). *Canedo* is a film with family resonances that works as observational document. The film shows the pilgrimage inherent to any biographical search and to the territorial rooting, since it is surrounded by the Galician family of one of its authors, Vicente Vázquez, while offering a structure as strong as open in its resolution. The piece moves from the appeal to the process of filmic construction, a meta-narrative start that situates the origin of the story (a story, for more details, about the return to the origins) in a family photo, to the follow up of the steps, shaped as significant spaces (sawmill, pulp mill, cardboard factory, press) which facilitate the cutting down of a tree (the background of that photo) and its progressive conversion to the format of a family book, a container to infinity of that initial image that, as a synthesis, gravitates around the video, the family gathering at the village of Quintela de Canedo (Ourense).

In the footsteps of this transformation, the ritual and the mechanical assault us. The diegetic sonorization (the belongings, vehicles, the crashing of wood, the drums of the father…) and several moments or memorable appeals (a rally car, a relative who practices martial arts, the cover inscription that shows the linotype of *Canedo*, the buried book) that build a thorough and content universe that hatches into a playful, celebratory final, a familiar party with the *verbena* song by Hidrogenesse (*El árbol*) as apotheosis, with the own Vicente Vázquez solo and his father's band from the '60s, Los Flavia, as an accompaniment.

The story of a symbolic tree that ends in the spot where it was cut, an exploration into tradition and the roots of affections and identity, a group portrait and approach to the places and processes of life with its subsequent phases; Canedo, in its last picture, the launch of a festive rocket, seems to open a period outlined fruitful for its authors, immersed in successive and successful projects, such as *90º*, which, in words of the duet, "explains some of the mysteries lurking in our work, the transmission of culture through stories, its power and limitations as the ultimate generator of meaning, and how it articulates the transcription of these contents among different representational languages. We have generated through various exercises of de-contextualization and re-contextualization a method that is essentially narrative that puts on hold the effectiveness of our forms of cultural transmission and code production".

Nichols, and before Barnow, suggest merging components that explain the delay and then the emergence and development of the documentary: an addition of trends, the addition of attraction films (the spectacular and exotic), experimentation (avant-garde), certain narrative maturity, accuracy and persuasion finally fitted to rhetorical strategies.

Arraianos (2012)

Arraianos was born as an open project and became a process extended in time. It began in 2007 and premiered at the Locarno Film Festival in 2012, in order to reach afterwards the theatres and the videographic market. A blend of representations (statism, antinaturalism, frontalilty, declamation, style features associated with Straub-Huillet) and non-fiction (the everyday habits of non-actors), the duration of the shots and the severity in the frame and the axis, the importance of the word in its purest form contribute, paraphrasing Comolli, to decipher cinema as we decipher a lost language. A film in which the text, the words (as the recital of a score), the silences, the bodies... matter.

Arraianos derived from a broad, abstract idea. It approaches a story of the past of uncertain origin, which houses the possibility of expansion of the myth, exemplified in the idea of a hiding place in the mists of history, in Galicia. There are three border towns, located in the so-called *Raia Seca*, between Ourense and Portugal, the Couto Mixto. Historically, they region had high degrees of autonomy (prerogatives, licenses), which precipitated its ending: the crowns of Portugal and Spain dismantled their privileges in the second half of the 19th century. The film *Arraianos* is the story of dissatisfaction; a denial on the ground, which will undo this approach firstly to the mysteries there placed in order to apply to the whole set, ultimately, to the alienation of the story and the territories linked to the myth.

A narrative of borders, being those boundaries understood both geographically and stylistically. This narrative that searched for remains in that place encouraged to explore those abstractions (identity, border, utopia, ethnographic authenticity, the myth itself or the social and historical remains) through subtle, non-standardized, clairvoyant aesthetic parameters. Since the beginning of the process, the presence of antinaturalism, representation and recitals (the traces of Straub and Huillet or Pedro Costa were not indifferent), lead to the need for a literary text as a starting point as a challenge, the feel of a first reception in the flesh, adjusting to the idea of a search or an open process, but maintaining certain basic assumptions: non-professional actors, representation, recitals, orality, non-realism.

The long process of research and documentation, full of readings, travelling, meetings, gatherings and collection of witnesses established by writer and director, shows how the experience of all the process, the accumulated knowledge (and the added advice by Galician literature professor Xosé María Dobarro) allowed to dive into a cultural and literary tradition, a series of texts and authors, from Méndez Ferrín or Dieste to Castelao, Varela Buxán, Riveiro Coelho or many ethnographic essays, that could be adjusted to the intentions that progressively developed.

By then, a figure of an intellectual sniper affiliated to the *reintegracionista* idiomatic movement appeared, Jenaro Marinhas del Valle (1908-1999). His theatre, precisely antinaturalist, comes impregnated with the intertwining of poetic, allegorical, philosophical or existential elements, stories of freedom, death and identity. Fitted to a modern conception, the attainment of an active viewer who moves from Brecht to Beckett, Ionesco or Camus, and a whole tradition of its own which, in different ways, reminds of Valle-Inclán, Cunqueiro, Dieste or Castelao. Despite the existence of several works of great interest, *A revolta, Loucura e morte de peregrino or A Gaiola*, the chosen one was be *O bosque* (1977), a play written years before its publication, still during the dictatorship, influenced by Dostoevsky, Strindberg, that integrates the existentialist trend and ends up by transforming into a native *Waiting for Godot*, a stranded boat of crazy men where the combination of thought, political action, lyricism and a conception of theatre as a travel, is the one that partially and after some thought, is considered to be optimal for the film. The language, the importance of the verb, of the recited, the parliaments, the representation, the musical character, the coexistence of Galician and Portuguese, acquire a body of its own within this text.

The script serves as a guide, as a firm text rehearsed for over a year with non-professional actors. In its various versions, the extreme refinement, selection and reblending of passages, give way to a voracious suppression of scenes. The hybridization between the everyday and the representation are part of the project since the beginning, and it grows during filming. Specifically, a second, more documental filmind will ease the romance of the meeting, the immediacy, the bond with nonfiction, the key of the resulting film.

Costa da morte (2013)

The last lucky link so far in this chain of titles, *Costa da Morte*, a documentary of unique beauty and production values, directed by Lois Patiño (Vigo, 1983). It began its unforgettable and successful run at the prestigious Locarno Film Festival in 2013, in a reaffirmation of the relative success of other recent Galician films. Patiño's career started with a series of documentaries based on portraits, the series "Rostros de Arena": *Profesor Tejero* (2008), *Rayito* (2009) and *Zuma* (2009). *Recordando los rostros de la muerte* (2009) is an intimate work, exploring the agony of a family relative with traces of aesthetic exploration. This film already exhibits a concern for landscape and for non-figurative elements. Video creation and short films that focus on natural spaces – such as the series *Paisajes or Montaña en sombra* (2012) exhibited at the Rome Film Festival –, signal the emergence of a telluric poet. In *Costa da Morte*, each carefully considered shot allows the visual to dominate, in a departure from standard narratives. Poetry and contemplation, the relationship between text, image and anthropological remains, combine to create a playful and beautiful work. The impact the film made following its premiere in Locarno is a continuation of the emergence of new authors, challenges and exciting proposals in Galician cinema.

Works cited

Cabo, José Luis. Jaime Pena and Ignacio Varela, *Audiovisual Galego* 2003, Santiago de Compostela: Xunta de Galicia-CGAI, 2003.

Castro de Paz, José Luis (coord.), *Historia do cine en Galicia*, A Coruña: Vía Láctea, 1996.

Comisión Técnica de Cinematografía e Artes Visuais (Consello da Cultura Galega), *Libro Branco de Cinematografía e Artes Visuais en Galicia*, Santiago de Compostela: Consello da Cultura Galega, 2004.

González, Manuel, *Documentos para a historia do cine en Galicia. 1970-1990*, A Coruña: CGAI, 1992.

Nogueira, Xosé, *O cine en Galicia*, Vigo: A Nosa Terra, 1997.

Audiovisual works cited

Orzán, oleaje. José Sellier. José Sellier, 1897. 35 mm.

Fábrica de Gas. José Sellier. Idem, 1897. 35 mm.

Entierro del general Sánchez Bregua. José Sellier. Idem, 1897. 35 mm.

San Jorge, salida de misa. José Sellier. Idem, 1897. 35 mm.

Matadero, salida de operarios. José Sellier. Idem, 1898. 35 mm.

Descarga de Carbón. José Sellier. Idem, 1898. 35 mm.

Botadura del acorazado Alfonso XIII. Empresa Salón París, 1913. 35 mm.

Ano Santo en Compostela. Manuel Cardoso Pereira. Invicta Films, 1915. 35 mm.

Miss Ledya. José Gil. Idem, 1916. 35 mm.

La casa de la Troya. Alejandro Pérez Lugín and Manuel Noriega. Troya Films, 1925. 35 mm.

La virgen del cristal. Saturno and Manuel Lois Piñeiro. Ediciones Sol Films, 1925. 35 mm.

Carmiña, flor de Galicia. Rino Lupo. Hispánica Film Ltd., 1926. 35 mm.

Maruxa. Henry Vorfins. Celta Films and Ernesto González, 1923. 35 mm.

A traxedia de Xirobio. José Signo. Vicus Film, 1930. 35 mm.

Nuestras fiestas de allá. José Gil. Galicia Cinegráfica, 1926. 35 mm.

Tierra de nuestros mayores. Manuel Arís. Hispanoamericana Cine Producción, 1959. 35 mm.

Galicia al día. Amando Hermida. Idem, 1956. 16 mm.

Así es Galicia. Irmáns Docampo. Carballal Films, 1956. 16 mm.

O carro e o home / El carro y el hombre. Antonio Román. PACE, 1940. 35 mm.

Mariñeiros. José Suárez. CIFESA, 1939. 35 mm.

La ciudad y el campo. Carlos Velo and Fernando Gutiérrez Mantilla. Ministerio de Agricultura y Fomento, 1934. 35 mm.

Felipe II y el Escorial. Carlos Velo and Fernando Gutiérrez Mantilla. CIFESA, 1935. 35 mm.

Castillos de Castilla. Carlos Velo and Fernando Gutiérrez Mantilla. CIFESA, 1936. 35 mm.

Galicia. Carlos Velo and Fernando Gutiérrez Mantilla. DESA, 1936. 35 mm.

El andamio. Rogelio Amigo. Carballal Films, 1958. 16 mm.

La Coruña, ciudad en la que nadie es forastero (1965), Ramón Saiz de la Hoya. Ayuntamiento de La Coruña, 1965. 35 mm.

Galicia hoy. Ramón Saiz de la Hoya. Comisaría del Plan de Desarrollo Económico y Social de Galicia, 1969. 35 mm.

Accesos a La Coruña. Ramón Saiz de la Hoya. Instituto Nacional de la Vivienda, 1971. 35 mm.

Malapata. Carlos Aurelio López Piñeiro. Carlos Aurelio López Piñeiro and Producciones Cine-Vós, 1980. 16 mm.

Urxa. Carlos Aurelio López Piñeiro and Alfredo García Pinal. Carlos Aurelio López Piñeiro and Xosé Xoán Cabanas Cao. 35 mm.

Sempre Xonxa. Chano Piñeiro. Producións Cinematográficas Piñeiro, SA, 1989. 35 mm.

Continental. Xavier Villaverde. Xavier Villaverde Asociados SL, Producciones Cine, 1989. 35 mm.

León y Olvido. Xavier Bermúdez. Xamalú Filmes and El Paso P.C., 2004. 35 mm.

Rafael. Xavier Bermúdez. Xamalú Filmes, 2008. 35 mm.

1977. Peque Varela. Idem, 2008. Digital.

Todos vós sodes capitáns. Oliver Laxe. Zeitun, 2010. 35 mm.

Las chimeneas deciden escapar. Oliver Laxe and Enrique Aguilar. Idem, 2006. 16 mm.

Suena la trompeta, ahora veo otra cara. Oliver Laxe. Idem, 2007. 16 mm.

París#1. Oliver Laxe. Idem, 2008. 16 mm.

Vikingland. Xurxo Chirro. Filmika Galaika, 2011. Digital.

Os señores do vento. Xurxo Chirro. Idem, 2008. Digital.

13 pozas. Xurxo Chirro. Idem, 2009. Digital.

36/75. Xurxo Chirro. Idem, 2009. Digital.

Cellular movie. Xurxo Chirro. Idem, 2010. Digital.

Une histoire seule. Xurxo Chirro and Aguinaldo Fructuoso. A Herbiña do Marraxo, 2014. Digital.

Canedo. Vicente Vázquez and Usue Arrieta. Idem, 2011. Digital.

Arraianos. Eloy Enciso. Artika and Zeitun, 2012. Digital.

Costa da Morte. Lois Patiño. Zeitun, 2013. Digital.

Profesor Tejero. Lois Patiño. Idem, 2008. Digital.

Rayito. Lois Patiño. Idem, 2009. Digital.

Zuma. Lois Patiño. Zeitun, 2009. Digital.

Recordando los rostros de la muerte. Lois Patiño. Idem, 2009. Digital.

Paisajes. Lois Patiño. Idem, 2011. Digital.

Montaña en sombra. Lois Patiño. Idem, 2012. Digital.

Cándida the Emigrant. The portrayal of the Galician diaspora in Argentinian cinema

Silvia Roca Baamonde

Buenos Aires was, in the early 20th century, the city with the largest Galician population in the world, well above that of any city in Spain.[1] At a time when the Argentinian film industry dominated the Spanish-language film market, it is fair to say that the construction of the social image of Galicians generated in the austral republic had major repercussions on how their portrayal was shaped on an international scale. It is from this perspective that the analysis of the key aspects of one of its most popular representations on film, Niní Marshall's Cándida the maid, is of great interest in the field of Galician Cultural Studies. By examining the films from which the series originated, this article approaches the role of the stereotype as a social organiser, the value of comedy as a critic of behaviour and the power of film to construct collective imagination.

Migrant stereotypes as a social control strategy

The Galician diaspora to Argentina, which was already evident in the colonial period, intensified in the last quarter of the 18th century and became a massive phenomenon in the second half of the 19th century.

The Alberdian dictum "To govern is to populate"[2] brought about a demographic strategy that favoured the settlement of communities of European emigrants with the aim of "escaping solitude, backwardness, poverty and despotism, rooted more in local customs than in governments" (Alberdi, 1915:223).

Argentinian migratory statistics show the arrival of more than two million Spaniards within the period 1857-1930 (Lojo, 2008). Galician migrants were the largest group and the word "gayego" soon became used to mean all Spanish people. Antonio Pérez-Prado argues that this extended usage of the word is a conscious negation of Galician identity:

> Sometimes, this abusive Hispanicisation of Galician people is part of the complex phenomenon in which simple-minded people negate all things Galician. At its most aggressive, this process sparked, and still sparks, countless *aldraxes* (insults) – of a more or less folkloric nature (Pérez-Prado, 1973:164).

María Rosa Lojo puts the negative connotations of the word down to "a mix of anti-peninsular sentiments and a relatively credible reflection of the community's social significance"' (Lojo, 2008:22) and emphasises the contrast between the size and the impact of the Galician group and its social esteem.

> An ethnic community without a state but with its own and very distinct identity and culture, whose importance in the construction of modern Argentinian society and their strong public presence clashes with the insufficient attention it has received from Argentinian historiography and with the partial and distorted collective knowledge that modern Argentinians still have of it (Lojo, 2008:21).

The construction of negative stereotypes in the heterogeneous Argentinian society as a result of the migratory process did not exclusively affect the Galician community. Xosé Manuel Núñez Seixas (2002:51-52) identifies "non-white races, Jewish Russians and Turks, Egyptians, vagrants, the sick and the illiterate", as well as Southern Italians, as the least desirable groups.

Paola Pereira emphasises the role that the country's media played in the assimilation of these representational models and revisits Anderson's theses to tackle the role that the media played as a system of social and cultural control in Argentina in the 1930s and 1940s, in a context in which immigration:

> posed a problem fundamentally linked to national identity, especially when the Argentinian intelligentsia became worried not only about the low level of integration of these groups, but mainly about the increase of social conflict – where unionised immigrants took centre stage in such a way that a discourse was constructed from different national powers, clearly linking labour unrest with European immigration. (Pereira, 2009:191)

The fear of a lack of governability and the advent of an unstable society lacking in social cohesion encouraged the development of discourses and strategies in favour of re-stabilising the pre-existing order. These arguments, on occasion, used positive and/or negative stereotyping of different ethnicities to delimit the acceptability of certain conducts and behaviours and set guidelines for their integration into an ideal Argentinian citizenry.

> One thing that played a role here was the hierarchy of values and ethnic preferences itself, of stereotypes and images of immigration that the receiving society had, which inevitably became a game of inverted mirrors, the respectable self-image that the ethnic leaders themselves wanted to create (Núñez Seixas, 2002:21)

The use of comedy as a censoring element, the categorisation of the laughable and the ridiculous in opposition to what was proper, gave particular importance to these discourses.

Galicians and the ridiculous. The case of Niní Marshall's *Cándida*

Caricatures, novels and farces based their parody on certain clichés about Galicians that different historians believe were borrowed from Spanish emigrants (Sempere, 2002; Fernández Santiago, 1995; Lojo, 2009). Drawing on these clichés, Pérez-Prado offers an indispensable description of the Galician icon proposed by the printed media:

> Gayegos, especially those from Galicia, were dirty, vulgar, strong-minded (sometimes), brutish (always) and coarse, but skilled for small businesses and clever enough. There was no reason to be scared of them. In characterisations and drawings they were represented with a big 'square' head – cubic, actually – and with a very characteristic feature: a thick, bushy, sinister unibrow, like eaves over 'Moorish eyes'. They were never clean-shaven – over their strong chin there was always stubble – while their hair resembled the bristle of a toothbrush (Pérez-Prado, 1993: 215)

As a humorous addition to these characteristics, and as a key element in the shaping of the public image of immigrants, the difficulties they experienced in expressing themselves correctly in Spanish – with constant interferences from Galician and a marked presence of dialectal features such as *rotacismo* (turning certain sounds into [r]), *gheada* (pronouncing the sound [g] similarly to the English sound [h]), *seseo* (turning certain sounds into [s]), etc. – are frequently used in literary texts but reach their peak in radio and film. Galician is perceived as a dialect of Spanish and, as Marcelino Fernández Santiago notes (1995:99), differences in pronunciation and vocabulary are interpreted as ignorance.

It is precisely these qualities that define the character of Cándida on her radio début. In 1935, Niní Marshall joined the cast of the series *El chalet de Pipita* (Pipita's Chalet) on Radio Municipal. According to Niní herself, she drew inspiration for the character from the maid that assisted her mother as a widow. The radio version of Cándida based her parody on puns and double entendres, constant mistakes, an exaggeratedly strong accent, excessive loudness, coarse language and constant linguistic interferences from Galician. Marshall became the loud and tactless voice of Galician maids. With radio appearances on different networks, Cándida won the affections of audiences in Buenos Aires and paved the way for her creator to write her own scripts and make the leap to film.

The Argentinian film industry was enjoying a golden age defined by a large number of popular comedies and the prestige of actors over directors and producers. Marshall accepted a contract with EFA to film a big-screen adaptation of *Cándida*, which would be directed by filmmaker Luis Bayón Herrera. Their fruitful collaboration led to a trilogy of films: *Cándida* (1939), *Los celos de Cándida* (Cándida's Jealousy, 1940) and *Cándida Millonaria* (Cándida the Millionaire, 1941). The success of these films led to the character's recognition and allowed the series to continue.[3]

The film version of the Galician "criadiña" (maid) incorporated a crafted physical comedy based on the actress' body language, her manner of walking and her clothing. Cándida's physical appearance (Fig.1) brings to mind the characteristics of the Galician icon described by Pérez-Prado and gives body and movement to the archetype of the outlandish maid that features in Mario Bellini's farce *Ramona* (1931) and Lino Palacio's homonymous caricatures.

Cándida (1939) offers one of the first critical examinations of the social conditions suffered by the female Galician emigrants who arrived in Buenos Aires in the 1930s. The film picks up the representation of Galicians that had been popularised in the printed media: coarse and clumsy, frugal (or, rather, stingy), barely literate and lacking in hygiene, although honest and obedient at work – usually in the service industry (Lojo, 2008). Like them, Cándida has come to serve. Dressed like a villager (Fig.2), she is dazed and confused by the city's size and is eager to start working.

> ATTENDANT: Why have you come to this country?
> CÁNDIDA: Me? To earn 40 pesos, a house and food.
> ATTENDANT: Nothing else?
> CÁNDIDA: Sundays off and…
> ATTENDANT: OK, fine, fine. Proceed to your check-up.
>   *Cándida* (Bayón Herrera, 1939)

The characterisation of the Galician emigrant, inherently associated with their professional occupation – which determined how they were assimilated into Argentina's social structure – encouraged a biased view of the community, but also contained elements of truth, which made the characters seem more believable. Indeed, Galicians who emigrated to Argentina took up positions in the service sector, commonly associated with urban or semi-urban services, in unskilled or semi-skilled jobs, in order to save up as much money as possible before moving back home. They settled mainly in urban areas and the Pampas coast, especially in and around Buenos Aires and in Avellaneda, as these population centres offered better opportunities for development to those who dreamt of going back. Though they did not come from the most impoverished regions and many of them were somewhat literate, most of them came from rural areas.

These factors contributed to establishing the stereotype and its internalisation by many members of the community. There would be many migrants who, in order to avoid being associated with these negative attributes, would try to hide their origins. Fernández Santiago (1995:108) calls them "whitewashed Galicians who conceal their origins in order to facilitate their integration into their new society". The Cándida films contain examples of this type of migrant. In the 1939 film, as in other titles from the series, the role is played by Jesús (Augusto Codecá), a stock clerk who tries to guide Cándida in her process of becoming an Argentine and makes ridiculous displays of his recently acquired position as an American:

CÁNDIDA: Ah, and the master has asked for a kilo of grass – I mean herbs. I guess they're for some animal.

JESÚS: No, they're for *mate.*

CÁNDIDA: For murder? They're poisonous, then?

JESÚS: No! For *mate.* It's the vice that we have here in the Americas.
    Cándida (Bayón Herrera, 1939)[4]

The character's failed attempts to smooth his reprehensible Galician manners result in supposedly hilarious scenes that demonstrate the efficiency of comedy in controlling behaviour. What one laughs at is opposed to what is desirable. A second reading of these scenes points to the Galicians' unsuccessful adaptation as the root cause of their lack of social mobility.

Los celos de Cándida (1940) is of great interest in the analysis of encounters between different cultures. The film portrays a Buenos Aires populated with immigrants. The protagonists are joined by a Castilian rogue, a Lithuanian model and a frivolous Italian. The contrasts highlight the Galicians' naivety, their coarseness and their lack of culture, which become obvious in their words and actions. In relation to this film, Pereira (2009) tackles the character's language as an element that defines their intellectual skills. In opposition to other bilingual characters, the constant interferences from Galician in the maid's speech highlight her inability to express herself at will in either language and, therefore, her incompetence.

Cándida is invariably paired with other Galicians. In this film, Jesús reappears as her partner. Focusing on the romantic adventures between these two characters, the film makes use of a key feature of the representation of the Galician community: their inbreeding. Affectionate relationships between Galicians, a constant in the films and in the literary tradition, together with the spaces they occupy – markets, kitchens, dances, etc. – do not at all reflect the emigrants' complex network of relationships, or their cultural, social and political involvement. Instead, they stick to common places that deepen their social stigma.

In *Cándida Millonaria* (1941), the last film in the trilogy, there are other Galician characters in the main cast but their presence explores new sides of the stereotype without calling it into question. A wealthy businessman, Marcial (Alberto Bello), an archetype of the new rich, enters the scene. He takes on Cándida as his maid and ends up marrying her. He is accompanied by his friend Benito (Alejandro Maximino), an archetype of the nostalgic Galician. Their relationships are limited to the affective level and are born out of common nostalgia for the land they left behind. In contrast to these characters, there are two other communities, the Argentinian high society and Marcial's servants, who are critical of Cándida's possible change in status:

CHAUFFEUR: You see, we used to be colleagues and... to be honest it's a bit embarrassing to have to open the car door for her.
ANA MARÍA: She's the one who should be embarrassed.
CHAUFFEUR: She should be, shouldn't she, madam?'
    Cándida Millonaria (Bayón Herrera, 1941)

The key narrative element of the film is the group's social climbing, personified by the newlyweds. The Argentinian middle class values Marcial's economic advancement but does not consider him one of their own, while the way they pass judgment on Cándida is in line with the portrayal of Galician women that Núñez Seixas identifies in printed media:

> They were given a number of particular characteristics: simple, ignorant, more or less coarse (despite going through a certain degree of upward social mobility), just as stingy – or more – than men and, occasionally, with a tendency to immorality or close to the dangers of prostitution (Núñez Seixas, 2002:82)

At the film's premiere on 17 September 1941, members of the Galician community protested against the ridiculing of women emigrants. The critics ignored their arguments, defended the actress's creative freedom and comic talent and lavished praise on the character's authenticity and complexity. "She wasn't like other Galician women. She was an exact Galician woman" (Echelet, 2004:49). The Galician community's protests were barely noticed against the mass media's uniform view.

The lack of alternative models to this type of emigrant, present in all three films and a constant in the literary tradition, is one of the key factors in the stereotype's endurance. Among the Galician immigrants in Argentina there was a long list of intellectuals – such as Alfonso Daniel Rodríguez Castelao, Rafael Dieste, Lorenzo Varela or Luis Seoane

– who intervened actively in the Buenos Aires cultural scene. The mark they left, like that of many other anonymous voices, has been forgotten or ignored by the mass media, and proposals that are inclusive of educated Galicians are few and far between. As Walter Lippman argues:

> The most subtle and dominant influences are those that manage to create and perpetuate an assortment of stereotypes. On the one hand we hear about the world before we see it, and on the other hand, we imagine most things before experiencing them. As a result, all of these preconceived ideas will almost fully dictate our whole perception process, unless education makes us fully aware of this. (Lippmann, 1922:87-88)

Given the lack of alternative proposals and the absence of tools to reinterpret the discourse established by the media, the icon of the provincial, coarse, rough, kind, hard-working Galician was firmly established in the Argentinian imagination.

The first trilogy in the series about Cándida the maid constitutes the film adaptation of a pre-existing stereotype in Argentina's literary tradition that is characterised by the individuals' marked physical and intellectual clumsiness and the community's inbreeding and social ambition. Marshall created a comic portrayal of Galicians based on the discrimination and negative attributes that affected some of the emigrants. The mockery of their way of being and behaving, in contrast to the Argentinians' civilised habits, becomes an argument in favour of the assimilation of the values of the receiving society. The portrayal of the emigrant community's working life, always associated with low-skilled jobs and limited opportunities for social mobility, confines them to a marginal and immutable place within the country's organisational structure. The fact that a more active, educated and politically-minded type of emigration was made invisible became a key factor in the consolidation and perpetuation of this image.

Notes

1 The 1910 census accounted for 306,850 Spaniards in the city; it is calculated that half of these were Galician. These numbers were well above those of any Galician city at the time, as none of them had a population larger than 60,000.

2 Juan Bautista Alberdi's key work, the 1852 treatise *Bases y puntos de partida para la organización política de la República de Argentina* (*Bases and starting points for the political organization of the Republic of Argentina*), became a guide for the writing

of the National Constitution of Argentina.

3   There would be ten films in total: *Cándida* (Bayón Herrera, 1939), *Los celos de Cándida* (*Cándida's Jealousy*, Bayón Herrera, 1940), *Cándida Millonaria* (*Cándida the Millionaire*, Bayón Herrera, 1941), *Cándida, la mujer del año* (*Cándida, Women of the Year*, Santos Discépolo, 1943), *Santa Cándida* (*Saint Cándida*, Amadori, 1945), *Una gallega en México* (*A Galician Woman in Mexico*, Soler, 1949), *Una gallega baila mambo* (*A Galician Woman Dances the Mambo*, Gómez Muriel, 1950), *Los enredos de una gallega* (*The Troubles of a Galician Woman*, Soler, 1951), *Una gallega en La Habana* (*A Galician Woman in Havana*, Cardona, 1955) and *Cleopatra era Cándida* (*Cleopatra Was Cándida*, Saraceni,1964)

4   In the original dialogue, Cándida's confusion is caused by the fact that "mate", the drink, sounds similar to the Spanish word "matar" (*to kill*).

Works cited

Alberdi, J.B. (1915): *Bases y puntos de partida para la organización política de la República de Argentina* [*Bases and starting points for the political organization of the Republic of Argentina*]. (Ed. Francisco Cruz) Buenos Aires: La cultura argentina. Available at: http://www.cervantesvirtual.com/obra/bases-y-puntos-de-partida-para-la-organizacion-politica-de-la-republica-argentina--0/

Blanco R.; Clemente, R. (2008): *Diccionario de Actrices del Cine Argentino 1933-1997*. [*Dictionary of Argentine Film Actresses 1933-1977*]. Buenos Aires: Corregidor.

Contreras, M. (2003): *Niní Marshall, el humor como refugio* [*Niní Marshall, humour as a refuge*]. Buenos Aires: Libros del Zorzal.

Di Núbila, D. (1959): *Historia del Cine Argentino*. [*History of Argentine Cinema*] v.1. Buenos Aires: Cruz de Malta.

Echelet, R. (2004): *Niní Marshall (La biografía)* [*Niní Marshall (The Biography)*]. Buenos Aires: La Crujía.

Farías, R. (2010): "Viejos Estereotipos y nuevos discursos: la visión de Galicia y de los gallegos en una fracción de la élite galaicoporteña a mediados de la década de 1940". [Old stereotypes and new speeches: the visión of Galicia and of the Galician people in a fraction of the Galician elite from Buenos Aires Arround the middle of the decade of 1940]. In: *Madrygal*, 13. (pp.51-61)

Fernández Santiago, M (2005): "Unha aproximación á consideración social dos inmigrantes galegos en Arxentina" ["An approximation to the social consideration of Galician immigrants in Argentina"]. In: *Grial*, nº.125 pp. 95-114.

Galán, E. (2006): "Personajes, estereotipos y representaciones sociales. Una propuesta de estudio y análisis de la ficción televisiva" ["Characters, stereotypes and social representations. A proposal for the study and analysis of TV fiction"] in ECO-PÓS v.9 nº 1 pp 58-81. Brasil: Universidad Federal de Río de Janeiro. In: http://e-archivo.uc3m.es/bitstream/10016/9475/5/galan_personajes_ECOPOS_2006.pdf

Lippmann. W (1922): *La opinión pública* [*Public Opinion*]. Madrid: Langre. (ed. 2003)

Lojo, M. R.; Guidotti de Sánchez, M.; Farías, R. (*2008): Los "gallegos" en el imaginario argentino. Literatura, sainete, prensa* [*"Galicians" in Argentinian stereotypes. Literature, farce and the press*]. A Coruña: Fundación Pedro Barrié de la Maza.

Lojo, M. R. (2009): "La Argentina gallega: Más allá de los estereotipos" ["Galician Argentina: Beyond Stereotypes"]. *Gramma*, XXII, 48 (2011), pp. 286-297. In: http://p3.usal.edu.ar/index.php/gramma/article/view/810/956#_ftn1

Mestmann, M. (2005): "Imágenes del inmigrante español en el cine argentino. Notas sobre la candidez del estereotipo" ["Representations of Spanish immigrants in Argentinian cinema. Notes about the ingenuousness of the stereotype"]. In: Secuencias, *Revista de Historia del Cine*, núm. 22, pp. 27-47.

Núñez Seixas, X.M (2002): *O inmigrante imaxinario. Estereotipos, representacións e identidades dos galegos na Arxentina (1888-1940)* [*The Imaginary Immigrant: Galician stereotypes, representations and identities in Argentina (1888-1940)*]. Santiago de Compostela: Universidade de Santiago de Compostela. Servizo de Publicacións e Intercambio Científico.

Núñez Seixas, X.M. (1999): "Algunas notas sobre la imagen social de los inmigrantes gallegos en la Argentina (1860-1940)" ["Some notes on the social image of Galician immigrants in Argentina (1860-1940)"]. In: *Estudios migratorios lationamericanos*. año 14 nº 42 (pp. 67-109). Buenos Aires: Centro de Estudios Migratorios Latinoamericanos.

Pereira, P. (2009): "Lenguas en contacto, el caso Cándida de Niní Marshall" ["Languages in contact: The case of Niní Marshall's Cándida"], en VV AA, in *Discursos, lengua, imágenes, la cultura gallega en paradigmas plurales* (Ed. Graciana Vázquez Villanueva. Buenos Aires : Universidad de Buenos Aires, Facultad de Filosofía y Letras ; [Santiago de Compostela] : Xunta de Galicia, Secretaría Xeral de Política Lingüística.

Pereira, P. (2007): "Cartas sin respuesta: intervenciones de gallegos a propósito de Cándida de Niní Marshall" ["Unanswered letters: Galician interventions in relation to Niní Marshall's Cándida"]. Paper read at the *VII Congreso Nacional y II Congreso Internacional de la Asociación Argentina de Semiótica. Rosario. 7 al 10 de noviembre de 2007* [*7th National Conference and 2nd International Conference of the Argentinian Association of Semiotics. Rosario. November 7th-10th, 2007*].

Pérez-Prado, A. (1993): "Imaxes da discriminación" ["Images of Discrimination"]. In *Grial*, T. 31, nº 118 pp. 212-221.

Pérez-Prado, A. (1973): *Los gallegos y Buenos Aires* [*Galicians and Buenos Aires*]. Buenos Aires: Ediciones La Bastilla.

Sempere, I. (2002): "Niní Marshall o la imagen de la gallega en el cine argentino" ["Niní Marshall or the image of Galician women in Argentinian cinema"], in VV AA, *Universitas. Homenaje a Antonio Erias Roel*. (Eds. Camilo Fernández Cortizo, Domingo L. González Lopo, Enrique Martínez Rodríguez). Tomo 2. Santiago de Compostela: Universidade de Santiago de Compostela, Servicio de Publicacións e Intercambio Científico.

Filmography

Cándida (Dir. Luis Bayón Herrera. EFA, 1939)

Los celos de Cándida [*Cándida's Jealousy*] (Dir. Luis Bayón Herrera. EFA, 1940)

Cándida Millonaria [*Cándida the Millionaire*] (Dir. Luis Bayón Herrera. EFA, 1941)

Cándida, la mujer de año [Cándida, Woman of the Year] (Dir. Enrique Santos Discépolo. Argentina Sono Film, 1943)

Santa Cándida [*Saint Cándida*] (Dir. Luis César Amadori. Argentina Sono Film, 1945)

Una gallega en México [Dir. Julián Soler. Filmex, *A Galician Woman in Mexico*] (1949)

Una gallega baila mambo [Dir. Emilio Gómez Muriel. Filmex, *A Galician Woman Dances the Mambo*] (1950)

Los enredos de una gallega [*The Troubles of a Galician Woman*] (Dir. Fernando Soler. Ultramar Films, 1951)

Una gallega en La Habana [*A Galician Woman in Havana*] (Dir. René Cardona. Pelimex y Argentina Sono Film, 1955)

Cleopatra era Cándida [*Cleopatra Was Cándida*] (Dir. Julio Saraceni. Filmex Argentina, 1964)

Literary and cinematographic parallels in the representation of women in the 1970s, during the Spanish and Portuguese dictatorships.

The will for absolute love in *Cartas de amor de una monja portuguesa* by Grau & Arquer (1978)[1]

Miren Gabantxo

The story of the five love letters of a 17th century nun

Cartas de amor de una monja was directed by Jordi Grau in 1978, after the success of *La Trastienda* (1975), his previous film, which portrayed full-frontal feminine nudity for the first time since Franco's death (in the person of the actress María José Cantudo). By request of the same producer, José Frade, Grau had also made *El secreto inconfesable de un niño bien* (1975) and *La siesta* (1976). These films, together with *Cartas de amor de una monja* (1978) form a non-homogeneous cycle of four commercial *destape* films[2] created under the auspices of the film producing company Frade S.A. This was the first film Grau was able to make without any kind of censorship, following a body of work of thirteen films that were closely monitored by the Film Censorship Bureau. However the thirteenth film, *La siesta* (1976), could be said to have been passed without censorship because the corresponding Censorship Committee cancelled, at the last moment, their demand to suppress parts of the film. The production context of the film *Cartas de amor de una monja* (1978) is therefore one exempt from censoring legislation.

Film censorship was suppressed by means of the Royal Decree 3071/1977, November 11th, which regulates everything concerning the production and exhibition of films. This decree only demands that the production company notified the *Dirección General de Cinematografía* (the General Film Directorate) of the filming start date. Also, in the case of foreign productions or co-productions between Spain and other countries that are to be filmed in Spanish territory, a special licence must be requested. Once the movie is completed, it will be necessary to obtain an exhibition licence, which is awarded by the Dirección General de Cinematografía after the release of a non-binding report by the Film Visas Committee, who will suggest the classification of the work. There are no representatives of the Catholic Church in any of these bodies (Minteguia Arregui, 2008: 10).

Cartas de amor de una monja (1978) is the most complex of the four films, because it uses the process of constructing a woman's sexuality (a nun's in this case, someone without sexual experience – in theory), to deconstruct *destape* films and formulate a new discourse about the representation of sexuality. Both the plot and the script of the film are indebted to various sources, but the connection with the literary work *Lettres Portugaises* – the famous letters written or translated into French to be read in the salons of Paris (Alcoforado, 1669) – is obvious. The authorship of these letters has been debated for more than three hundred years; it isn't clear if they were really written by the Portuguese nun Mariana Alcoforado, if the text was written originally in French or Portuguese, or if a man called Gabriel de Guillerages made up a translation, as the writer and researcher Carmen Martín Gaite believes was the case.

> Is there a woman in love out there who hasn't written or at least wished to write "a Portuguese letter"? What usually happens, though, is that she will tear it up after writing it, or keep it and not send it. And if Guilleragues guessed that, he guessed a great deal. Because he understood, simultaneously, that his invention was likely to make many anonymous authors of love letters feel quite specifically identified (Martín Gaite, 2000:31).

There is abundant debate among researchers about the text's anonymity and authorship. From the 1950s onwards the general consensus agreed upon was that Guillerages was its author (Spitzer, 1954). Spitzer couldn't have imagined that Guillerages would become a mere footnote to a text that didn't need an author and would receive multiple interpretations in the course of its life.

More relevant than the real authorship of *Lettres Portugaises* is the figure of Mariana Alcoforado, who started off as "an anonymous textual shadow" only to become "a personal identity and a genealogy, both familiar and national, that makes her (…) a nationally representative epitome of femininity, of national identity, in the eyes of the Portuguese" (Klobucka, 2000: 19). The mysterious question of authorship became extremely important with regard to the reception of the book *Novas Cartas Portuguesas* because, "As Três Marias" chose *Lettres Portugaises* (in Andrade's 1969 translation) as a matrix text, precisely because of the symbolic weight of Mariana's figure and the female image that emanated from her: the stereotypical abandoned woman, begging and submissive, alternating between love and hate and articulating a discourse of over-whelming passion for the gentleman – who will reciprocate the passion, but then depart and never return. And it is precisely this relationship of love and devotion, servitude and self-victimization that the three authors in Portugal and the cinematographers Grau & Arquer in Spain will (dis)assemble and re(assemble) three centuries later, stylizing the frontiers and limits of the subject, both in terms of its subject matter and of the language itself.

Lettres Portugaises was a hugely popular text in France during the reign of Luis XIV, the Sun King – a time of great literary and political splendor in the country. Some researchers corroborate the existence of Mariana Alcoforado and insist that the authorship of those letters can be ascribed to the Portuguese nun[3] (Vélez Pareja, 1996). These are, in essence, five love letters gathered together in a volume that was considered to be a masterpiece of the erotic genre. In them, a nun in love writes down her her feelings towards her object of desire: a handsome soldier, the Marchese of Chamilly, who has abandoned her.

Female sexuality: As três Marias

Underlying the subject of these letters and their literary and cinemato-graphic representations is the concern with the control of female sexual impulses. Many religions, even today, repress sexual freedom with strict rules. The afore-mentioned canonical title awoke the imaginations of many creative people in its own epoch, and continues to do so to this day, inviting artists to recreate it in various ways.

In Portugal, in 1971, in the midst of Salazar's dictatorship, Maria Isabel Barreno, Maria Teresa Horta and Maria Velho da Costa, three intellectuals, wrote and co-published the volume *Novas Cartas Portuguesas*. The book was a playful collection featuring works in various literary genres. The works are principally epistolary, but there are also poems and short stories, and all surround the figure of the nun Mariana Alcoforado. In April 1972, the book was published with the support of Estudios Cor and under the literary guidance of Natalia Correia, who, despite being under enormous pressure to censor parts of the book, published it whole. The story surrounding its publication and first reception was echoed in media outlets of the time. The first edition was confiscated and destroyed by the censors of Marcello Caetano's government three days after it hit the shelves; a judiciary process was opened against the three authors because the content of the book was deemed "pornographic and an attack on public morality." The trial opened on October 25th 1973 and after a series of incidents, and following the April 1974 Revolution, never came to take place. The Spanish translation did not become available until 1975.

> Em voz uníssona (em falas que se embaralham na scrita, sem se identi-ficarem individualmente), as "três marías" investem contra todos os valores consagrados pela dição (a pureza, o interdito ao sexo, o horror ao corpo, a proibição do aborto, o silêncio sobre o prazer do sexo, etc.), expressando a grande crise ético-existencial que vem do início do século e recrudesce neste limiar do 3° Milênio. Crise, em cujo bojo, sem dúvida, está se forjando uma "nova mulher", ressentida pelas "três Marias", mas ainda oculta em interrogações agônicas.
>
> Colônia do homem, a mulher? ... se a mulher nada tem, se existe só através do, se mesmo seu prazer por aí é pouco e viciado, o que arrisca ou que perde em revoltar-se? [...] Só de nostalgias faremos uma irmandade e um convento, Sóror Mariana cinco cartas. Só de vinganças, faremos um Outubro, um Maio e novo mês para cobrir o calendário. E de nós, o que faremos?" (Novaes-Coelho, 1999: 120).

Book censorship in Portugal wasn't commonly exerted, but it came down quickly on any perceived challenge, so the book was removed from circulation and the three authors, together with their editor, were prosecuted for offences against public morality. Feminine eroticism was thus considered pornographic.

The case became more popular abroad than in Portugal and international pressure, as well as the advent of the Carnation Revolution in April 1974, rehabilitated the authors. *Novas Cartas Portuguesas* is a literary game in line with the experimental tendencies prevalent at the time in which it was written, the early seventies, and the game is not limited to the mixed genres, or to the reference to a previous work from which characters and situations are derived. The game is mainly in the language itself. "As Três Marias" are three female intellectuals writing epistolary prose in late 17th century mode, mixing it with satirical and humorous poetry, with explicitly erotic descriptions, avant-garde fragments, and great doses of irony and humour. Leaving aside the fact that some parts are better than others, this is a valuable book, an incredibly daring one for its time, and a subject of study in academic circles. Moreover, a new annotated edition of *Novas Cartas Portuguesas* has recently been published, the fruit of research carried out by the Margarida Losa Comparative Literature Institute at the Faculty of Letters of the Universidad de Oporto.[4]

Film analysis

In their film, Grau and Arquer seem to be saying that there is no future for a woman who tries to be free or think differently, something applicable to the clerical society of the 17th century, and this in turn could be understood as a call to female rebellion, a call for feminism to be understood as unfinished business for 20th century Spanish society. In this sense, Grau and Arquer's proposal is a cinematographic retelling of *Lettres Portugaises*, written a few years after the literary version penned by "the three Marias," *Novas cartas portuguesas* (Barreno, Velho da Costa et al., 1972). Both Grau and Arquer and "the three Marias" revisited the key 17th century text that is *Lettres Portugaises*. On the one hand, this was because of the symbolic value ascribed to Mariana herself. On the other, it was because of the female image that emerged from her: the stereotype of the abandoned woman, begging and submissive, alternating adoration with hatred and practising a discourse of overwhelming passion for the man (the gentleman/chaplain), who will initially

reciprocate the passion, but will then leave, never to return. It is this relationship of love and devotion, of servitude and self-victimization which
the three Portuguese intellectuals, Barreno, Horta and Velho da Costa,
and the Catalan couple Grau and Arquer would deconstruct and reconstruct three centuries later, pushing both the subjects addressed and the
language used (be it literary or cinematographic) to their limits.

Another cinematographic version of *Lettres Portugaises* was made in
parallel, around the same time, by the Spanish cinematographer Jess
Franco, which could be placed in the category of *nunsploitation*. Jess
Franco's version only resembles Grau's in that they both take place in a
nunnery. In Jess Franco's version the female protagonist is a young,
innocent girl forced to live in a convent were Satanism and sado-
masochism reign against her will. It is not a *destape* film, but a pornographic, violent film that received an "S" rating in Spain. Franco had a
generous budget, a team of German technicians and German, Italian
and Portuguese creative directors. This movie had problems being
shown in Spain because its main actress, who played the young nun,
Susan Hemingway, was under age. Franco was the director of this piece,
entitled *Cartas de amor de una monja portuguesa*, and wrote the script
with his producer, Erwin C. Dietrich (who wrote under the pen name
Manfred Gregor) and the dialogue expert Christine Lembach.

Cartas de amor de un monja portuguesa was filmed in Switzerland
and Portugal and premiered in Spain in 1978, the same year as Grau's
film of a similar title: Cartas de amor de una monja. The original
German title of Jess Franco's film was Die Liebesbriefe einer portugiesis-
chen Nonne, but it appeared under other titles for its distribution in the
international market. In this context, José Frade, producer of a great
number of destape genre movies, trusted that director Jordi Grau would
film Cartas de amor de una monja (1978) turning the sexual voltage up a
notch from his previous films, El secreto inconfesable de un chico bien,
La trastienda and La siesta:

> Then I proposed a script that I had written with Gemma to him, it was
> called *El Examen*. He wanted to do a sentimental thing and I objected.
> Then I put to him that we should do *Cartas de amor de una monja*, with
> Gemma, and he accepted, because I told him it's based on a famous
> erotic book. […] Frade thought that I was going to make a practically
> pornographic movie, but the truth is that it's a film that shows a lot of

respect for religious feeling, for religious heterodoxy. It didn't go down well because in 1977, politically, the vibe was very right-wing and anti-church too. Right-wingers thought it was blasphemous and left-wingers thought it was too soft. But it's a film I like, and there it is (Grau Solá and Gabantxo Uriagereka 2004).

The adaptation of a canonical literary text to 1978 cinema

It is important to reflect on the identity of the co-scriptwriter of this film: she is Jordi Grau's wife, the Catalan actress and writer Gemma Arquer, who on occasion signed her work as Gemma Grau. Although through-out her husband's cinematographic career she took part in many of the other laborious aspects involved in the creative process of making movies, this is the only time that she shared a scriptwriting credit with him. They both knew of the relevance of the canonical title *Lettres Portugaises* (de Andrade, 1969)[5] and also knew of the scandalous *Novas Cartas Portuguesas* (Amaral, Barreno et al., 2010).[6] It is evident that both the original text and the experimental version by "as tres Marías" are worthy of respect and that Arquer and Grau had no intention of treating the said texts in a vulgar way in order to write their script; additionally, they were brought up Christians (they both belonged to Catholic parish groups in their youth) and felt an inherent respect toward religious feeling.

It is interesting to pause to consider Gemma Arquer's role, because the original text was supposedly written by a woman and dealt with female sexual desire. Even in the 17th century, *Cartas portuguesas* was a subversive book; in the first place, because it was written by a woman at a time when most women did not write, indeed could not write; and secondly, because the woman who wrote it was a religious woman who supposedly felt no sexual desire. Therefore, the literary text was doubly subversive and in this sense the film is too, because a parallelism was established. It is as if the text had an internal force that was in essence female and subversive, while existing in the context of a patriarchal system into which Grau's film was also inscribed in 1978.

Undoubtedly the epistolary form – I once wrote – must have been the first and most suitable of literary expressions for women. The person to whom I most like to speak about the tribulations of the soul is the person responsible for those tribulations, who supposedly is interested in receiving a reply that is more elaborate than a rejection or a sharp amen. But if the ideal receptor of the message disappears or has never existed, the need for interlocution, for trust, drives us to invent him. Or, in other words, it is the passionate search for the "you," that connecting thread of female discourse (Martín Gaite, 2000).

Following that idea, it could be said that Grau and Arquer in this film tried to go beyond mere *destape* with sex scenes that were rather daring in tone. What underlay those images was a whole declaration of principles against the banalisation of sex; in other words, against the *destape* genre. It was also a very harsh critique of the church and of the denial of the body and sexual desire by some religious orders, who zap the life out of women like Mariana or the adolescent novice nun burnt at the stake by the Inquisition as a punishment for her sexual awakening. It is fitting to underline at this point that using the 17th century to explain these ideas serves as a safety shield for Arquer and Grau, in that the viewers are free to interpret whether the situations portrayed are similar to the reality of 1978 Spain. Consequently, the movie could also be seen as a criticism of the patriarchal, Catholic-repressive system internalised by large swathes of Spanish society in 1978. As can be observed, the film is subversive at various levels.

Novas Cartas Portuguesas, the breakthrough text by María Isabel Barreno, María Teresa Horta and María Velho da Costa, written in 1971, offered important aesthetic and feminist readings that were recognised beyond the frontiers of Portugal. The text, hybrid in character, played with the canonical 17th century text *Lettres Portugaises* to create a new discourse about female representation, subjectivity and desire in 1970s Portugal. Unsurprisingly, news of the scandal reached the neighbouring country, Spain, where the Catalan couple of artists Jordi Grau and Gemma Arquer, deconstructed the said literary text to create a film about absolute love, a film that was no less scandalous than the book, and showed that parallel discourses were taking place among Portuguese and Spanish intellectuals in the 1970s, at a time of openings after the dark years of the dictatorships in both countries.

Notes

1 Translated by Amaia Gabantxo.
2 *Destape* literally means "uncovering"; *destape films* were a genre of their own in the

Spanish cinema of the 1970s, and a very successful commercial sub-genre at that. They showed naked women on film and addressed sexual issues for the first time (although sex acts were not shown). They were a rection to Francoist ideology and censorship, and a sign of the newly found freedom that followed the dictator's death. (Translator's note)

3   For this purpose, Ignacio Vélez-Pareja consulted the fifty-six titles associated with the letters or their translations kept at the Library of Congress of the United States, as well as the seventy-three copies of this work at Harvard University (among them were translations into German, French, Hebrew, Dutch, English, Italian, Portuguese, Finnish and Russian), until he found a 1888 text of great importance for the culmination of this historic-literary work: *Soror Mariana, a freira portugesa* (Cordeiro, 1891).

4   Universidad de Oporto, "Novas Cartas Portuguesas Três Décadas Depois" project. [Horta, M.T., Barreno, M.I. y Velho da Costa, M. (2010). *Novas cartas portuguesas – Ediçao anotada*. Lisboa: Ana Luísa Amaral ed., Publicaçoes Dom Quixote].

5   Of the many versions of the 17th century literary text *Lettres portugaises*, it is believed that one penned by the Portuguese erudite Eugénio de Andrade, translated from the French, is most accurate.

6   The last edition is from 2010, and includes a commentary by the authors themselves about the *Novas cartas portuguesas* from 1971, which Marcello Caetano's dictatorship removed from Portugal's bookshosps.

Works Cited

Alcoforado, M. (1669). *Lettres d'amour d'une Religieuse portugaise* (1ª ed.). París: Barbin, Claude.

Alcoforado, M. (1969). *Cartas portuguesas.* [*Lettres portugaises*] (E. de Andrade Trans.). Lisboa: Assirio & Alvim.

Amaral, A. L., Barreno, M. I., Horta, M. T., & Velho da Costa, M. (Eds.). (2010). *Novas cartas portuguesas – Ediçao anotada* (1972ª ed.). Lisboa: Publicaçoes Dom Quixote e autoras.

Barreno, M. I., Horta, M. T., & Velho da Costa, M. (1974). *Novas cartas portuguesas* (2ª ed.). Lisboa: Futura.

Barreno, M. I., Velho da Costa, M., & Horta, M. T. (1972). *Novas cartas portuguesas* (1ª ed.). Lisboa: Cor.

Horta, M.T., Barreno, M.I. y Velho da Costa, M. (2010). *Novas cartas portuguesas – Ediçao anotada*. Lisboa: Ana Luísa Amaral ed., Publicaçoes Dom Quixote.

Klobucka, A. (2000). *The Portuguese nun: formation of a national myth* (1ª ed.). Lewisburg, USA: Bucknell University Press.

Martín Gaite, C. (Ed.). (2000). *Lettres portugaises/ Cartas de amor de la monja portuguesa Mariana Alcoforado [Lettres portugaises]* (C. Martín Gaite Trans.). (1716 ed.). Barcelona: Círculo de Lectores.

Minteguia Arregui, I. "La evolución del ejercicio de la censura cinematográfica durante el régimen Franquista", p.10, *El Aula de Cristal*, Universidad de León. <www3.unileon.es/dp/ade/minteguia.pdf> (visited 02/01/2013)

Novaes-Coelho, N. (1999). *O discurso-em-crise na literatura feminina portuguesa*. Via Atlântica, 1(1), 120-128.

Spitzer, L. (1954). "Les Lettres portugaises". *Romanische Forschungen*, 65, 91-135.

Subcomisión-Clasificación (1978), Expediente de clasificación de la película: *Cartas de amor de una monja*, caja 81.285– expediente 280/77, Archivo General de la Administración (AGA), Alcalá de Henares (Madrid).

Vélez Pareja, I. (1996). *El Hábito de la pasión: cartas de amor de Sor Mariana [Alcoforado]*. Santa Fe de Bogotá: Altamir, Ediciones-Centro Editorial Javeriano (Ceja).

Audiovisual resources

Grau Solá, J. (1985). *Cartas de amor de una monja* [VHS]. Madrid: Constan Films.

Grau Solá, J. (2004). *Cartas de amor de una monja* [DVD]. Valladolid: Divisa Home Vídeo.

Grau Solá, J. & Gabantxo-Uriagereka, M. 2004, Interview (raw material from the unpublished thesis Jordi Grau. Cine, amor y muerte), by Miren Gabantxo-Uriagereka, University of the Basque Country, UPV/ EHU, 2012.

Pere Gimferrer and Cinema: Between Hollywood and Iberian Avant-Garde

Lídia Carol Geronès

The aim of this article is to review Pere Gimferrer's theoretical essay written in Spanish, *Cine y literature*, paying special attention to the author's vision on Iberian cinema. The combination of film (image based art) and literature (word based art) is essentially, for Pere Gimferrer, a dual experience. *Cine y literature* is perhaps one of the least studied works of the Barcelonan poet, even though he has already published three different editions.[1] In this re-working process, that has lasted some 30 years, aside from the notorious affection Gimferrer feels towards film, the writer's personal interest emerges as the main idea of the book. Put simply, he tackles the fertile relationship between word and image as manifested in literature and cinema.

Included in his first writings about film one finds reviews of cinematographic adaptations of literary works, which, as will be demonstrated with specific examples, could be considered the preamble of the theoretical themes that will later be developed in *Cine y literatura*. Before publishing poetry, which first appeared after 1963, Pere Gimferrer began issuing film reviews for the magazines *El Ciervo*, *Film Ideal* and the newspaper *Tarrasa Información*.[2] This collaboration remained constant until the end of the sixties, especially with *El Ciervo*. From these first reviews we can recall the negative assessment in the Barcelonan magazine given to *Tom Jones* by Tony Richardson (1963), a film that reflects an:

> autocomplacencia constante, afán gratuito de lucimiento, movimientos de cámara intempestivos e inútiles que impiden ver prácticamente nada con claridad, traición total a Fielding desde el momento en que se parte del falso supuesto de que Tom Jones es un folletín que hay que superar

> inoculándole distanciación crítica. La realidad es que ni el libro de
> Fielding tiene nada que ver con el folletín, ni la cinta de Richardson con
> la distanciación, que por fortuna es algo más que el viejo truco escénico
> de reclamar con guiñones y chistes de almanaque la complicidad del
> público, lo cual justamente le coartara en vez de dejarle en libertad de
> juzgar los acontecimientos propuestos (Gimferrer, "La admirable
> novela de Fielding" 16)

However, the evaluation of Miguel Picazo's big screen adaptation (1964)
of Miguel de Unamuno's novel *La tía Tula* is very positive: "la cinta debe
su importancia [...] a dos razones fundamentales: una puesta en escena
[...] extremadamente escrupulosa, de precisión maníaca y rigor casi
artesanal, y una narración de planos largos [...] que respetan la continuidad de la realidad filmada, sin violentarla mediante rupturas
llamadas a conferirle este o aquel sentido" (Gimferrer, *Sobre La tía
Tula*" 16). Also, within the newspaper *Tarrasa Información* (and the
same year 1965) there are examples, both negative and positive, of this
process of bringing imagery into a literary piece, despite the fact that
Gimferrer focuses his attention on the director's work and never on
specific films. The first positive case is Alexandre Astruc, an "eminencia
gris de 'Cahiers du cinéma' [que] alcanzó rápida celebridad en la raya de
los veinte años con su artículo-manifiesto acerca de la 'cámara-stylo',
donde preconizaba que, en el cine moderno, debía poder escribirse con
la cámara directamente sobre la pantalla como con la pluma sobre el
papel, vale decir concediendo libertad y primacía a la continuidad
espacial por encima de los recursos de montaje. (Gimferrer, "El mundo
de Alexandre Astruc" 7). The negative reviews are those concerning
Richard Brooks' adaptations of *Lord Jim* (1965) by Joseph Conrad and
The Brothers Karamazov (1958) by Fyodor Dostoyevsky because,
according to Gimferrer:

> Lord Jim resulta tan insuficiente con relación al mundo de Conrad
> como *Los hermanos Karamazov* lo fue respecto a Dostoievski. No le
> pido a Brooks que ilustre una tradición literaria; sí creo legítimo
> exigirle, en cambio, que no se le escape lamentablemente de entre las
> manos cuanto de mágico, misterioso y poético encierra el espíritu de
> Conrad. [...] En suma: se ignora a Conrad como se ignoró a
> Dostoievski. (Gimferrer "Presencia de Richards Brooks" 7)

Following the publication of the last edition of *Cine y literatura*,
Gimferrer commented on this primary passion for cinema: "Empecé a

leer 'Cahiers du Cinema' a los 14 años cuando me la prestó un amigo. He seguido con ese interés, aunque vi que no podía ser director o guionista" (Fernández, 2012). In the light of this remark, we can affirm that before dedicating himself to literature, Gimferrer aspired to have a career in the world of film. In fact, at the inaugural conference "Literatura i cinema" (1990) at the Sabadell Film Club, he recalled how from the immediate post-war until 1968 some generations (which include film makers like Godard and Truffaut or Antonioni and Pasolini) have been the latest generations of artists to vacillate between choosing the literary career or being a film director. He was aware of a double interest among many filmmakers:

> Si bé hi ha alguna excepció in les generacions anteriors –Eisenstein, per exemple, un intel·lectual amb una formació molt variada-, la majoria dels realitzadors, els grans clàssics del cinema, no eren gent de gran cultura humanística. Fritz Lang, posem per cas, que era un home molt intel·ligent, arquitecte i escultor, i un gran director, no tenia una gran cultura literària. [...] Em fa l'efecte, en tot cas, que els primers intel·lectuals del món del cinema que, en general, dubten entre cinema i literatura són els de la generació de Godard –o els d'una mica abans, Rossellini i Antonioni-, fins a la de Bertolucci. (Gimferrer, 1997: 345)

Such passion on the part of the author for the two arts comes from a very young Gimferrer, and it is most likely the reason why the result of *Cine y literatura* is not just an objective history of cinema, but a very personal theoretical essay about the art of a poet who loves that art. In fact, if the writer's position in his theoretical analysis is analysed in detail, we can confirm finding a deliberate subjectivity that is not new, but rather a common trait in most of Gimferrer's essays, from *La poesia de J.V. Foix* (1974) to *Valències* (1993), including *Lecturas de Octavio Paz* (1983) and *Les arrels de Miró* (1993), to mention just a few. As Enric Bou points out, "molts dels seus escrits assagístics [...] en espanyol [o en català] tenen una relació de deute, crònica de lectures, homenatge a escriptors i artistes que li són significatius. L'assaig esdevé el negatiu que explica el positiu de l'obra de creació estricta" (Bou, 1997:7).

If we wished to follow a chronological order leading up to *Cine y literatura*, even though the first edition dates back to 1985 we would have to acknowledge that the appendix "Cine y surrealismo" was written much earlier, in 1965. In those years Gimferrer did not just go to film clubs or to the cinematheques and wrote film and book reviews for the magazines previously mentioned; he was also very familiar with the avant-garde group *Dau al set*.[3] It is in this context that the brief essay "Cine y surrealismo" was written, and Gimferrer decided to add it to the second edition of *Cine y literatura*. As the title implies, the essay aims concisely to trace the relationship between cinematographic art and surrealism. Thanks to this essential bond between the art of words and the art of images in movement we can understand why "Cine y surrealismo" precedes the theoretical work found in *Cine y literatura*.

Cine y literatura revolves around a simple yet radical thesis. Despite the evident formal differences, films are recorded and constructed with real elements from reality. Literature, on the other hand, can omit certain parts of reality in its process of creating stories by using a completely arbitrary selection process. The two arts do have, in fact, a point in common: to tell or narrate a story, to present certain actions, to develop a plot. According to Gimferrer, at a very precise moment in cinema's history, with the developments in film technique (thanks to the American filmmaker D. W. Griffith), cinema was no longer limited to narrating a story in theatrical style but was able to present a series of actions, and the composition of what is represented by the actors (exactly as the novel worked, primarily in the 19th century), as composed of a sequence of actions in the form of a written narrative. In other words, with the birth of filmmaking technique, following Griffith, both literature and cinema tried to follow the same trend: telling something through words or moving images. This is the main argument in the essay *Cine y literatura* that Gimferrer analyses from four different perspectives that correspond to the four chapters of the book.

In the first chapter, "Lenguaje literario y lenguaje cinematográfico", the author, using different examples from history of cinema and literature, tries to highlight (as he had already expressed in "Cine y surrealismo") the practical differences between the novel and cinema, but, above all else, he identifies the common denominator shared by the two regarding their overall objective: telling a story. With the passing of time, some aspects of this story may well have changed, both in cinema and literature alike, but, at base, the common starting point of both is the same. Both involve the composition of a story. From the narrative language point of view, cinema has only seen two time periods: one before Griffith and another after him. The second follows the modules of the 19th century narrative, which is none other than the development of one of the exploration routes proposed by Cervantes; namely, telling a story scene by scene.

In the second chapter, "De la novela al cine", Gimferrer focuses his attention on the cinematographic adaptations, suggesting, just as he did in his reviews during the sixties, some criteria for better understanding and judging (as well as creating) the cinematographic adaptation of a (great) novel. The history of the cinematographic adaptations of famous novels provides an eloquent indication of sterile loyalties and infidelities – and yet traditions – that are still fertile. In fact, the relationships between novels and adaptations to film should be primarily discussed not on the basis of the similarities in the language used, but instead on the similarities in the aesthetic result obtained.

In the third chapter, "Teatro y cine", again based on different examples that illustrate his thesis, the Catalan poet discusses the distance between narration (cinema and literature) and the word (theatre). Expressed in his own words: "el teatro, tal como se venía entendiendo desde los griegos hasta Brecht, por ejemplo, no se halla hoy tanto en los escenarios, […] en las que la palabra desempeña un papel mucho más importante que en cualquier recreación escénica actual" (94).

The original reconstruction that Gimferrer develops throughout these three first chapters discussing the ancient relationship between the arts is brought to a close in the fourth and final chapter with an elegant elegy for a genre that is as timeless as it is necessary: the screenplay. If the screenplay is true evidence of the written link between the language of cinema and the language of literary narratives, Gimferrer stresses the need not to refute but to reinforce his earlier thesis that, although it is usually based on a written text, in the end it is solely the film that has to be evaluated, appreciated, and even, in some cases, loved. Cinema, understood as the final product, the fruit of an intention to tell, narrate, or express something, is, as Gimferrer suggests, as compelling as poetry when it lives through what it is able to convey and transmit.

When we direct our attention to the changes between the first and second editions of *Cine y literatura* we notice that, as far as content is concerned, the essence of the text is essentially the same. There are no radical changes, aside from, on the one hand, the addition of the appendix "Cine y surrealismo" as we have mentioned above (which is a 1965 text), and, on the other, the removal of the photographs with their corresponding commentaries or notes whose function was concisely to repeat what the text affirms. We do not know what the motives were that led to such a decision. It could simply have been due to the copyright costs of the images or legal concerns involving their reproduction but, in any case, they do not change the substance of the book. Gimferrer shows more examples of films that further elaborate the ideas argued in the text. For example, in the last chapter, when he discusses the relationship between the film's original script and its effective production, he states that "el guión es también a su modo, un género literario y si se descarta que el film vaya a existir adquirirá una extraña y desazonadora autonomía," whereas in the first edition we read: "no parece probable que nadie filme nunca el guión de Federico García Lorca, *Viaje a la luna*, o el guion de Juan Larrea y Luís Buñuel *Ilegible hijo de flauta*, o el guión de Salvador Dalí *Babaouo* o el guión de Carl Theodor Dreyer sobre la vida de Jesucristo que el gran cineasta danés no pudo nunca rodar" (1985: 143). In the second edition he rewrites this fragment in the following way: "Se ha filmado el guión de Federico García Lorca Viaje a la luna pero no lo ha hecho un cineasta profesional sino un pintor (Frederic Amat en 1998) y parece poco probable que alguien filme el guion de Juan Larrea y Luís Buñuel Ilegible hijo de flauta, o el proyecto de Vicente Huidobro, Cagliostro, publicado en libro, o el guión de Carl Theodor Dreyer sobre la vida de Jesucristo que el gran cineasta danés no pudo nunca rodar" (1999: 141). It its clear that Gimferrer essentially updated the situation in relation to the production of films from some artists' screenplays. In the third editions this fragment also changes. Interestingly enough, the part about Dalí is removed, and even more surprisingly, it is not mentioned (even though Gimferrer could have known) that Manuel Cussó-Ferrer brought this screenplay, written by the surrealist painter from Ampordà, to the big screen in 2000. The additions made between the first and second editions are generally similar. Nonetheless, two film directors stand out: Kenji Mizoguchi and Manoel de Oliveira.

Gimferrer has consistently shown a special sensitivity and keen interest in the Japanese director since his beginnings as a writer, as can be noted in his 1965 *El Ciervo* article "Mizoguchi en la filmoteca".

Amongst the rich, personal compilation that Gimferrer makes of the films of the great directors in his magazine reviews, the name of Mizoguchi is prominent. The director becomes an exemplary figure together with only a few others like Carl Theodor Dreyer, Raoul Walsh or John Ford in creating films that did not aspire to reveal the beauty of everyday life, but instead wanted to evoke the subliminal hidden sense behind existence, "descubrir nuestro secreto esencial mediante la aprehensión de las apariencias" (Gimferrer, "Mizoguchi" 16). This special affinity with the Japanese recording style was recently reflected in four poems, similar to Haikus, that Gimferrer dedicated to the Japanese filmmaker in his last compilation of poetry written in Catalan, *El diamant dins l'aigua* (2001).

Regarding Oliveira, and following the case of Iberian cinema, Gimferrer refers to his films as perfect examples of indirect and therefore very good adaptations of literary works. As Gimferrer wrote in the second edition, "el trabajo de Oliveira es muy vario y complejo: pero en él destaca siempre la preponderancia del plano fijo como unidad [...] frente al movimiento de cámara, reducido al mínimo indispensable" (50) which enabled him to create, paradoxically, some indirect literary adaptations that are more faithful than others that overtly refer to a specific novel. "Por ejemplo [...] en *A divina comedia* (1991) [...] es, en el fondo, una inteligente, libérrima y estilizadísima adaptación de *Crimen y castigo*, escenificada por los reclusos de un manicomio y trambin en *El valle Abraham* (1993) se inspira en *Madame Bovary*, pero retiene de ella solo los nomres de pila de los protagonistas, alguna situación y – a modo de contraseña – hace aparecer en la pantalla a la heroína leyendo el libro de Flaubert en una secuencia" (60).

The main addition to the recent third edition is a list of one hundred and twenty five films that Gimferrer selected as being "a mi juicio representativas de la historia ecléctica del cine que este libro no pretende ser, pero que sí puede apuntar o sugerir" (7), limiting himself to one film per director. He is also aware of recent developments in film, particularly the impact of digital media, which allows lower production costs, and the possibility of continued creative production: "el coste menor de filmar en digital producciones baratas permite rodajes muy largos con diálogos total o parcialmente improvisados por actores no profesionales: tal es el caso de Pedro Costa [...] o de Albert Serra [...] y el fenómeno no ha hecho más que empezar" (140). In addition, and without moving further from the last chapter of the book, Gimferrer points out a possible antithesis between classic cinema (capable of excellent results even basing itself strictly on a written script) and the *other* cinema, that which improvises without a script, or, if does stem from one, completely alters it.

In conclusion, in *Cine y literatura* Gimferrer underlines the bold idea that there is an intimate link between the narrative structures of cinema and the novel. Such a connection emerges thanks to Griffith movies, re-adapting to the screen the style of 19th century novels. However, following this reconstruction of the history of cinema (albeit in an indirect fashion) Gimferrer suggests the possibility of taking a different path from the one begun by Griffith, by denying and altering it, continuing the path initiated by Méliès. Through this unusual and unconventional path, Gimferrer demonstrates particular attention towards Iberian cinema of the past, suggesting that authors such as Buñuel, with his surrealistic cinema, Portabella, with his poetic anachronisms, Serra, with his lengthy improvisation plans, and Oliveira, with his films made with words that create the action, have managed to keep another cinematographic tradition alive. *Cine y literaura* outlines the specific elements of cinematographic language, and tries to explain how ideas and concepts stemming from different disciplines are reformulated in cinema. As is well known, the French philosopher Deleuze in his seminal books *Time-image* and *The Movement-image* tries to find, within the history of cinema, concepts that pertain to philosophy (specifically the anti-Cartesian philosophy of Bergson) or those which pertain to the post-Copernicus sciences. Gimferrer, adopting a similar attitude to that of Deleuze, points out how many concepts, ideas, and artistic practices in film, with its limited visual language, were taken from the intrinsically verbal language of literature, a language that cannot show on a physical level but simply suggests by evoking an imagined reality. To understand the aim of Giferrer's *Cine y Literatura* we should recall the words of the French philosopher who, in an interview given to the writers of *Cahiers du Cinema* (and found in number 357, March 1987), explains the possible relationship between philosophy and cinema in the following way: "The encounter of two disciplines happens not when one begins to reflect on the other, but when one [discipline] is convinced of having to solve a problem, on their own and with their own resources, that is similar to a problem that also arises in the other [discipline]." (Deleuze, 2002:120). It appears that Gimferrer also positions himself along this line, finding precisely in the area of cinematographic adaptations a specific instance where the two arts can face the same problem. In this sense, the cinematographic adaptations of novels serve, most importantly, to underline the close bond between these two languages that, ostensibly, seem so distant.

Notes

1   First edition: *Cine y literatura*, Editorial Planeta, Barcelona, 1985; second edition: *Cine y literatura*, Seix Barral, Barcelona, 1999 and third edition: *Cine y literatura*, Austral, Barcelona, 2012.

2   It should be noted that it is before 1962, the poem book Malienus, but it was published in 1988 by the Editorial Visor de Madrid, who compiled his Castilian poetic work (1962-1969).

3   "Antes del comienzo estricto de su colaboración, el poeta [Brossa] y Portabella formaban parte, junto con el escritor Pere Gimferrer, el fotógrafo Leopoldo Pomés, los músicos Mestres Quadreny y Carlos Santos […] de un cenáculo que organizaba sugestivas sesiones cinematográficas en casa del pintor Tàpies" (Riembau-Torreiro 75).

Works Cited

Bou, Enric "Pere Gimferrer: una poètica en acció" *Obra Catalana Completa. Assaigs crítics* 5, Barcelona: Edicions 62, 1997. 5-14.

Deleuze, Gilles *Divenire molteciple. Nietzche, Foucault ed altri intercessori* Verona: Ombre corte, 2002.

Fernández, Víctor "Entrevista a Pere Gimferrer" *La Razón*. Web. 7 June 2012.

Gimferrer, Pere "Mizoguchi en la filmoteca", *El Ciervo* 132 February 1965: 16.

– "La admirable novela de Fielding, saboteada por Osborne y Richardson en aras del free cinema", *El Ciervo* 133 March 1965: 16.

– "Sobre La tía Tula", *El Ciervo* 134 April 1965: 16.

– "Traducción de Foc al Càntir de Joan Brossa, *Papeles de Son Armadans*, 109 April 1965. 88-95.

– "El mundo de Alexandre Astruc", *Tarrasa Información* 25 November 1965: 7.

– "Presencia de Richards Brooks", *Tarrasa Información* 29 December 1965: 7.

– "Cine fantástico y terrorífico" E*l cine, la enciclopedia del séptimo arte*, 3, Barcelona: Buru Lan S.A. de Ediciones, 1973. 1-92.

– *Cine y literatura*. 1rst ed. Barcelona: Editorial Planeta, 1985.

– "Literatura i cinema" *Obra Catalana Completa. Assaigs crítics* 5, Barcelona: Edicions 62, 1997. 340-360.

– *Cine y literatura*. 2nd ed. Barcelona: Seix Barral, 1999.

– *Cine y literatura*. 3rd ed. Barcelona: Austral, 2012.

Riembau, Esteve and Torreiro, Casimiro, *La Escuela de Barcelona: el cine de la «gauche divine»*, Barcelona: Anagrama, 1999. Print.

PART III

NATIONAL IDENTITIES TELEVISION AND STAGE

Impossible sutures: Loss, mourning, and the uses of Catalonia's immigrant past in TV3's *La Mari*[1]

Josep-Anton Fernàndez

Few issues in Catalan culture are as contentious and pregnant with contested meanings as immigration. This is partly because the antagonisms related to immigration have a triple temporal dimension: the past, in that the narratives of 20th-century migratory processes and their legacy are a stake in symbolic struggles; the present, with regards to discourses, representations, and policies dealing with recent waves of immigration; and the future, insofar as both immigration and immigrants are important elements in the formulation of competing projects for Catalan society within the current phase of the conflict between Catalonia and Spain. The complexity of this issue is compounded by the scarcity of representations, both literary and audio-visual, of Spanish-speaking immigration within Catalan culture.

Indeed, as authors like Salvador Cardús have argued, one striking characteristic of Catalan culture is the paradox of enjoying an extremely rich migratory history that contrasts with a hard-to-explain poverty of representations ("The Memory of Immigration in Catalan Nationalism").[2] In contrast with Spain, Catalonia has been a net importer of population for centuries, as geographer Marc Aureli Vila and historians Josep Termes and Martí Marín Corbera have shown. Demographer Anna Cabré has famously argued that without the migratory waves of the 20th century, Catalonia would have fewer than two and a half million inhabitants, instead of the seven and a half million it has now (26). Immigration in Catalonia, says Cabré, is a process that begins in the context of industrialisation with a very early reduction of the birth rate and a crisis in the traditional system of patrimonial transmission (the *hereu* in Catalan, the *mayorazgo* in Spanish) (211-14). Starting with migrations from Catalan rural areas to urban and industrial areas, the attraction of a quickly developing Catalonia then extended beyond its own borders (Cabré 215-16). In 1930, 27% of the Catalan population was born outside Catalonia, a percentage larger than that of Argentina (Cabré 183, 178). After the great immigration wave of the 1950s to 1970s, Catalonia experienced an enormous demographic transformation, to the extent that by the end of the 20th century only 25% of Catalans had four grandparents born in Catalonia, or to put it another way, 75% of Catalans had a migrant origin (Cabré 164). At the start of the 21st century, there has been another wave of immigration, this time from outside Spain, in which over a million people have settled in Catalonia. The proportions of this latest wave are equally massive: if in 2001 the percentage of foreign registered residents was 4.05% of the population, in 2010 it had jumped to 15.95% (Idescat). Clearly, immigration is one of the most important aspects of Catalonia's social and cultural history, and it could be claimed that it is the true "fet diferencial de Catalunya", the one element that singles Catalonia out as a different nation within Europe. (How many cases exist in Europe with this demographic makeup, yet have managed to preserve a subordinated language and a sense of being a distinct society, in the absence of its own state?)

Yet strikingly, as I claimed earlier, representations of Spanish immigration are few and far between in Catalan culture or, if you prefer, in Catalan-identified cultural production. True, there is Francesc Candel's *Els altres catalans*, Montserrat Roig's *L'òpera quotidiana*, Maria Barbal's *Carrer Bolívia*,[3] and two classic films, Rovira Beleta's *Los Tarantos* and Josep Maria Forn's *La piel quemada*. But these are exceptions to a general trend, and the wave of immigration in the second half of the 20th century remains largely unrepresented. We can thus speak of a phenomenon of relative invisibility of immigration in Catalan culture. For sociologist Salvador Cardús this invisibility is a consequence of the subordinate position of Catalan nationalism, which lacks proper instruments to craft symbolic adherence to the nation, and which has produced a political tradition whose discourses have obeyed a defensive strategy and therefore have emphasized "cultural roots" as a way to preserve identity (Cardús, 2005:41). My own hypothesis is that when this political tradition obtained the instruments of a quasi-nation state, and so-called "cultural normalisation" started being deployed, the categories that defined Catalan identity until the Restoration of the constitutional monarchy experienced a process of fragmentation and redefinition that dissolved the consensus over what being Catalan was (Fernández, 2008:232-45). This exceeded the capacity of the symbolic, rhetorical, pragmatic, and institutional resources available to Catalan society to represent itself, resulting in what we could call a process of national deconstruction (Fernández, 2008:246-50). In this context, the issues of Spanish immigration and Catalan identity became a site of social antagonism, and the Andalusian diaspora particularly the locus of intense political and symbolic competition.[4]

It was not until the end of the 1990s that attempts at the representation of immigration were successfully made, the most important perhaps being Maria Barbal's novel *Carrer Bolívia* (1999). Narrating the history of the experience of immigration is necessary for the cohesiveness of the national community; having the power to do so entails the possibility of building a hegemonic position in the definition of Catalan identity; but this possibility always meets the limits of intense competition from Spanish-language cultural industry and the regulatory power of the Spanish state. Television is a case in point. As Josep Gifreu argued throughout the 1980s and 90s, television had a major role to play in the construction of an "espai català de comunicació" (a Catalan communication space), as the main instrument, both economically and symbolically, in the nation-building project of post-Franco "normalització" (normalisation) (*Comunicació i reconstrucció nacional; El meu país*). But this was, and remains, a project fraught with difficulties arising from the complex position of the Catalan language, a large availability of choice for viewers (mostly in Spanish), and the ongoing conflict between Spanish and Catalan nationalisms.

In this context, the Catalan public broadcaster, Televisió de Catalunya, becomes, in Enric Castelló and Hugh O'Donnell's words "un espacio de conflicto discursivo sobre la identidad" (a space of discursive conflict over identity) (Castelló and O'Donell 2008:178). It is on the basis of this discursive conflict that TVC performs that most problematic of tasks, "la recuperación de la memoria histórica" (the recuperation of historical memory) (*ibid.*) through fiction, comedy, and documentary. In this respect, TVC is what Francisca López calls an "agente historiador" (historical agent) that "contribuye a perfilar y organizar el discurso público sobre el pasado" (contributes to define and organise public discourse about the past) (Castelló and O'Donell 2008:15), responding to "la importancia que tiene – tanto para los productores como para el público – la creación de 'pasados usables' mediante la representación de momentos específicos relevantes para la situación presente" (the importance for both producers and audiences of the creation of "usable pasts" through the representation of specific moments which are relevant for the present) (Castelló and O'Donell 2008:16). However, the creation of "usable pasts" that allows audiences to understand the present and imagine their own future necessarily operates within the uncertainties of both present and future, and the consequences of these uncertainties in political, symbolic, and subjective terms.

A drama series like Televisió de Catalunya's *La Mari* (Jesús Garay, 2003) is an excellent example of the construction of a "usable past" by a public broadcaster in order to negotiate complex social antagonisms. Written by Pau Garsaball, directed by Jesús Garay, and produced by In Vitro Films in alliance with Televisió de Catalunya, Canal Sur, Ràdio Televisió Valenciana, and Televisión de Galicia, *La Mari* presents, in two episodes of 120 minutes, the story of the eponymous character, an Andalusian woman, played by Ana Fernández, who emigrates to Barcelona. The first episode, "Alosno" (the name of Mari's village), starts in 1961 with the death of her husband, which prompts Mari move to the Barcelona district of Verdum. In the convent where she first stays, Mari meets Reme (Ruth Gabriel), a vivacious young Andalusian woman whose liberal morals challenge Mari's strict observance of conventions, and who will become Mari's best friend. She also meets Robles (Juli Mira), a communist militant who will act as Mari's surrogate father, and his wife Amparo (Anna Lizaran)who is traumatized by the death of her son. When Reme dies as a consequence of a backstreet abortion, Mari decides to leave the convent where she was staying because of the cruel reaction of the religious community to Reme's death. She moves in with Robles, starts to work as a cleaner and a maid for an upper-class Catalan-speaking family, and meets Genara (María Galiana), a mother-like figure who will encourage Mari to learn to read and write, and will eventually help her get her own apartment. Mari's teacher at adult school is

Ivan (Carlos Hipólito), a left-wing priest who will become her confidant and who is permanently tortured by his crisis of faith as well as by his impossible love for Mari. Through Genara and Ivan, Mari gets involved in the political and social mobilisations against Franco's regime. The first episode ends in 1966 with Mari finally fulfilling her long-standing desire of bringing her mother and two children to Barcelona.

The second episode, "Poble Sec" (a traditional working-class neighbourhood in Barcelona), starts with the arrival of Mari's mother and children to Barcelona's railway station, and immediately takes us to 1971, with the family settled in Mari's flat in Verdum. Rosa, Mari's mother, has failed to adapt to the new environment, and longs for her village. Meanwhile, Ivan persuades Mari to become a teacher at the adult school, where she meets Enric (Ramon Madaula), a lower-middle class, Catalan nationalist who participates in the resistance against Franco but is ambivalent about the social struggle in the Spanish-speaking working class districts of the city. Their romance develops while Mari becomes more involved with the anti-Franco political struggle, especially after Robles is arrested and tortured. After the death of her mother, Mari and Enric marry and move to Poble Sec. On the same day that Franco dies, Mari announces that she is pregnant. The episode ends with the couple taking their newborn daughter to Mari's village, Alosno.

La Mari was a major success both in Catalonia and in Andalusia. The first episode, broadcast at prime time on TV3 on 4 June 2003, achieved an audience of 771,000 viewers and a share of 31.5%, and the second episode, broadcast the following day, reached 798,000 viewers and a share of 31.1% (Baget Herms). On Canal Sur, the series was shown on 1 and 8 May, and obtained a share of 29% and 21% respectively (Fernández Labayen and Gómez González 236). The series has been re-run on TV3 on a number of occasions, including Christmas Eve 2004 and on May Day 2008, when it reached a share of 13.5%. It was shown once again during the Easter vacation in 2010, as a warm-up for the second season of the series, which brings the action to 1987 (Busquets).

La Mari has achieved an iconic status in the Catalan imagination, having been described as an "epopeya de la gran migración de los 60" (an epic of the great migration of the sixties) (Madueño, "Entrevista a Pau Garsaball"). It is thus unsurprising that this series should have both the power to attract large audiences that seek an effect of recognition in fiction, and the inability to please everybody. While some criticise the series for its "assimilationist" discourse that privileges the figure of the "good immigrant" (Fernández Labayen and Gómez González), others attack its reproduction of the stereotypes of the poor, left-wing, Spanish-speaking immigrant vs. the nationalist, bourgeois Catalan; while some praise its "faithful" depiction of the social reality of immigration under Francoism and the recuperation of the memory of this period, others castigate it for its "sugary", melodramatic tone; finally, its use of Spanish on a Catalan-language channel and its problematic depiction of social uses of language have also been contentious issues.

Clearly it is important to analyse the ideological processes involved in the production of meanings in a series like this. However, such an analysis will be severely limited if it does not take into account what the series might be helping audiences work through. The representation of the loss and mourning involved in the immigrant experience in the 1960s might facilitate a process of working through other losses and mournings in Catalan society at the start of the twenty-first century: a context of rapid social change and new developments in the conflict between Spanish and Catalan nationalisms. If this is the case, what uses of the (immigrant) past is *La Mari* making, and to what effect? What kind of incompleteness or lack, what kind of social antagonism is *La Mari* trying to suture over? If this suture is at once necessary and impossible, how does it fail? What are the effects of its failure?

Television, says John Ellis in his seminal *Seeing Things*, "imbues the present moment with meanings. It offers multiple stories and frameworks of explanation which enable understanding and, in the very multiplicity of those frameworks, it enables its viewers to work through the major public and private concerns of their society" (Ellis, 2000:74). Television, argues Ellis, mediates the viewer's act of witnessing the world, and processes the witnessed material "into more narrativized, explained forms" (Ellis, 2000:78). This process is what Ellis calls "working through", a term borrowed from Freud's essay "Remembering, Repeating, and Working Through". The term refers to the painstaking process in which the patient goes over the material again and again in order to overcome his resistances. According to Ellis, television follows a similar process: "It works over new material for its audiences as a necessary consequence of its position of witness [...] making and remaking meanings and exploring possibilities". Like analysis, television's working through is inconclusive: "It renders familiar, integrates and provides a place for the difficult material that it brings to our witness" (Ellis, 2000:79), but it "comes to no conclusions" (*ibid.*) in a process of "non-totalizing speculation" (Ellis, 2000:80) that tends towards "uncertainty and openness" (Ellis, 2000:82).

If we accept that television operates a process of working through, in cases in which the material that is worked over is a fiction of the past (a past marked by issues of otherness and identification) it becomes necessary to enquire what the resistances involved in the process are, and what repressed content the narrative stands for. This is especially relevant in *La Mari*, a narrative punctuated by loss and mourning, but also by work and politics, and by sexual desire and its dangers. However, determining whose loss, whose mourning, and whose desire it is might not be a straightforward task, as the promotional dossier released by the broadcaster makes apparent. The dossier title reads, *Tu ets part de la seva història* (*You Are a Part of Her Story*). This interpellation seeks to elicit a strong identification on the part of the viewer with a certain story and with a certain history, with a past. Who is this "tu" (you)? In the blurb's description, there is a slippage from the second person to the third: Mari embodies "el coratge de milers de milers de dones que, com ella, van lluitar per obrir-se camí lluny de la seva terra" (the courage of thousands of women who, like her, fought to find their own way far from their homeland); and so, thousands of Catalans "formen part de la seva història" (are a part of their story) (Televisió de Catalunya 1). The inter-pellated "tu" seems to be at once specifically those members of the audience who are former migrants, and generally the entire Catalan audience.

As we will see later this slippage is interesting and valuable, but it signals a discursive gap that needs to be analysed. In order to do so, it might be helpful to take into account two points regarding historical fiction in TV3 and the position of immigration in Catalan cultural discourse. Regarding the first, Enric Castelló and Hugh O'Donnell argue that TV3's historical fictions tend to narrate "una historia popular" (a popular history) (Castelló and O'Donnell, 2009:194), "en minúscula" (in lower-case letters) (Castelló and O'Donnell, 2009:195), due to the impossibility of narrating "una Historia en mayúsculas, basada en los dirigentes y las élites" (a History in capital letters, based on leaders and elites) (Castelló and O'Donnell, 2009:194), since these heroes are no longer perceived as active referents by a majority of society. The gap opened by this narrative impossibility – itself a consequence of "la heterogeneidad de la 'nación'" (the heterogeneity of the "nation") – is compensated by "el discurso de la convivencia e incluso del pactismo" (the discourse of peaceful coexistence and even of pactisme [the Catalan tradition of political compromise in the exercise of power and sovereignty]) in order to achieve an effect of identification (Castelló and O'Donnell, 2009:195). Thus, the gap open at the level of the fiction is sutured over at the level of political discourse.

The second point, regarding immigration, is made by Salvador Cardús: "Fins ara", he says, "més en el discurs que en l'experiència, hem associat immigració a estrangeritat amenaçadora" (until now we have associated, in discourse rather than in actual experience, immigration with a threatening foreignness) (Cardús, 2009:13). The subordination of Catalan culture and nationalism – the same subordination that makes a history of leaders and elites impossible – emphasizes the trope of cultural roots as a defensive reaction, and so immigration is perceived as a threat to the survival of the nation. Immigration, says Cardús, thus becomes "un cos estrany" (*ibid.*), a foreign body that cannot be integrated into Catalan cultural discourse. To put it in more explicit psychoanalytic terms, immigration is an un-symbolised trauma in Catalan culture.

What, then, is being worked through in *La Mari*? How should we understand a narrative like this, so focused on loss and mourning? I think the answer to these questions might be found, firstly, in the way loss and mourning are represented in relation to sexual desire, politics, and work; secondly, in the way language and language uses are presented; and lastly, in the treatment of the metaphor of the roots.

Let us begin with the representation of loss. From the outset, *La Mari* is punctuated by death and separation. The first episode begins with the death of Mari's husband in the highly symbolic space of the village's mines, and subsequently she suffers a double separation from her family and children, and from her familiar landscape: the panoramic shots in the credits sequence show the hills around the village, full of trees and devoid of any human presence, suggesting the loss of a *locus amoenus*, of a paradise. These shots contrast later on with other panoramic shots of the hills around Barcelona where Verdum is located, hills that are filled with poorly built blocks of flats and streets with no sewers. The reality of loss involved in the experience of migration is thus visually conveyed to the audience through a contrasting representation of rural and urban landscapes. However, lack is already inscribed in Mari's original landscape: after the death of her husband, we see a tracking shot following the funeral procession against the background of the mine's gigantic hole.

A more significant loss for the purposes of my argument is perhaps that of Reme, Mari's first friend in Barcelona. Reme, a happy-go-lucky young woman who is ready to enjoy life to the full, guides Mari into the secrets of social and sexual availability. She is therefore an agent of knowledge, but also a subject of naïveté. On the one hand, when Mari expresses her surprise at hearing a language she does not understand, Reme says, "Es catalán, pero no lo habla casi nadie" (it's Catalan, but almost nobody speaks it). On the other hand, she violates moral conventions by having sex with a boyfriend who will persuade her to have a backstreet abortion that will later kill her. In a scene in which both women leave the convent on their way to town, Mari is shown wearing black clothes (the conventional mourning dress), while Reme's outfit corresponds to what the nuns in the convent and Francoist moral codes would consider appropriate. They turn a corner, and Reme, as though peeling off a layer of skin, removes her outfit to reveal other, less modest clothes that mark her sexual availability. She then puts on her earrings, two long metal studs with a red tip. Mari reacts in shock, and Reme jokingly challenges her to finally come out of mourning.

Here we encounter two symbolic elements that will recur throughout the two episodes: mourning dress codes and Reme's earring (the single earring that Mari will manage to keep after Reme's death, and which she will wear at her own wedding, a symbol of her loss). If the latter represents the dangers of *jouissance* and is a painful remnant and reminder of loss, the former becomes a site of tensions, as it both protects and separates Mari from the realisation of sexual desire. Other female characters – her older friend Genara, for example – pressure her to come out of mourning and stop wearing black clothes. These elements suggest that there is a strong tension in *La Mari* between sexual availability, promiscuity, reproduction, and work. The existence of such tension should not come as a surprise: as we know, Freud famously describes mourning as a kind of work in which the subject, confronted with the loss of a loved object, spends large amounts of energy in order to relinquish this object, divesting from a libido that can then be placed in other objects (Freud, 2005:204-5).

This process is vividly dramatized in *La Mari*. Halfway through the first two-hour episode, shortly after Mari decides to wear "normal" clothes again – thus making herself available – death strikes again and takes her father away. After she receives a call from the village with the news of her father's death, we see Mari sitting in the bedroom she is renting from her friends Robles and Amparo. Mari, dressed again in black, has taken a break from packing her suitcase, and is being consoled by her friends and her mentor Genara. She decides not to travel to Alosno for the funeral, and to stay instead in Barcelona in order to work and save money to bring her mother and two children with her. In a medium shot against the background of her sparsely decorated room, Mari delivers a grief-stricken monologue: "Tengo que trabajar, tengo que trabajar mucho, tengo que trabajar, tengo que trabajar mucho, mucho… Traérmelos conmigo, tengo que traérmelos conmigo…" (I've got to work, I've got to work a lot, I've got to work, I've got to work a lot, a lot… Bring them [my mother and children] here with me, I've got to bring them here with me). This is followed by a sequence of shots in which close-ups of Mari's hand, rubbing a cloth with a soap stick or scrubbing the floor of a staircase, alternate with shots of Mari cleaning and close-ups of a hand lighting a candle against the background of a family photograph and effigies of the Virgin Mary, taking a lottery ticket and tearing it. At one point in this sequence – in which each shot dissolves into the next – we see a desk where two hands count money and place some banknotes in an envelope with the name "Alosno" written on it; we then see a close-up of the candle and the religious images, this time accompanied by a folded handkerchief where Reme's earring rests, and a hand placing a new lottery ticket on the mantle. Finally, we return to Mari's hand washing the floor.

The constant repetition in this sequence – both in speech ("I've got to work") and in action (the performance of work and ritual remembrance) – and the rhythm of the non-diegetic music (a flamenco-inspired guitar tune, serious yet uplifting) evoke the process of slowly working through traumas and resistances in psychoanalysis. The dissolving transition between each shot suggests the dissolution of the attachment to Mari's lost objects, and brings to mind Adam Phillips's beautiful definition of mourning as "a process of detachment that releases hidden energies" (Phillips, 1999:132). It is ultimately through work that Mari overcomes the loss of Andalusia and integrates into Catalan society. But this is not a seamless process: as the "cupón de los ciegos" (lottery ticket) she keeps replacing and tearing up, there is an element of contingency at work here.

This element of contingency stems from the emergence of sexual desire, visually suggested in the above sequence by the presence of Reme's earring. There is indeed a narrative pattern in the series in which coming out of mourning marks the irruption of a desire presented as dangerous, be it because it might lead (as with Reme) to unwanted pregnancy and illegitimate reproduction, be it because it leads to deception by dominant males, as is the case of Julio, the *falangista*, wife-beating *alcalde de barrio* (neighbourhood boss) who keeps the local population under control and charms and seduces Mari.

We can thus find in *La Mari* a tension between desire and work, in which desire is associated with availability, expenditure, chaotic promiscuity, the private, and the subjective, whereas work is associated with discipline, investment, orderly reproduction, the public, and the political. This tension will be resolved through education and political involvement: Mari's romance with Enric (played by well-known Catalan actor Ramon Madaula) will be sealed during a political protest, thus rendering possible a synthesis between desire and work (which, as I have pointed out before, is the quintessential Catalan value).

However, the dangers of promiscuity reappear after the work of mourning is done. The left-wing, socially committed priest, Ivan, who will become Mari's mentor, teacher, and confidant, is tortured by his attraction to her. There is of course a limit to promiscuity, and this limit is relevant in the context of immigration, because what is at stake in it is mixing populations and social reproduction. How far should the "integration" of immigrants go, and how should it be carried out? In other words, how promiscuous can Catalan society be vis-à-vis its immigrants, and how should this promiscuity be managed? What is at stake here is the capacity of Catalan society to remain a society open to outside populations while retaining its difference in national and cultural terms; that is to receive migrants without dissolving itself into undifferentiation.

When it was first broadcast, the series elicited a debate about these issues in Catalan society, regarding specifically the wave of immigration that was taking place at the time. *La Mari* thus facilitated a process of working through an enormously complex social concern. But this in turn revealed the existence of another antagonism. In an interview with scriptwriter Pau Garsaball published by *La Vanguardia*, Eugeni Madueño says:

> La Mari refleja el proceso de integración y progresiva incorporación al mundo catalán de los inmigrantes de los 60. ¿Porqué los de ahora han de ser distintos? "La gracia es que al final todos somos un mismo pueblo, que es posible llegar a serlo", dice el guionista. Y añade: "La mitad de los seis millones de catalanes han llegado de fuera, así que por suerte todos somos más hijos de la mezcla que no descendientes directos de Guifré el Pilós". (Madueño, 2003)

Making reference to the Fòrum Universal de les Cultures, held in Barcelona in 2004, Garsaball once again links the migration of the nineteen-sixties with the most recent migratory wave, while turning his protagonist into a Catalan archetype: "El proceso de integración de 'las Maris' no se consigue debatiéndolo en un evento como éste, sino haciéndote amigo de ellas, ayudándolas a encontrar piso y trabajo', dice. Lo extiende a lo que sucede con los nuevos inmigrados" ("The integration process of the 'Maris' isn't best achieved through a debate in an event like this, but rather by befriending them, helping them get accommodation and a job", he says. This also applies, he says, to the situation of new immigrants) (*ibid.*).

In another article, also published around the time the series was broadcast, Madueño refers to how *La Mari* was discussed in the Catalan parliament, and positions himself in the debates about language policy and immigration that were common during that period. Reproducing the false dichotomy between social justice and language policy, Madueño claims: "Primero las personas y luego la cultura. El catalán se ha de exigir en la escuela, y en la calle promoverlo; no imponerlo. Es lo más inteligente para garantizar la convivencia y hasta la conciencia nacional" (People come first, culture comes later. Catalan must be compulsory in school, and it should be promoted, not imposed, in the streets. This is the most intelligent policy in order to guarantee peaceful coexistence, and even national consciousness) (Madueño, 2003). The closure of a gap (the "integración" of the "Maris" into cultural discourse) opens up another gap, related to language policy and the relationship or lack thereof between social and nationalist issues.

The cliché of the "imposition" of the Catalan language rears its ugly head once again thanks to Madueño's article. However, this cliché also prompts us to examine the issue of language in relation to immigration, because of the pivotal role of language in the discourses of Catalan identity. We should not underestimate the pressure that a series like *La Mari* exerts on these discourses as well as on linguistic normalisation policies, considering that it is a series spoken mostly in Spanish and broadcast by a corporation whose statutory role is to contribute to the "normalisation" of the Catalan language. On the other hand, the series features several instances of bilingual conversation that, I would speculate, are aimed at providing models of linguistic behaviour for the audiences; but these occurrences of bilingual conversation violate sociolinguistic norms of the period (that is, a Castilian-speaker must be addressed in Castilian). This, in turn, makes the representation of social reality in *La Mari* less credible.

Yet there is in the series a link between language and subjectivity as well. Indeed, Catalan is for Mari the incomprehensible language of desire, right from her arrival in Barcelona. On her first day at the convent, she is helping in the kitchen and an attractive young man comes in to deliver the bread. He comments in Catalan on how beautiful she is (and therefore, he says, she should not become a nun). These statements baffle Mari because she does not understand a word. Subsequently Mari's lack of understanding, her resistance to Catalan, will be repeated over and over.

Interestingly, it is through a shibboleth that Mari starts to develop a relationship with the Catalan language. In the second half of the first episode, Mari's self-improvement crusade is well under way, and she has joined adult school, where she has learned to read and write. For this, she has had the encouragement of Ivan, the left-wing priest, who has become her friend and confidant. At one point we see them in church,

Ivan behind the confessional's screen, Mari at the other side, modestly dressed and wearing a veil. Rather than listening to Mari's confession, Ivan is helping her with her mathematics homework. The following dialogue takes place between the two, in a series of alternating medium shots of both characters in which Ivan is always seen from the point of view of Mari and shown through the screen of the confessional:

IVAN: Atiendes o no?

MARI: No… Yo he venido a confesarme.

IVAN: Ya estamos otra vez. Pero qué manía de confesarte, Mari. Si no tienes ni tiempo de hacer pecados.

MARI Me viene bien hablar.

IVAN: Para hablar están los bares, los paseos, las casas, pero no los confesionarios.

MARI Aquí es mejor. No me voy a ir contigo a un bar…

IVAN: ¿Por qué no? Además pago yo.

MARI (*laughs*): Cómo se nota que no eres catalán…

IVAN: Uy, ¿quién lo ha dicho? I tant! Para que te enteres, guapa, yo soy de Vic, provincia de Barcelona, tierra de cerdos y de curas.

MARI (*embarrassed*): Contigo no doy una…

IVAN: Mira, hoy vas a tener lo que siempre estás pidiendo. Te vas a llevar tu penitencia por hablar mal de los catalanes.

MARI No… Eso no vale…

IVAN: Repite conmigo. Setze jutges d'un jutjat mengen fetge d'un penjat.

MARI ¿Qué?

Subsequently, Ivan humorously prompts Mari to repeat the tongue-twister bit by bit, while she struggles with the voiced fricatives and affricates that Castilian speakers find difficult to pronounce in Catalan. The penance for Mari's anti-Catalan prejudice is thus to engage with the Catalan language through a shibboleth. A shibboleth is a site of conflict, a linguistic device aimed at policing ethnolinguistic barriers. Like the confessional's screen that separates Ivan from Mari and makes them unavailable to one another, but also mediates the communication between them, a shibboleth is a border, a cut – but also a seam, an edge that in *La Mari* closes the gap between the protagonist and the Catalan language. It is in fact through repetition of the shibboleth that Mari becomes committed to learning Catalan. But the symbolic role of the shibboleth also affects the political sphere. In the second half of the second episode, a lovers' quarrel takes place between Mari and Enric, because she has to cancel the date that was supposed to be the occasion for the consummation of their relationship. Mari has to cancel because she wants to take part in a lock-in in church to demand a trial for her friend Robles, who is in prison. Mari and Enric encounter a fundamental disagreement: she cares about "las personas" (people), while he cares about the Catalan nation, and Mari is at fault, he says, because she does not speak Catalan. At this point she storms out of the bar where the conversation takes place, not before spurting the shibboleth back at Enric. It is therefore through the shibboleth – the cut but also the seam – that the discursive gap between social issues and nationalist issues is laid bare, and therefore open to analysis.

The shibboleth is thus a site of suture. Suture is a concept from Lacanian psychoanalysis that refers to the lack of correspondence between the subject and the Other, that is the symbolic, which prevents the closure of the subject as self-identical, as a full presence. As Jacques-Alain Miller puts it:

> La suture nomme le rapport du sujet à la chaîne de son discours; on verra qu'il y figure comme l'élément qui manque, sous l'espèce d'un tenant-lieu. Car, y manquant, il n'en est pas purement et simplement absent. Suture par extension, le rapport général du manque à la structure dont il est élément, en tant qu'il implique position d'un tenant-lieu. (Miller, 1966:39)

Suture thus designates the relation of the subject to lack – but it also implies a "filling-in" of this lack, the possibility of coherence (Laclau and Mouffe, 1985:88n1). The concept of suture has a long tradition in film studies, but here I am interested in how it has been applied to politics, particularly by Ernesto Laclau and Chantal Mouffe. They describe hegemony as a process in which the openness of the social, determined by "the unfixed character of every signifier", is attempted to be filled in order to achieve social closure (tantamount to a society without antagonisms) (Laclau and Mouffe, 1985:88n1; see also 125-27). But "such closure of the social", the attempt to bridge and ultimately close the gap "between intrasocial differences (elements *within* the social space) and the limit that separates itself from non-society (chaos, utter decadence, dissolution of all social links)" (Žižek, 2001:32), is bound to fail. Like the construction of meaning and the constitution of the subject, this is a process that is at once necessary and impossible.

In *La Mari* we see this process at work at both the subjective and the political levels. Regarding the former, it obviously has to do with the protagonist's relationship with language. She has learnt to read and write through adult literacy classes and, momentously, has been able to send a letter to her children. Finally, at the beginning of the second episode, she is persuaded by Ivan to start teaching at adult school. She starts her first class by teaching her illiterate students how to write her name: "Voy a empezar por escribir mi nombre. Me llamo Mari, como ya sabéis, de María. Así que me cojo una eme, una a, una erre y una i. Así. Ahora lo junto tó y me sale Ma-ri, Mari" (I'll start by writing my name. As you know, my name is Mari, as in María. So I take an em, an a, an ar and an i. Like this. Now I put it all together and I get Ma-ri, Mari). She utters these words to her attentive students as she writes each letter on the blackboard, then connects them with a line, and finally writes her name below; meanwhile Ivan has been watching her performance through the glass in the classroom's door. The scene ends with a medium shot of a confident Mari on the left of the frame, addressing her students, with the blackboard behind her, displaying the letters "m", "a", "r", and "i", and the word "Mari" underneath (significantly, the lines linking each letter that we could see earlier in Ivan's POV shots have now disappeared).

This shot provides us with a visual metaphor of suture as bridging the gap between the arbitrariness of the signifier (the word "Mari") and the subject as the signified (the newly confident Mari standing in front of the blackboard and facing the students, and who now feels in command of language). Suture, however, also operates at the intersubjective and sociopolitical levels. There is a constant visual reference in the series to the impossibility of intimacy: this is shown, for example, in the confessional's screen that separates Ivan and Mari in the scene I discussed earlier (significantly, towards the end of the second episode Ivan confesses his love to Mari, and their hands attempt to touch through this same screen). This impossibility of intimate contact and completeness also affects the social body as such, as we can see in the scene, halfway down the second episode, which shows the exit from the lock-in that has taken place in the local church in protest at the arrest of Robles.

The tension in the neighbourhood is palpable, as the police have gathered outside the church where the protest is being held. After discussing whether to end the lock-in, the protesters decide to come out of the church. In this scene, the sense of confrontation created by the reverse-angle cutting is emphasised by close-up shots of the protesters exiting the church and standing outside the door, strongly contrasting with the long shots of the barrier of anonymous, potentially brutal policemen in grey uniform, holding truncheons. The tension is resolved after an exchange of glances between Ivan and the police commander, as the latter gives a silent sign to his men to let the protesters pass. In a climactic conclusion enhanced by epic-sounding background music, the barrier of policemen opens up, allowing the neighbours to come forward. Finally, we see a tracking shot of the protesters walking towards the left of the frame, past the policemen, until they reach their anxious neighbours who hug and cheer them.

In this scene, it is the Francoist police who separate the social body from itself, but they are also what connects it. It is not by chance that visually this scene is highly reminiscent of Juan Genovés's painting *El abrazo* (1976), which shows the backs of a number of people painted in brown tones opening their arms and rushing to hug their loved ones, against a completely white background, as though floating in the air. I mention this painting because one of the issues being worked through in *La Mari* is, I would argue, the nostalgia for the presumed, lost imaginary completeness of the Catalan political body in the resistance against Francoism, the period we call "resistencialisme". This period was characterised by what Jaume Lorés called "ideologia marc" (framework ideology), an implicit political discourse that, whilst erasing or suturing enormous and fundamental ideological antagonisms, allowed all (democratic) political sides in Catalonia to work together under the unifying principles of Catalan nationalism.[5] This reading is strongly suggested by a dialogue between Mari and Ivan at the end of the series, in which he tells her about his decision to quit the priesthood: "Franco se acaba," says Ivan, "y el clero se acabará con él. El Evangelio dará paso a los convenios colectivos y a los sindicatos. ¿Y sabes lo que temo? Que también eso sea mentira. Que los partidos se llenen de gente sin fe en lo que predican. Como yo." ("Franco is dying, and the clergy is dying with him. The

Gospel will give way to collective bargaining and the trade unions. And do you know what I fear? That this too will be a lie. That the parties will be full of people without faith in what they preach. Like me.")

Finally, to end my analysis of *La Mari*, I wish to look at how this series treats the metaphor of roots. As I mentioned earlier in this essay, Salvador Cardús attributes the difficulties of representing the experience of immigration into Catalan cultural discourse to the emphasis placed by Catalan nationalism on the metaphor of the roots. This emphasis, says Cardús, has to do with the sense of cultural vulnerability that stems from the political subordination of the Catalans, which led them to view the past as a guarantee of continuity of their culture and nation (Cardús, 2009: 8). At the same time, multiculturalist postulates as proposed in Catalonia have established "l'imperatiu moral d'haver de respectar, i fins i tot de preservar, les 'arrels culturals' de les persones que havien migrat" (the moral imperative to respect, even to preserve, the "cultural roots" of the migrants) (Cardús, 2009:10), which in fact condemns immigrants to a permanent uprooting that makes their process of taking root in their new country more difficult (*ibid*.). Against both of these discourses, Cardús proposes an inversion and a displacement of the terms of the metaphor of the roots, and to link these with the future and not with the past:

> De manera que, si l'origen és la llavor [...], les arrels ja no són el passat, sinó exactament el contrari: són el futur. Efectivament, allò que proporciona futur és la capacitat d'arrelament, amb independència de l'origen. És l'arrelament el que fa possible que qualsevol origen tingui una realització social concreta en un territori determinat, que qualsevol projecte esdevingui una realitat històrica localitzada. La vinculació de la imatge de l'arrel amb el futur, i no amb el passat, permet fer visibles tres processos socials fonamentals per al nostre esdevenidor. En primer lloc, posa de manifest la nostra històrica capacitat d'adaptació. [...] En segon lloc, la imatge de l'arrel com a futur ens recorda que no s'arrela per sempre ni tan sols en el cas de no moure's de lloc, sinó que les arrels són parts vives que segueixen treballant per mantenir forta i ufanosa la planta. Tercerament, posar l'accent en l'arrelament fa més comprensibles els processos que viuen els "nous catalans" i sobretot els aproxima als dels "catalans de tota la vida" [...], també ocupats a seguir acomodant-se als nous temps. (Cardús, 2009:11)

Unsurprisingly, *La Mari* stresses the experience of uprootedness and taking root of the "new Catalans", and it does so, predictably, through discursive and visual reference to flowers and plants. For instance, when Mari leaves Alosno at the start of the first episode, her sister gives her a red carnation (red as the tip of Reme's earring) as they bid each other farewell at the station. The carnation cut away from the plant in the pot thus becomes a symbol of Mari's uprootedness. However, the symbol of the plant and the flower is here related not only to the migrant's origins but also to the feelings of nostalgia for their homeland. Half way down the first episode, when Mari meets Genara, the two women are having a conversation about their villages and their new life in Barcelona. Mari confesses her nostalgia for her *pueblo* and for elements such as food. At this point Genara shows Mari a pot of geraniums that are planted on earth from her plot in the village, then another pot with geraniums growing on Catalan earth, and says: "Cuando se lleva mucho tiempo fuera, una aprende que la tierra es igual de buena en todas partes. [...] Pues ésta la he plantado aquí con tierra de aquí. Y está tan hermosa como las otras". (When one has been away for a long time, one learns that the soil is equally good everywhere. This one I've planted on soil from here. And it's as beautiful as the others). Genara then proceeds to offer this pot of geraniums to Mari as a gift. This action is mirrored at the end of the second episode, after Mari has married and moved to Poble Sec. She is visited by her friend Luz, who confides that she is moving back to her village. Like Genara had done some years before, Mari gives her friend a pot with a plant:

MARI: Así te acuerdas de nosotras.

LUZ: ¿Y tú, Mari, no volverás nunca?

MARI: ¿Adónde? ¿Dónde está mi casa? ¿En Alosno, en el Verdum, o aquí [Poble Sec]? ¿La casa de uno está donde descansan sus muertos o donde están sus vivos? A mis hijos no hay quien les saque de aquí. Y a Enric, a ver...

For Mari, thus, the sense of belonging is not derived from the place of origin, but rather from where roots (affection, relationships, practices) have taken. The uncertainty she expresses in the dialogue ("Where is my home?") contrasts with the certainties provided by the nostalgia for the homeland, as we see towards of the end of the series, when Mari takes her homesick mother back to Alosno. The re-encounter with the village and with Mari's sister is sensual as well as emotional. The three women embrace one another, celebrate their familiar scent ("¡Ay qué bien huele! ¡Ay mamá, ay mi madre!" ("Oh you smell so good! Oh mum, oh mother!"), says Mari's deeply moved sister), touch the bodies and objects they love. Before entering the house, we see a close-up of the hand of Rosa, Mari's mother, caressing the white wall of her house before the camera pans to the left and settles on the face of the jubilant woman. Later, in a delicately filmed scene, we follow Rosa, who has told her daughters that she has much work to do. We see her in a long shot, framed by the white walls of the cemetery where her husband rests, before she places a bunch of carnations (not red, but white) in his grave. Then we see her sitting on a stone fence against the background of the village, bathed in the afternoon sun and the song of the cicadas. Cut to a point of view shot of the landscape, with bushes, fields with olive trees and hills on the horizon. Cut to a medium close-up of Rosa, dressed in mourning, who is watching the landscape and smiles. She brings a branch of rosemary to her face, inhales its aroma, closes her eyes, exhales, and brings the branch to her heart, as the camera tilts down following her body until it settles on her bare feet, which lovingly caress the soil. Finally, we see the woman in her dimly lit bedroom. Sitting on the bed, she takes a wedding photograph from the bedside table, caresses the photo of her late husband, brings the picture to her heart, and lies down in the foetal position.

The sensuality of these scenes, in which the sense of smell plays a major role, indicates the power of nostalgia as an effect of the recalling of the memory of very fundamental experiences. This is also the case with respect to the sense of touch, and to physical contact (caressing the walls, touching the photograph of a loved one, caressing the native soil with one's feet) as an attempt to achieve an impossible union with lost objects. The foetal position in which Rosa falls asleep, on the other hand, suggests a return to an imaginary completeness, but also anticipates the woman's death. Moroccan-born Catalan writer Najat El Hachmi points out at the end of her autobiographical essay *Jo també sóc catalana*, as she narrates the death of her grandfather, that the word for "to die" in the Amazigh language is "to return home" (El Hachmi, 2004:194). Similarly, in *La Mari* the satisfaction of nostalgia, fulfilling the desire to return home, is associated with death.

Returning to one's roots leads to death; nostalgia kills. Roots are thus the object whose loss is worked through in *La Mari*. However, and as a conclusion to this essay, I would like to suggest that these roots that are relinquished through the slow and patient work of mourning are not the Andalusian ones. Rather, the object being mourned through the fiction is, I would claim, the attachment to the idea of cultural roots in Catalan cultural discourse.

The series ends with Mari and Enric travelling to Alosno so that Mariona – Mari's newborn daughter, the fruit of orderly, legitimate reproduction – can be introduced to her roots. In the dialogue, Mari and Enric make a pact: he will teach Mariona to dance *sevillanas*, and Mari will teach her Catalan. Therefore little Mariona will unwittingly become the outcome of a cultural dialectic between native Catalans and Andalusian immigrants that will supersede their opposition. In this pact, a suture of discrete cultures is being proposed in order to exorcise the excessive promiscuity of immigration as the limit of social cohesiveness in Catalan society; that is, to avert the danger for a nation of immigrants like Catalonia to dissolve itself into undifferentiation and lose its national and cultural difference. This unity has the effect of concealing something that remains repressed in Catalan cultural discourse: the fact that all Catalans are immigrants; indeed that we are all the product of the social promiscuity at which Catalonia has excelled for generations.

Thus *La Mari* allows Catalan audiences at a time of massive immigration to work through the loss of the idea of cultural roots, the loss of the idea of purity of origins, and the loss of an imaginary completeness of a political body that has become fragmented and demystified in the period of cultural normalisation. In this respect, the series contributes to the discursive dissolution of the distinction between *autòctons* (native Catalans) and immigrants that Salvador Cardús has proposed (Cardús, 2005:42-43). However, this process of dissolution of certain attachments requires the work of mourning. In his essay on the metaphors of identity, Cardús evokes the quintessential singer-songwriter of Catalan anti-Franco resistance, Raimon, in his critique of the appeal to cultural roots in the discourses of Catalan nationalism: "Hem cantat, convençuts, allò de 'qui perd els orígens, perd identitat'. I tanmateix, el contrari també és cert: la identitat es recrea i sobreviu a condició de revisar els orígens" [We have sung our sincere belief that "he who loses his origins loses a part of his identity". However, the opposite is true too: identity is recreated and survives on the condition that origins are revised] (Cardús, 2009:11).

Yet this task of revising and rewriting identity can only be performed if the work of mourning is done, and so perhaps Raimon's famous line could be rephrased thus: "Qui perd els orígens, si fa el treball del dol, guanyarà identitat" (he who loses his origins will gain identity, should he do the work of mourning). In *La Mari*, through the fiction of the loss of an Andalusian migrant's origins, Catalan audiences work through the loss of their own attachment to the idea of a Catalan identity centred around a full origin. If this is true, then the promise of a new beginning that arises from loss suggests that our analyses of Catalan identity require thinking the place and the role of mourning in its discursive constitution, in order to describe an idea of a decentred Catalan identity built on an empty origin and to deploy the social, cultural, and political potential of this idea.

Notes

1 This essay is part of the research project "Functions of the Past in Contemporary Catalan Culture: Institutionalisation, Representations, and Identity", carried out by the research group Identi.Cat (Llengua, cultura I identitat en l'era global) at the Universitat Oberta de Catalunya, and funded by the Spanish Ministry of the Economy and Competitiveness (FFI2011-24751).

2 I make a similar point in *El malestar en la cultura catalana*, especially chapter 6.

3 On Barbal and Roig, see my article "Thou Shalt Not Covet Thy Roots: Immigration and the Body in Novels by Roig, Barbal, and Jaén".

4 In this respect the Partit dels Socialistes de Catalunya (PSC) has been widely perceived as maintaining a relation of patronage (*clientelismo*) with Spanish immigrant organisations through its popular culture commission, Crisol. The activity of the Federación de Entidades Culturales Andaluzas en Catalunya (FECAC), especially the Feria de Abril, has been especially controversial; the organisation *Els Altres Andalusos* (The Other Andalusians) has accused the FECAC as well as the Junta de Andalucía of making a commercial and political use of the nostalgia of the Andalusian diaspora. See Cabrera, Morón, Riera et al., *Els altres andalusos*.

5 On the figure of Jaume Lorés, his concept of ideologia marc and its role in contemporary Catalan culture, see Fuster-Sobrepere.

Works cited

"Alosno." *La Mari*. Writ. Pau Garsaball. Dir. Jesús Garay. OK Records, 2010. DVD.

Baget Herms, Josep Maria. "Después del éxito de La Mari." *La Vanguardia* 7 Jun. 2003: Vivir en Barcelona, 8.

Barbal, Maria. *Carrer Bolívia*. Barcelona: Edicions 62, 1999.

Busquets, G. "TV3 estrena la segona part de La Mari." El Punt [Barcelona], 6 Apr. 2010. Web. 18 June 2012. http://www.elpuntavui.cat/noticia/article/-/20-comunicacio/154145-tv3-estrena-la-segona-part-de-lla-marir.html?tmpl=component&print=1&page=

Cabré, Anna. *El sistema català de reproducció*. Barcelona: Proa, 1999.

Cabrera, Lluís, Pedro Morón, Marta Riera et al. *Els altres andalusos: La qüestió nacional de Catalunya*. Barcelona: L'Esfera dels Llibres, 2005.

Candel, Francesc. *Els altres catalans*. 1964. Barcelona: Edicions 62, 1968.

Cardús i Ros, Salvador. "The Memory of Immigration in Catalan Nationalism." *International Journal of Iberian Studies 18.1 (2005), 37-44.*

Cardús i Ros, Salvador. *Tres metàfores per pensar un país amb futur*. Barcelona: Institut d'Estudis Catalans, 2009. PDF file.

Castelló, Enric, and Hugh O'Donnell. "Historias de Cataluña: Ficción y memoria histórica en la televisión pública catalana." *Historias de la pequeña pantalla: Representaciones históricas en la televisión de la España democrática*. Ed. Francisca López, Elena Cueta Asín and David R. George, Jr. Madrid and Frankfurt: Vervuert, 2009. 175-96.

El Hachmi, Najat. *Jo també sóc catalana*. Barcelona: Columna, 2004.

Ellis, John. *Seeing Things: Television in the Age of Uncertainty*. London and New York: I.B. Tauris, 2000.

Fernàndez, Josep-Anton. "Thou Shalt Not Covet Thy Roots: Immigration and the Body in Novels by Roig, Barbal, and Jaén." *Romance Quarterly* 53.3 (2006), 223-35.

– *El malestar en la cultura catalana: La cultura de la normalització 1976-1999*. Barcelona: Empúries, 2008.

Fernández Labayen, Miguel, and Ángel Custodio Gómez González. "Memoria, identidad y construcción social de la inmigración en La Mari." *Historias de la pequeña pantalla: Representaciones históricas en la televisión de la España democrática*. Ed. Francisca López, Elena Cueta Asín and David R. George, Jr. Madrid and Frankfurt: Vervuert, 2009. 217-42.

Freud, Sigmund. "Mourning and Melancholia." *On Murder, Mourning and Melancholia*. Trans. Shaun Whiteside. London: Penguin, 2005. 201-18.

– "Remembering, Repeating, and Working Through." *Beyond the Pleasure Principle and Other Writings*. Trans. John Reddick. London: Penguin, 2003. 31-42.

Fuster-Sobrepere, Joan. "La crisi del resistencialisme: Jaume Lorés i el concepte *d'ideologia marc*." Paper presented at the International conference "Resistencialisme i normalització: Usos del passat i discursos culturals en la Catalunya contemporània", Universitat Oberta de Catalunya, Barcelona, 14 Dec. 2012. Unpublished.

Gifreu, Josep. *Comunicació i reconstrucció nacional*. Barcelona: Pòrtic, 1989.

– *El meu país: Narratives i combats per la identitat*. Lleida: Pagès, 2001.

Idescat. *Evolució de la població total i estrangera: 2000-2012 Catalunya.* Institut d'Estadística de Catalunya (Generalitat de Catalunya), 2013. Web. 7 Sep. 2013. http://www.idescat.cat/poblacioestrangera/?b=0

López, Francisca. "Introducción: El pasado en la pequeña pantalla." *Historias de la pequeña pantalla: Representaciones históricas en la televisión de la España democrática.* Ed. Francisca López, Elena Cueta Asín and David R. George, Jr. Madrid and Frankfurt: Vervuert, 2009. 9-25.

Laclau, Ernesto, and Chantal Mouffe. *Hegemony and Socialist Strategy: Towards a Radical Democratic Politics.* London and New York: Verso, 1985.

Lorés, Jaume. *La transició a Catalunya (1977-1984): El pujolisme i els altres.* Barcelona: Empúries, 1985.

Madueño, Eugeni. "Lecciones de La Mari." *La Vanguardia* 7 Jun. 2003: Vivir en Barcelona 2.

– "Entrevista a Pau Garsaball, guionista de La Mari: 'En Cataluña se ha formado un solo pueblo'." *La Vanguardia* 13 Jun. 2003: Vivir en Barcelona 7.

Marín Corbera, Martí. "Ritmes i composició migratoris: Les xifres d'un fenomen complex." *L'Avenç* 298 (2005): 24-31.

Miller, Jacques-Alain. "La Suture: Éléments de la logique du signifiant." *Cahiers pour l'analyse* 1.3 (1966), 37-49. PDF file.

– "Suture (elements of the logic of the signifier)." Trans. Jacqueline Rose. *The Symptom* 8 (2007), n. pag. Web. 5 Jun. 2012. Orig. publ. in *Screen* 13 (1978).

Phillips, Adam. *Darwin's Worms.* London: Faber and Faber, 1999.

"Poble Sec." *La Mari.* Writ. Pau Garsaball. Dir. Jesús Garay. OK Records, 2010. DVD.

Roig, Montserrat. *L'òpera quotidiana.* 1982. Barcelona: Edicions 62, 1991.

Televisió de Catalunya. *La Mari: Tu ets part de la seva història.* TVC, n.d. PDF file.

Termes, Josep. *La immigració a Catalunya i altres estudis d'història del nacionalisme català.* Barcelona: Empúries, 1984.

Vila, Marc Aureli. *Les migracions a Catalunya.* Barcelona: El Llamp, 1984.

Žižek, Slavoj. *The Fright of Real Tears: Krzsystof Kieslowski between Theory and Post-Theory.* London: British Film Institute, 2001.

Standardising the foreign, localising the national. Conflicting strategies toward the development of a Catalan oral standard in dubbed films and TV series

Asia Lindsay, Peter Castellani and Josep Soler-Carbonell

In this article, we will focus on the relationship between language and the media, with particular reference to the type of language that features most commonly in the Catalan media. The historical minoritisation that the language suffered during the Franco regime (1939-1975) left the language community deeply Castilianised and with no standard variety to serve as a linguistic model. Later on, after the Catalan Broadcasting Corporation was established in 1983, the urge for such a variety was amplified. At that time, mass-media outlets were not only filling a gap in providing television and radio channels in Catalan, they were also serving a pedagogical function. On the one hand, the entire demographic composition of the country had changed significantly during the previous decades, with a large percentage of the non-Catalan speaking population having settled on a permanent basis in Catalonia's urban centres. On the other hand, nearly all of the Catalan-speaking population had been schooled exclusively in Spanish, and as a consequence the responsibility of the Catalan media to spread a given linguistic model was even greater. At the same time, however, the political tension between the various Catalan-speaking regions (in particular Catalonia, the Valencian region and the Balearic Islands) has also proved a barrier in the establishment and promotion of a common standard variety.

In this article, we will offer an overview of the type of language that features in audiovisual products, contrasting what has been observed in the case of animated films dubbed into Catalan (Vila i Moreno et al. 2007) with what is to be found in domestically produced TV series and films. Our analysis will find resonances with Barambones' (2012) research on the Basque language. In his study, the author finds that there is more room for dialectal variation in locally produced series or films than in dubbed movies, which tend to be largely homogenised and make extensive use of the standard language variety.

The Catalan oral standard and the political fragmentation of the linguistic community

The creation of an oral standard and its problematic relationship with mass-media communication has been at the centre of language debates in Catalan-speaking territories for at least thirty years now. The reason for this lies in the powerful link that exists between language and identity, which has informed ideological debates triggered by the treatment of particular language forms in the media.

Historically, the elaboration of an oral standard represented a key part of the *normalització lingüística* or "language normalisation", the recovery process which the language has been undergoing since the death of Franco. This can be seen in the emphasis placed on language normalisation by the most important language policies of recent times, particularly since the *Llei de Normalització Lingüística* of 1983 (for a thorough review of language policies in the Catalan-speaking area, see Strubell and Boix 2011). However, it was not until 1990 that the Philological Section of the *Institut d'Estudis Catalans* (IEC) put forward its *Proposta per a un estàndard oral de la llengua catalana* ("A proposal for an oral standard of the Catalan language"), which sought to codify an oral standard with which every speaker of the language could identify. This *Proposta* is divided into two volumes: *Phonetics* (1990) and *Morphology* (1992). The IEC's proposal for an oral standard is defined as compositional and based on polymorphic solutions. This means that it strives to highlight the forms that are widely shared by the demographically larger dialects (*central, valencià* and *balear*) while including enough elements from the range of geographical variants to ensure that the standard achieves the desired referential function. This supradialectal variety aims to reduce the prevalence of a single dialect over the rest while shaping a common variant by which all speakers in the territory feel represented.

Needless to say, such objectives are complex in nature, and although they have found active support from outside Barcelona (Bibiloni, 1997), they have also been strongly criticised from within Catalonia's capital. Albert Pla Nualart (2010) stands out as one of the opponents of such a proposal. He has suggested that the "compositional" model put forward by the IEC has to be reconsidered, arguing instead for a polycentric option, i.e. one in which each of the varieties, or at least the three demographically largest Catalan dialects, would devise its own oral standard independently. In his opinion, any attempt to create a polyphonic oral standard would merely add to the already extensive list of difficulties that Catalan faces on the road to linguistic normalisation.

The fact that it took nearly a decade for the IEC to publish the *Propostes* after the passing of the first Language Normalisation Act in 1983 is already indicative of the complexity of the question at hand. Not surprisingly, one of the stumbling blocks has been the tendency for one dialect to dominate in the most influential mass-media outlets (TV3 and Catalunya Ràdio especially). *Català central*, which is spoken in the provinces of Barcelona, Girona and Tarragona, features far more prominently in printed works and audiovisual media (films and series), which has led to many speakers viewing it as the standard form. The status it enjoys can be attributed to several factors, not least the number of speakers – which is higher than that of any other dialect – and the standing of Barcelona as a city. The dominance of *català central* has triggered a power struggle that has been particularly noticeable in the political sphere. One example dates back to the government of Jaume Matas in the Balearic Islands, when there were calls for an autonomous television channel (IB3) to be founded as a means of protecting the local variety of Catalan from the influence of *català central*. Since its launch, however, the channel has sought to foster a "bilingualist" image, in keeping with the ruling party's dominant ideology, and broadcasts in both Catalan and Spanish to similar degrees.

Similarly, the current president of the Balearic Islands José Ramón Bauzá, also of the *Partido Popular*, has strived to underline the linguistic differences and the uniqueness of the Balearic variants, although he has tended to concentrate his efforts more on the education system. In 2010, he stated that: "Quan recuperem el Govern, tots els llibres de text no s'editaran en català, sinó en cada una de les modalitats lingüístiques del català (mallorquí, menorquí, eivissenc i formenterenc)." ("When we return to power, our textbooks will not be edited in Catalan, but in each and every one of the Catalan linguistic modalities [sic] (Mallorcan, Minorcan, Ibizan Catalan and Formenteran Catalan)") (Source: *Diari ARA*, 03/10/2013). In early April 2013, Bauzá announced that from the 2013 academic year, school textbooks would be available in Balearic Catalan in order to avoid "la pancatalanització als llibres de text utilitzats fins ara" ("the pan-Catalanisation of textbooks used thus far") (*Diari ARA*, 09/04/2013).

Another key example of political tension is to be found in Valencia. Starting in 2007, the then president of the region, Francisco Camps of the Partido Popular, decided to prevent TV3 (a *public* television station) from broadcasting in the region 26 years after their programmes were first shown thanks to the invaluable work of language and cultural activists (most notably *Acció Cultural del País Valencià*). In February 2011, the last TV relays in the area were shut down and the Valencian Government threatened *Acció Cultural* with fines of up to 120,000 euros per month. However, some progress has recently been made towards reverting the situation. At the time of writing, the Catalan and Valencian governments have signed an agreement of media reciprocity which will enable the inhabitants of the Valencian Country to once again view Catalan media channels, while also allowing the population of Catalonia to enjoy those from Valencia (Canal 9 and its related channels). Historically, the political elite in the region has seen the presence of TV3 as a significant cultural link with Catalonia and a potential driving force behind the unification of the Catalan language. For that reason, the elite has tended to pitch the "protection" of Valencian language and identity against a perceived Catalan influence (much like Bauzá's current policies in the Balearics), with TV3 and the rest of the Catalan media constituting a significant threat in that regard. This ideological trend is closely linked to a wider-ranging and more profound movement (itself strongly associated with the *Partido Popular* in Valencia), that of *Blaverisme*, characterised by an anti-Catalan ideology and the proclamation of linguistic secessionism.

Apart from this political and ideological fragmentation, there is another important challenge that Catalan must overcome if it is to establish an oral standard. It relates specifically to the audiovisual industry and the need for programming to satisfy certain artistic ideals. In the case of television series, the acting must avoid sounding scripted, a task made harder if there is a standard by which to abide. Programmers must also resist the temptation to include calques from Castilian, as this would severely hinder any move to standardise the language. Frekko (2009) documents and discusses a lack of "resources" most commonly perceived by language professionals – the idea that Catalan is missing particular registers so it cannot function as a "normal" language. This notion is important for the purposes of our paper, as we shall argue next.

Language diversity and audiovisual artistic products

For a long time, dialectal variation has been exploited in the media for artistic purposes. In *Pygmalion*, the 1912 play about a phonetics teacher who makes a bet that he can teach a Cockney market girl to pass for a duchess at an ambassador's garden party, Bernard Shaw uses dialectal variation to highlight the class differences between Higgins, the upper-class phonetics teacher, and Eliza Doolittle, the lower-class flower seller. The play draws attention to how decisive accent is in differentiating socioeconomic classes and types of character in the media.

This exploitation of dialectal variation has been pursued in animated films, particularly those by Disney. For example, in Lippi-Green's seminal work (Lippi-Green, 1997), she discusses the racist implications of the dialectal variation used in Three Little Pigs. In the film, the wolf dresses as a Jewish peddler and contrives a Yiddish accent in an attempt to get into the pigs' house. Disney later admitted that this was in bad taste and upon re-release the scene was changed, but it was only the visual representation that was different. The accent remained the same for many years until the dialogue was finally changed, with the wolf then being given a standard "cartoon voice."

Animated films dubbed into Catalan

Clearly, this use of dialectal variation in English can prove very problematic when films come to be dubbed into Catalan, a process that frequently results in the vast majority of variation – particularly ethnolectal and sociolectal varieties – being reduced, as there is often no way of transferring connotations of an accent in one language to another. It is not possible to equate a British accent to a central Catalan accent, or a Texan accent to a Mallorcan one. This is the stance taken in the Televisió de Catalunya's *Linguistic Criteria for Translating and Dubbing*. In fact, they go even further, suggesting that when original versions contain significant dialectal variation (which is usually the case in British or Italian productions, for example), then "és millor inventar una parla diferenciada exclusivament per mitjà de trets lèxics senzills de captar i que no es puguin atribuir a cap zona concreta del territori català." ("It is better to use invented speech composed exclusively of non-complex lexical traits which cannot be attributed to any specific Catalan dialectal area")(Televisió de Catalunya, 1997:18).

In Vila i Moreno et al. (2007), the authors find evidence to suggest that translators and film-dubbers follow these guidelines. The study is particularly revealing because it focuses on four animated films: *Shark Tales*, *The Jungle Book 2*, *Finding Nemo* and *Shrek 2*. In all these films, dialectal variation is actively exploited for artistic purposes, making translation a complex matter. Ultimately, the variants invented by Catalan dubbers provoked consternation among the viewing public. In *Shark Tales*, for instance, the two jellyfish Ernie and Bernie speak Jamaican English in the original, thus complementing their Rastafarian appearance. Understandably, there is no Catalan equivalent of Rastafarian English and the dubber compromised by creating a new accent, using features from different dialects, including north-western, central and *Terres de l'Ebre Catalan* (Vila i Moreno et al., 2007:397).

In other instances, Catalan dubbers looked to the Castilian versions and mimicked their solution. This can be seen in the case of the vultures in *Jungle Book 2*. In the original, they speak various dialects, including British and Caribbean English. In the Catalan version, all the vultures speak invented Catalanised Latin American dialects, i.e. Catalan with Mexican, Argentine and Caribbean features. This mirrors the Spanish version of the film, and highlights the uneasiness that dubbers feel in playing with the regional variation available in Catalan.

Domestically produced TV series and films
In locally produced TV series and films there is a perceivably higher

degree of language variation, and more accents are present in such productions. That said, it is also true that *català central* tends to be the most
frequently heard dialect in these products too. In a recent poll conducted
by the newspaper *ARA* (January 2012, N=10078), the two most popular
Catalan series ever were found to be *Plats Bruts* (42%) and *Porca Misèria*
(17%). Both series feature at least some degree of dialectal diversity. In
Plats Bruts (1999-2002), Pau Durà (from Alcoi, Valencia) plays Pol, a
bartender. In *Porca Misèria* (2004-2007), Juli Mira (also from Alcoi)
plays Doctor Joan Grimau. Both characters speak in a non-central
variety of Catalan.

Remarkably, however, it would also appear that occasionally, actors
who are native speakers of Valencian or Balearic dialects reshape their
speech and tailor it to *català central*. In a recent prime-time series,
Kubala, Moreno i Manchón (2012-2013), Pep Molina, also from Alcoi,
played the character of Blai, the bartender. In the programme, he
sometimes mixes linguistic features typical of Valencian Catalan with
those typical of the Central dialect. An active linguist documented this
case and other ones in her blog, *Do de Llengua* (2012). In her opinion,
Pep Molina's approach is not successful: "El resultat és deplorable, una
barreja que no és ni valencià ni català central (ni barceloní)" ("The result
is terrible, a mixture that is neither Valencian nor Central Catalan (nor
Barcelonan Catalan)"). Most readers who commented on the blog post
strongly agreed with the author's appraisal of the situation and blamed
TV3 for a supposed misrepresentation of Catalan dialects. The blogger
sent her remarks to TV3 as part of a complaint and obtained the
following reply from Ernest Rusinés, head of the Linguistic Advisory
Committee for Catalan TV:

> Thank you for getting in touch with us and for following our pro-
> grammes. The point that you raise is a valid one, but under no circum-
> stances is it the result of an assessment carried out by our linguists. The
> fact is that actors, quite often and for different reasons, try to alter their
> original accent if it differs from the Central one. This is, of course,
> unnecessary when the script does not require it: we repeat this message
> to our actors as often as we can. However, your valid comment has led
> us to reflect on the matter and to insist on our message in order to
> prevent actors' own accents from becoming hidden unnecessarily.[1]

Rusinés's response is relevant to our analysis here because he contradicts a statement that he had made previously. In *Les veus del Pamano* (2009), an adaptation of the much-celebrated novel by Jaume Cabré (2004), the pervasive accent throughout the film is the Central one, which is incongruous given that the story takes place in post-Civil War Pallars, in the Pyrenees. In this case, Rusinés responded quite differently to widespread criticism of the fact that it was mostly the Central variant that was spoken, with the local one, Pallarès, being spoken by just a few pupils in the village school. Indeed, he sought to justify it, a response that American linguist and anthropologist Susan DiGiacomo (2010) found astonishing. Rusinés stated that: "Central Catalan, simply by demographic size, has to have a very important specific weight and presence in our national mass media." One of the arguments that he put forward to try and justify the pervasive presence of Central Catalan in this film was that the actors were chosen on the basis of their acting skills, rather than their accent. Had accent been the most important consideration during casting, they would have had to restrict themselves to Pallarès-speaking actors and the quality of the whole film would have suffered.

Needless to say, this argument does not hold water, and there is proof that actors can be trained to speak convincingly with a particular accent in the recently aired prime-time series *Gran Nord* (2012-2013), which, ironically, is also set in the Pyrenees. However, in this case, the vast majority of the local characters employ the Pallarès dialect, even though the actors themselves are not originally from Pallars. Of the 16 main characters, only three do not speak the dialect. Naturally, Central Catalan is still present in the series. Anna and Pep are the two *Mossos d'Esquadra* around whom the main plot develops, and they feature prominently as speakers of *català central*.

In this article we have discussed the type of language present in Catalan audiovisual products, contrasting dubbed films with domestically produced TV series and films. In the case of dubbed films – particularly animated movies (Vila i Moreno et al. 2007) – a homogenising trend that makes extensive use of Central Catalan seems to be the most common practice. By contrast, locally produced TV series and films appear to offer greater scope for the inclusion of different Catalan dialects, which is similar to the Basque case (Barambones 2012). However, this possibility seems to be relatively underexploited, and when variation is used for artistic or humoristic purposes, it may draw criticism from the audience, as was the case with *Lo Cartanyà*, a sitcom that sought to exploit the nord-occidental dialect. In our view, negative feedback is indicative of the uneasiness that is still felt with regard to the internal dialectal variation of the language, which helps explain why dubbers and translators opt for homogenising solutions when adapting foreign-language films into Catalan. At the heart of this uneasiness lie the ideological debates that continue to affect the Catalan-speaking community and that are sometimes exploited by an anti-Catalan political elite from outside Catalonia.

Gran Nord offers a useful example of good practice, highlighting the fact that actors are naturally capable of producing different accents with the correct training. This approach should be taken more often, and particular effort should be made to convince actors who speak a regional dialect not to tailor their accent to conform to Central Catalan. At present, it is crucial to have a natural and flexible variety that can serve as an oral standard, but if the Central dialect is favoured as a matter of course, the presence and visibility of other dialects in the media will be strongly hindered.

Pla Nualart (2010) suggests that Catalan faces a number of challenges in its quest for "linguistic normalisation," making it essential to create a fully representative oral standard with which speakers of all variants feel comfortable. Given the issue of political fragmentation, it seems wise to propose that the most widely spoken dialects develop their own oral standard. However, that does not mean that Central Catalan should be favoured uncritically in media as influential as TV3 and the Catalan Broadcasting Corporation in general. Such an approach is likely to play into the hands of anti-Catalan groups who attack Catalan audiovisual products for being too "Catalan." Providing greater scope for language-internal dialectal variation in both domestically produced TV series and dubbed products (foreign films and series) would be a productive route to explore.

Note

1   Translation by the authors.

Works cited

Barambones, Josu. *Mapping the Dubbing Scene. Audiovisual Translation in Basque Television*. Bern: Peter Lang, 2012.

Bibiloni, Gabriel. "Sobre l'estàndard composicional." In *Jornades de la Secció Filològica de l'Institut d'Estudis Catalans a Mallorca* (18 i 19 d'octubre de 1996). Barcelona-Palma: Institut d'Estudis Catalans-Universitat de les Illes Balears, 1997. Web. 26 May 2013.

Cabré, Jaume. *Les veus del Pamano*. Barcelona: Edicions Proa, 2004.

Diari ARA. "Bauzà, el 2010: "Suprimirem la normativa de normalització lingüística." 3 October 2013. Web. 13 October 2013.

Diari ARA . "Bauzá garanteix llibres de text en "balear" per al curs vinent." 9 September 2013. Web. 13 October 2013.

Diari ARA . "Els lectors escullen 'Plats Bruts' com a millor sèrie en català de tots els temps." 21 January 2012. Web. 26 May 2013.

DiGiacomo, Susan. "Quines veus del pamano?" *L'Avenç* 354 (2010): 12-13.

Do de Llengua. TV3 respon (sobre els dialectes), 17 May 2012. Web. 26 May 2013.

Do de Llengua . Els dialectes i TV3, 29 February 2012. Web. 26 May 2013.

Frekko, Susan. "'Normal' in Catalonia. Standard language, enregisterment and the imagination of a national public." *Language in Society* 38 (2009): 71-93.

Generalitat de Catalunya. Llei 7/1983, de 18 d'abril, de normalització lingüística. Web. 26 May 2013.

Institut d'Estudis Catalans. *roposta per a un estàndard oral de la llengua Catalana*. I *Fonètica*. Barcelona: Institut d'Estudis Catalans, 1990.

Institut d'Estudis Catalans. *Proposta per a un estàndard oral de la llengua Catalana*. II *Morfologia*. Barcelona: Institut d'Estudis Catalans, 1992.

Lippi-Green, Rosina. *English with an Accent: Language, Ideology and Discrimination in the United States*. London: Routledge, 1997.

Pla Nualart, Albert. *Això del català. Podem fer-ho més fàcil?* Barcelona: Editorial Columna, 2010.

Rusinés, Ernest. "Les veus de 'Les Veus del Pamano'." *El Punt Avui*, 1 December 2012. Web. 26 May 2013.

Strubell, Miquel and Emili Boix-Fuster (Eds.). *Democratic Policies for Language Revitalisation: the Case of Catalan*. Basingstoke: Palgrave Macmillan, 2011.

Televisió de Catalunya. *Criteris linguistics sobre traducció i doblatge*. Barcelona: Edicions 62, 1997.

Vila i Moreno, Francesc Xavier, Sarah Cassel, Núria Busquet Isart, Joan-Pau Callejón i Mateu, Toni Mercadal Moll, Josep Soler Carbonell. "Sense accents? Les contradiccions de l'estàndard oral en els doblatges Catalans de pel·lícules d'animació." *Revista de Llengua i Dret* 47 (2007): 387-413.

The funny others on our screens: Stereotype, self-loathing and resistance in the audiovisual representation of Wales and Galicia

Marta Pérez and Daryl Perrins

The people of Wales and Galicia share much in common in terms of their historical relationships with their respective neighbours, England and Spain, notably: a peripheral position, neatly expressed on maps of Iberia and the United Kingdom, which generates similar patterns in the development of stereotypes and the configuration of a repertoire of comic tropes. English and Spanish popular and high cultures have created strong comic archetypes for Welsh and Galician alike, characters that can be traced back to at least the early modern period. In this article we will consider the role these archetypes have played in the twentieth century and how they have become symbols not only of stereotype and self-loathing but also resistance in the postcolonial epoch.

In the case of Wales and Galicia, these representations share enough features to make possible a comparative analysis of the commonalities of both national stereotypes and the strategies that both cultures employ in response. Our research on national stereotypes is necessarily comparative, as the study of national images "addresses cross-national relations rather than national identities" (Leerssen, 2007:29). This paper, therefore, focuses on examples taken from the most successful comic performances and characters in Welsh/British and Hispanic/Galician media in the last few decades in order to show which stereotypes remain active.

Although there is a glut of research surrounding the comparative analysis of humour, most of such work is focused on jokes from a linguistic perspective, aiming to prove the effectiveness of form, through the dynamics of jokes and laughter, performance and audience reaction (Aarons, 2011; Ritchie, 2003). While this research represents a significant step forward in the recognition and understanding of the science of humour, it neglects important elements such as the socio-historical context of performance. With few exceptions, see Wagg (1998), there is seldom an analysis from an academic perspective that could highlight the social uses of humour.

The cultural comic script – a changeable form

As Christie Davies (1999) explains, traditional ethnic jokes tend to fall into binary narratives of ethnic character groupings. The dominant culture defines the "lesser" or "junior" culture as either the "stupid" or the "canny" "other", while, importantly, at the same time keeping a "neutral" comic status. In this sense, Davies indicates that

> The most common ethnic jokes of the modern world are about alleged canny (i.e. shrewd, calculating, thrifty) and stupid groups. Every country has its own "stupid" and "canny" groups about whom it tells jokes (Davies, 1999:83).

Davies concentrates on "ethnic" designations, therefore limiting his pattern to national and intra-national cultural contexts. "Canny" and "stupid" stereotypes work inwards as identifiers, from whole countries or regions to local jokes, concerning the particular "stupidity" of a distinct locality. Identity is not just a matter of territory or an ethnic definition. Humour about minorities, class-based groups, urban cultures and so on, cannot be analysed solely within this binary pattern. We would therefore claim that the concept of the "ethnic script" is quite limiting for our purposes. From now on we will instead use the term *cultural comic script* to refer not only to the comic relationships between countries and national identities, inter-relationships like Scots, English, Welsh and Irish in the British Isles, but to other modes of identification, modes that Davies (1999) describes in terms of circles of influence. In his attempt to elaborate a comprehensive theory for the creation and development of ethnic jokes, Davies describes four circles of influence in comic relations pulsing out from the consensual centre ground of the dominant culture. From a hypothetical centre, any given cultural stereotype about another identity is measured in terms of distance or proximity on the time-space axis. This is an expression of how far away that group is from the dominant culture in terms of either history or geographical space. In the first circle, the one closest to the centre, the given culture creates jokes about its very closest neighbours.[1] In this orbit, Davies identifies the comic "close-relations" we analyse here, namely the pattern established in the relationship between the different nationalities that make up the unions of Spain and the United Kingdom. If we apply Davies' pattern of comic satellites to Spain and the UK, we can identify the Catalans and the Scots as the "canny" in jokes, while the Galicians and the Welsh represent the "stupid".

These circles are a starting point for analysing humour as part of a series of dynamic patterns that can evolve in time and change depending on the relation between the teller of the joke and its object. The comic script changes historically as the relations between different identities – and so stereotypes – also mutate. The Welsh and Galician people both share a geographically and economically peripheral position that has established them in comparison with the centre as provincial and "stupid". As Leerssen contends,

> the centre, whom positively valorized, will count as a locus of refinement, progress, energy and dynamism, often contrasted with the opposite, negatively valorized image of the periphery as uncouth, static, passive and backwards (Leersen, 2007:280).

This tension between centre and periphery is deepened by the existence of a minority language, which in comparison to the centre defines English and Spanish respectively as the only recognised state *lingua franca* and allows myths around insularity and minority language communities to form in the minds of outsiders. The perspective of provincialism also sanctions a common sense consensus to develop in the dominant culture that legitimises "these people" as the ones to laugh at. With this provincialism being established very early in the development of the nation states of Spain and England (later the United Kingdom), the identification of Wales' and Galicia's populations as the "stupid" of the jokes was made possible, in a comic relationship that was far from being equal.

The evolution of the national stereotypes of both nations also runs a parallel course. In this sense, Wales and Galicia were until the turn of the 17th Century described as proud, aggressive, boastful and quarrelsome (Davies, 1999; Caramés, 1993). Writers like Cervantes and Shakespeare contributed to the spread of these assumptions, which do not derive from familiarity with either Galician or Welsh peoples but rather from the sketching of characters for their easy identification in narratives that are classic texts in the construction of Spanish and English identity and in particular of their respective boundaries. The caricatures that evolved for both nations after this period appear historically to reflect the influence the Galician and Welsh populations had in relation to the political centre of power. And as their influence waned in the respective capitals of the UK and Spain, the stereotype changed to reflect their relative lack of agency. Throughout the twentieth century Welsh and Galician representation underwent a two-fold process. On the one hand, they were incorporated into the media of the dominant culture, while on the other both audiences and the creators of humour in both emerging nations began to react against the increasing reduction of their identities to simple and archaic forms. During this period cinema, television and radio developed a repertoire of comic types that othered Welsh and Galician characters from the centre ground. In the British media by the middle of the 20th century, the Welsh were increasingly being characterised as provincial and often "stupid". During the middle of the century a raft of films were made that, as Kate Woodward argues, offered "a shorthand view of Wales". These include; *The Proud Valley* (Pen Tennyson, 1940), *How Green was My Valley* (John Ford 1941), *Valley of Song* (Gilbert Gunn, 1953) and the comedy *Only Two Can Play* (Sidney Gilliat, 1962). As Woodward notes "it is these Orientalized images, created by large American and English studios during the middle years of the last century, that have taken root permanently in the international imagination" (Woodward, 2006:54). The Ealing Comedies in particular were pivotal at the time in defining the UK's Celtic periphery from the locus of the South East of England and while *Whiskey Galore* (MacKendrick, 1949) has become the cinematic acid test of Scottish canniness, *A Run for your Money* – a film which Woodward defines as "probably, the film that most orientalises Wales" (Woodward, 2006:56), which has innocent brothers Twm and Dai coming to London to watch the rugby match between Wales and

England to fall foul of scheming women, spivs and the demon drink–can be seen as a central comic narrative in defining the Welsh stereotype against the other near neighbour as sketched out by Christie (1999). As the film historian Dave Berry concludes; "there was no moral toughness, deviousness or shading in the miner's characters in *A Run for your Money* comparable to the defiant Scots in *Whiskey Galore*" (Berry, 1994:214).

Both Spanish and South American media also employed caricature in their fictional depiction of Galicians. In Spain these roles were often performed by Galician actors. One such Galician performer was Xan das Bolas, famous for his various supporting roles playing unenlightened Galician characters from the 1940s to the 1970s. In South America this trait is best exemplified through the character Cándida. Cándida was a Galician maid played by the Argentinean Niní Marshall. From her first appearance in *Cándida* (1939), this illiterate and stubborn woman faces the difficulties of being a newcomer in Buenos Aires. Most of the comic situations derive from the communicative limitations of the language spoken by Cándida – a mixture of Galician and her recently acquired Spanish, together with her ignorance in contrast to the cosmopolitanism of the Argentinean characters.

In the last few decades, the citizens of these emerging nations armed with a new found autonomy and a burgeoning national consciousness have been interrogating these stereotypes. In Galicia, television has become the main battleground in which notions of national representation have been contested. In February 2005, for example, the popular show *Los Serrano* (Telecinco, 2003-2008) had to remove the character of waitress Loli, because of the negative audience response to the character's portrayal as a filthy and poorly educated Galician. The Galician media and the Galician trade union Comisión Intersindical Galega (CIG) denounced her depiction as discriminatory for women and for Galicians in general (Vertele, 2005). In Wales, we can look at the muscular response to Anne Robinson's comments made on the BBC television comedy show Room 101 broadcast in March 2001. Anne Robinson, a guest on the show hosted by Paul Merton, made derisive comments about Welsh people and the Welsh language, stating: "What are they for?" and "I never did like them." Robinson stirred up a furore in Wales where there was a backlash against her comments. Welsh MPs for example called for Robinson to be hauled in front of the Welsh Affairs Select Committee to apologise for her "racism". Robinson was also investigated by The North Wales Police after complaints of racism were filed. The ire of Welsh academia was also raised, Kevin Williams writing in *Planet*, for example, can be seen to speak for many when he argues that the reaction to the comments in Wales "is a reflection of a new found national vigour that indicates that we [Welsh] are no longer going to put up with the litany of anti-Welsh jibes that have littered our history" (Williams, 2001:37).

Addressing the comic "other"

It is important to note however that the imbalance in the relationship between the centre and the periphery that Davies proposes in his comic script has not been corrected with social or legal action. Indeed this imbalance forms a tension that is often exploited by Welsh and Galician media who recreate these comic relations with the other in dynamic fictions where these stereotypes can be worked through on home ground.

A contemporary example of this process, appears in the hit BBC situation comedy[2] *Gavin and Stacey*. As John Jewell suggests,

> much of the comedy in Gavin and Stacey derives from the representation of Wales and the cultural differences between Barry and Billericay. As Raymond Williams argued, in terms of the relationship between England and Wales we have moved on somewhat from the old perspectives of England as conqueror, colonizer, exploiter and big neighbour (Jewell, 2009:62).

Replacing the crude but well-known historical English archetypes that revolve around notions of the upper class and the inheritance of power are the Shipmans. The Shipmans are a historically working-class Essex family, the inheritors of Margaret Thatcher's legacy in the South East of England and of the ex-Prime Minister John Major's "classless society", now clearly upwardly mobile in their Dorma Bungalow. Given that this was written by Ruth Jones, a Welsh woman, together with the Englishman James Corden and was made for a British audience by Baby Cow Productions (the company fronted by Steve Coogan), we would argue that it has a double sided perspective that works on both a socio-economic level of recognition (nouveau riche v. traditional working class) as well as a pan-national level of identity, and this is at the heart of its UK success. *Gavin and Stacey* is essentially a British comedy, which uses the differences between South Wales and South East England as the primary social and national conflict necessary to propel the sitcom's narrative along. The conflict revolving around the relationship between Gavin from Billericay and Stacey from Barry is presented as a mixed marriage in the style of the LWT sitcom *Mixed Blessings* (1978-1980) about a black and white couple. In *Gavin and Stacey*, family conflict highlights the differences, but also allows dialogue through them. As Uncle Bryn, the character played by Rob Brydon, puts it after a heated exchange: "look at yourselves, just look at yourselves. We live in a cynical world, a cynical, cynical world and tonight we have the chance to build a wonderful family that spreads across two nations".

In contrast, Galician humour does not generally develop such a relationship between Galicians and Spaniards. In the oral tradition there are no records of humorous tales about the Spanish, just an insignificant proportion of stories about Andalusians who are the butt of the joke (Llinares García, 1999). The Spanish are portrayed only as authority figures – namely the doctor, the chemist, the Mayor and so on, as opposed to the lower classes represented by the Galician people who are often sailors and/or farmers. Perhaps the finest examples of these portraits are to be found in the cartoons of Alfonso Daniel Castelao. One of the fathers of the Galician nationalist movement, Castelao drew a series of cartoons for regional newspapers during the 1920s and 1930s, under ambiguous titles such as *Things* or *Things of life* (Castelao, 2001). These cartoons made explicit the tension between the rural and urban ways of life in a society where language often makes the divide between the two communities far more distinct. Although all the characters were from Galicia, Castelao reflected the social tension between poor Galician speakers and their rulers who expressed themselves in Spanish. Here, the carnivalesque frame of the cartoon re-connected the Galician people with the historical carnival practice of using humour as a brief liberation from the established social order. In Castelao's cartoons, published in newspapers such as *Galicia*, *Diario de Vigo* and *Faro de Vigo* during the 1920s, common people were ironic, even sarcastic, while the ruling classes were grave and stiff. The "other" in Galician humour is therefore an insider from the ruling classes or an absent figure. We could only find one exception to this trend of hiding the enemy, in the TV show *Air Galicia*, a satirical programme broadcast on the public Galician television station, Televisión de Galicia (TVG). For the first time in the Galician media, a *Madrileño* appears to be the "stupid" one in the tale, fooled by the attitude of the locals when in Galicia as a tourist. This localised response is an example of *retranca*, a rhetorical feature of Galician language that tries to hide the real intentions of the speaker (Piccardi, 2004). With these examples in mind, we could claim that Welsh humour has developed recent strategies to counter the stereotypes constructed by the dominant culture. Galician culture, on the other hand, has internalised the caricature and included it in the national comic repertoire. It has not always been this way, as popular culture has included some forms of rebellion, particularly against the dominant near neighbours.

"I want to laugh like common people": Peasants and Proles on Stage

Performance has been a rather neglected subject from the very beginning of research into humour, although it is a central aspect of comedy (Mills, 2009). There have been, however, some reviews of the history of specific genres, such as stand-up comedy (Mintz, 2005), in which there is an attempt to define their frame and their boundaries.

Stand-up comedy "like other genres of verbal art, is characterised by a hyper-awareness of how something is said" (Chun, 2004). Despite the idea that comedians are supposed to challenge the accepted social norms, the social role he or she uses

> is almost always establishing agreement, consensus with his or her specific audience. This is done by developing rapport and understanding between the comedian and the audience, but also by keeping the comments within the frame of acceptability of the particular group (Mintz, 2005:577).

Nonetheless, the general agreement necessary for humour is far more complex, particularly when dealing with ethnic identities. Ideologies at play may often appear contradictory, as comedians sometimes incorporate negative racial stereotypes into their performances in a way that can be understood as self-mockery or even self-hatred. This is usually framed however as "safe" via the unspoken rule in Western comic culture that decrees that only someone from an ethnic identity can make jokes about that ethnicity. An example of this can be taken from Margaret Cho's stand-up show. Cho is an Asian American comedian who, according to Chun (2004), employs a hyper-mock Asian mode of speech to perform general stereotypes associated with an oriental in America. At the same time she is a Korean who plays with this stereotype and in particular satirises the language used by newly arrived Asians. As such "she engages in racial crossing practices without symbolically crossing racial boundaries herself, performing the speech of a *racialized other* who is not necessarily a *racial other*" (Chun 2004:264). Here we have two elements to consider in terms of performance, firstly character – an Asian self for Margaret Cho – and, secondly, a matter of language – a comically developed accent. Both derive from the stereotype, which is present in American society, but this acquires a second meaning when Cho performs it (Chun, 2004).

When considering stereotypes, frame is a key factor for the performance of humour, as Jaffe sustains:

> Like the performer, the audience could both identify and not identify. This is particularly important for comic performances like this one that involve insider play with stereotypes that are often also used by outsiders (…). The outsider's critical eye and voice are temporarily silenced in the performance, but they are never completely gone (Jaffe, 2000: 50).

In this vein, it is important to consider who is impersonated in Galician and Welsh comedy, how do they behave? How do they talk? This is an especially important question for two countries with minority languages; Galician and Welsh have withered on the vine for centuries yet both have gone through a recovery in the last three decades.[4] Although the recent creation of minority language public media and a raft of legislation have contributed to the development of parity across the languages spoken in Wales and Galicia, the minority tongues are still at a clear disadvantage when placed beside the world languages of English and Spanish respectively.

Therefore, when dealing with humour about Galicians, in characters such as those we have mentioned above, language is also a key factor. For, just as Margaret Cho creates a mock Asian, Spanish and South American comedians developed a mock Galician based on the linguistic mistakes of the Spanish spoken by Galician people. The heightened language of mock Galician is therefore perhaps the best way to identify a Galician character in South America, for instance, along with certain occupations directly related to the immigrant community. Again Cándida is a good example, as her language mistakes constitute the most important comic aspect of her character, together with a liberal dose of pratfalls. This "mock Galician" persona uses what is sometimes called *Castrapo*, i.e. Spanish spoken in a Galician accent with extensive use of Galician vocabulary and grammar.

Galician comedians use language in quite a different manner as they combine Galician and Spanish. Here we can talk about what Jaffe calls codeswitching, this is a "second strategy, in which performers implicitly undercut this logic of clear-cut boundaries [between languages], by making use of the bilingual repertoire in ways that validate mixed language practices and identities" (Jaffe, 2000: 39). Jaffe talks about Corsican radio programmes in which French and Corsican mix in a non-hierarchical manner. For the researcher, the violation of language boundaries is a sign of the de-legitimising of the status of the language in power – in this case, French – or at least a questioning of this supposedly clear barrier. A more accurate denomination for this humour based in language switching is what Canakis (1994) calls "diglossic humour" to refer to the mixture of the different varieties of Modern Greek in literature for humorous affect. The interaction of these varieties not only creates a comic effect but also a "self-contained comedy of manners reflecting social aspirations within Greek society" (Canakis, 1994: 228).

Codeswitching is a relatively common strategy in the most recent Galician humour. Double-acts[4] like *Os Tonechos* [The Tonechos] and *Nucha e mucha* [Nucha and Mucha] perform in Galician but insert some sentences in Spanish – often a punch line or a repetitive expression that is recognisable by the audience. There is also an extreme example of diglossic humour in the Galician context in the character called Señora de Palmírez. It is important to note that Palmírez, a character to laugh at, not to laugh with, speaks *Castrapo* in a context where the audience is mostly composed of Galician speakers. Also, she performs *Castrapo* in a programme on the official Galician language channel – Televisión de Galicia – where Galician is the only official language. This performance of the different language competencies also dramatizes the struggle between rural and urban Galicians, as the use of Galician is normally considered a residual form of rural culture. Making fun of a woman who speaks Spanish in order to climb the symbolic social ladder is a comic strategy previously unknown in the Galician tradition.

In the Welsh context we take into account the figure of the seasoned comic entertainer Max Boyce, a man who divides opinion in recent scholarship which considers Wales within a postcolonial context. He is considered a Welsh institution by a large proportion of the population, for whom he is engaged in the process of re-imagining representation of what Ed Thomas calls "old colonial Wales, the Wales of stereotype" (quoted in Blandford, 2005:177). For Kevin Williams he is "yet another professional Welshman", and proof that "when confronted by the English the Welsh often revert to stereotype" (Williams, 1991:19). Boyce indulges in his own mock-linguistic strategies via an exaggeration of a South Walian dialect of English sometimes called "Wenglish" because it includes words and phrases from the Welsh language. In his perfor-mances, Boyce mimics this dialect that was associated with coal mining and uses it to help create the persona of the mother-centred valley "boyo". But with coal mining long gone, and "Wenglish" along with it, Boyce's hyper-vernacular keeps this dialect alive as an example of Welsh *hiraeth*, a word without direct translation in English which is often equated in use and meaning to the Portuguese *saudade*; both represent nostalgia and longing for a sense of nationhood found in the past. Max Boyce's persona thus reproduces the naïve, beer-swilling, Mam-loving, choral-singing, homesick, rugby-obsessed caricature already found in *A Run for Your Money*.

Although shorn of its heavy industry, the South Wales that Max Boyce inhabits is quickly established via the traditional Welsh working class environment in *Gavin and Stacey*. For while located in the port of Barry, in the Vale of Glamorgan, the mise en scène of the show distilled in the terraced street at an angle, together with the accents of the majority of the cast is instantly recognisable to a UK-wide audience as "the Valleys", the ex-coal mining area to the north. This area of Wales has become, as Brett Mills argues, "a synecdoche for Wales" (Mills, 2008:56), due to the comparative raft of images available from the films of the mid-20th century onwards. The representation of place therefore operates through both the visual and verbal vernacular of "the Valleys", a performance of class which, as John Jewell notes, "is demonstrated by terraced housing, neighbours talking to each other in the street and people entering Stacey's mother's house through unlocked doors and helping themselves to food on the table" (Jewell, 2009:63). In many ways it is a world unchanged from Richard Hoggart's definitive depiction of working-class life in 1950s Northern England found in the book *Uses of Literacy* and, therefore, when compared with the upwardly mobile world of Essex, it fits into a wider British narrative of the North/South economic and cultural divide. The representation of the performance of class is most extreme in the figure of Nessa. She marries the identities of Welsh and working class through her nationalism, which is signposted by the red dragon tattoo on her arm, and by her world weariness. The latter is signalled through her detached masculine performance, which relies for example on the use of masculine modes of communication like the grossly exaggerated anecdotes she tells, over modes which are perceived as feminine, like gossip. She is, as John Jewell explains, "a breakthrough female character in British sit-com history" (Jewell, 2009:46).

Class and social position are also important elements of Galician comic performance. Galician characters are often working class or lower-middle class people who aspire to climbing the social ladder. However the overarching social feature in Galician comedy characterisation is rural origin. There are two possible readings of this characterisation; first it reflects the audience for this humour, as the demographics of viewers who most watch Televisión de Galicia suggest a middle-aged or older rural woman (Rodríguez, 2003). In this sense, this particular Galician television audience can identify with characters who are recognisable to them and who also share their provincial and broad sense of humour. Secondly,

> From Aristotle on and in contrast to tragedy, comedy was for centuries the most appropriate genre for representing the lives, not of the ruling classes, of those with extensive power, but of the middle and lower orders of society, those whose power was limited and local, and whose manners, behaviour and values were considered by their betters to be either trivial, vulgar or both (Neal and Krutnick, 1990:31).

This tradition is followed in Galician comedy, with central characters largely taken from the lower classes, and with those from higher social categories playing the bosses etc., whom they are in conflict with.

The situation comedy *A casa dos Tonechos* [Tonechos' Place][5] is perhaps the best illustration of this tendency, as the central characters are a father and a son, both unemployed and lazy, living off the mother's wages and the grandmother's pension. The father is always in his pyjamas while Tonecho junior wears a crash helmet over his head all day. They spend most of their time avoiding physical work and instead try to earn easy money through the buying and selling of second-hand goods. As in the classical sitcom narrative, the characters do not evolve and the situation remains the same at the end of the show with the characters back to square one without any narrative development.

Another major success on the Galician comedy scene in recent years is the above-mentioned *Nucha e Mucha*, a double-act of male actors impersonating two rural spinsters who perform folk music with comic lyrics. Codeswitching here does not only affect language, but also gender, via cross-dressing. The comedic basis for *Nucha e mucha* is the dialogue between these two sisters who talk about their lives in an imaginary Galician village. Again, the key for identification here is an imagined shared proximity to a peasant life style and working conditions, highlighted by the comedians convincing imitation – in both dress and behaviour – of two old Galician countrywomen.

In conclusion, we can say that both Wales and Galicia share peripheral and, more importantly, provincial profiles within the cultural comic script. This position is secured within the political sub-national frameworks of the Galician Autonomous Community and the Principality of Wales respectively. This satellite status in part explains the continuance of the designation of both identities as "stupid" following Davies' comic script model. This comic designation has its origins in the early modern period. These caricatures appear to harden and settle as time progresses and, by the 20th Century, have been given fuller currency via mass media; notably in cinema. In the last few decades, a period of rising national consensus in both cultures, there has been an increasing awareness of the ideological purpose behind these comedic stereotypes and therefore counter rationales have begun to develop. We have shown that situation comedy has become a site of renegotiation in media. However, there is also clear evidence of a clear and ongoing undercurrent of self-hatred. In particular, we have tried to demonstrate that in stand-up comedy there was a continued inhabitation by performers of personae that mimicked the colonisers' historical sketch of the near neighbour and "lesser" culture. For both identities, we have found language to be a defining element in the comic relationship between the centre and the peripheral culture. Indeed, here we have found evidence to suggest that comedy performers, especially in the Galician model as a bilingual nation, engage in "codeswitching" or "diglossic humour" to reflect the tension between the two languages experienced by their audience. Central also to the characterisation of both cultures is the relative poverty and the designation of class. In Galicia, a largely rural society, the caricatures of cultural types are mostly designated as coming from a pre-industrial peasantry. In Wales, overwhelmingly a post-industrial society, the designation is always working class. And this working-class comic archetype must be situated in South Wales and in particular be representative of the former coal mining area, an area characterised by features which act as a synecdoche for the whole nation, in the rest of the UK and beyond.

Notes

1 Davies (1999) completes his explanation with three other circles: in the furthest circle from the centre he includes those jokes about entirely unknown cultures that are portrayed in a very simplified manner, for instance, cannibals of the South Islands. In the next circle moving inwards, there are those jokes, which we can call "historical", created from actual events and cultural differences, for example, jokes about cowardly Italians in World War II. In a closer circle still, Davies includes jokes about recently arrived migrants who are seen as underdeveloped or inferior.

2 We will use equally the full name situation comedy or the abbreviation sitcom to refer to this TV genre.

3 According to the 2001 UK census, 582,000 people in Wales claimed to be able to speak Welsh. This represents 20.8% of the total population. The number and the percentage of Welsh speakers is increasing. In 1991 there were 508,000 speakers, or 18.7% of the population (Thomas, 2007). The situation of Galician is slightly better than Wales as 30% of the population regularly used it in 2008. Nonetheless, the *Instituto Galego de Estatística* [Galician Statistics Institute] indicates that the percentage five years before was a 43% (Fraga, 2010).

3 Most of the comedians included as examples in this section first found success on the variety programme *Luar*, broadcast on Televisión de Galicia.

4 *Os tonechos* started their career in Luar in short sketches that evolved into an independent TV programme. *O show dos Tonechos* [Tonechos' Show] was first screened in 2005 and consisted of a variety show that included a brief sitcom called *A casa dos Tonechos*.

5 *Nucha e Mucha* are Marcos Pereiro and Xosé Antonio Touriñán, a double-act that debuted on Luar in 2007.

Works Cited

Aarons, Debra (2011) *Jokes and the Linguistic Mind*, London: Routledge.

Bakhtin, Mikhail (1974) *La cultura popular en la Edad Media y Renacimiento*, Barcelona: Barral.

Beller, M.; Leerssen, J. (eds.) (2007) *Imagology. The cultural construction and literary representation of national characters*, Amsterdam: Rodopi.

Berry, Dave (1996) *Wales and Cinema: the First Hundred Years*, University of Wales Press.

Blandford, Steve (2005) "Dramatic Fictions in a Postcolonial Wales" in Aaron J. and Williams, C. (ed.) *Postcolonial Wales*, University of Wales Press.

Canakis, Costas (1994) "Diglossia as an agent of humor in the writings of Elena Akrita", *Journal of Modern Greek Studies* 12 (1994), 21–237.

Caramés Martínez, Xesús (1993), *A imaxe de Galicia e os galegos na literatura castelá*, Vigo: Galaxia.

Castelao, Alfonso d. (2001) *Things*, Aberystwyth: Planet.

Chun, Elaine W. (2004) "Ideologies of legitimate mockery: Margaret Cho's revoicings of Mock Asian", *Pragmatics*, 14:2, 263-289.

Davies, Christie (2005) "European ethnic scripts and the translation and switching of jokes", *Humor. International Journal of Humor Research*, 18:2 (2005), 147-160.

Davies, Christie (1999) "Change and continuity in one of Europe's oldest comic ethnic script", *Humor. International Journal of Humor Research*, 12:1 (1999), 1-33.

Fraga, Xesús (2010) "O número de galegofalantes baixa, pero segue a manterse maioritario", In: http://www.lavozdegalicia.es/galicia/2010/04/16/0003_8421321.htm (last accessed: October 2013).

González Pagés, Julio César (2008): "Una gallega llamada Cándida". In: http://www.migraventura.net/sabias-que/una-gallega-llamada-candida (last accessed: March, 2012).

Jaffe, Alexandra (2000) "Comic performance and the articulation of hybrid identity", *Pragmatics*, 10:1, 39-59.

Leerssen, Joep (2007) "Imagology: history and method", in M. Beller and J. Leerssen (eds.) Imagology. The cultural construction and literary representation of national characters,17-32.

Leerssen, Joep (2007) "Centre/Periphery", in M. Beller and J. Leerssen (eds.) *Imagology. The cultural construction and literary representation of national characters*, 278-280.

Littlewood, Jane; Pickering, Michael (1998) "Heard the one about the white middle-class heterosexual father-in-law?" in Stephen Wagg (ed.) *Because I tell a joke or two. Comedy, politics and social difference*, London: Routledge, 291-312.

Llinares García, Mar (1999) "Xogos de identidades na cultura popular galega", in M. Gondar Portasany (coord.), *Galicia fai dous mil anos. O feito diferencial galego III. Antropoloxía*, Santiago de Compostela: Museo do Pobo Galego, 103-119.

Lojo, María Rosa (dir.) (2008) *Los "Gallegos" en el imaginario argentino. Literatura, sainete, prensa*, A Coruña: Fundación Pedro Barrié de la Maza.

Jewell, John (2009) "Gavin and Stacey: Character, Region and Welsh Identity in Series One", *Cyfrwng: Media Wales Journal*, Volume 6, 2008, 61-74.

Mariño, Henrique (2004) "Rosa Díez: 'Zapatero es gallego, en el sentido peyorativo del término'". In: http://www.publico.es/espana/297725/rosa-diez-zapatero-es-gallego-en-el-sentido-mas-peyorativo-del-termino (Last accessed: September, 2013).

Mills, Brett (2008) "Representations of the Welsh in Contemporary British Sitcom", *Cyfrwng: Media Wales Journal*, Volume 6, 2008, 47-60.

Mintz, Lawrence E. (2005) "Stand-up comedy", in Maurice Charney (ed.) *Comedy: a geographic and historical guide*. Volume 2, Westport: Praeguer, 575-585.

Neale, Steve and Krutnik, Frank (1990) *Popular film and television comedy*, London: Routledge.

Núñez Seixas, Xosé M. (1999) "Algunas notas sobre la imagen social de los inmigrantes gallegos en la Argentina (1860-1940)", *Estudios migratorios latinoamericanos*, 42, year 14, (1999), 67-109.

Piccardi, Alice (2004), "A retranca como acto lingüístico", *Cadernos de lingua*, 26 (2004), 99-108.

Ritchie, GD. (2003) *The Linguistic Analysis of Jokes*, London: Routledge.

Rodríguez, Octavio (2003) "Audiencias TV en Galicia". In:

http://www.slideshare.net/octaviorodriguez/audiencias-tv-en-galicia-2003(March 2012).

Stead, Peter (1985) "Wales in the Movies", in Tony Curtis (ed.), *Wales: The Imagined Nation; Studies in Cultural and National Identity*, Brigend: PoetryWales.

Thomas, Peter Wynn (2007) "Welsh today", In: http://www.bbc.co.uk/voices/multilingual/welsh.shtm1 (last accessed March 2013)

Vertele (2005) "Críticas a "Los Serrano" por el tratamiento dado a la mujer gallega". In: http://www.vertele.com/noticias/criticas-a-los-serrano-por-el-tratamiento-dado-a-la-mujer-gallega/ (Last accessed: October 2013).

Wagg, Stephen (ed.) (1998) *Because I tell a joke or two. Comedy, politics and social difference*, London: Routledge.

Williams, Kevin (2001) "The Wider Significance of Anne Robinson's Remarks", Planet. The Welsh Internationalist, 147, June/July 2001, 37-44.Williams, Kevin (1993) "And Even the Welsh?" *Planet. The Welsh Internationalist*, 104, Feburary/March 1993,16-19

Woodward, Kate (2006) "Traditions and Transformations: Film in Wales during the 1990s", *North American Journal of Welsh Studies*, Vol 6, 1 (Winter 2006), 48-64.

Woolard, Kathryn (1987) "Codeswitching and comedy in Catalonia", Papers in *Pragmatics*, n° 1, 106-122.

The importance of being Basque – the aesthetic construction of Non-Basque identity[1]

Beatriz Zabalondo

NON-BASQUE[2]
There was a Basque writer of Biscay,
Who proposed something funny one day:
– Don't bother writing Basque,
So let's write in non-Basque,
This will be the new Basque writer's way!
　　　Hitzen ondoeza (1997), J. Sarrionandia

We want to start this article by stating our agreement with the following argument: "A text is a communicative action that can be realized by a combination of verbal and non-verbal means" (Nord, 2005: 16). Audiovisual texts make use of various code systems to frame meaning, namely: language – mostly oral, but also written – music, colour, camera angle, cutting, etc. Thus, the resulting text will convey a meaning that goes beyond the meaning transmitted by each of the individual codes employed, bolstered by the influence of each one on the others. Without wishing to dismiss the importance of the words themselves in the meaning of audiovisual texts, image and sound are just as important.

The starting point of this study, *Le Bleu de l'Océan*, is a French mini-series produced by TF1 channel and set in the Northern Basque Country, more specifically in the Larrun mountain region, Biarritz, Donibane Lohitzune (Saint-Jean-de-Luz), Donostia (San Sebastian), etc. and shot almost entirely at these locations. It is a five-episode soap opera, each episode having a duration of 100 minutes. It was first shown in February-March 2007 on Euskal Telebista's Channel One (ETB1),[3] which is aimed at Basque-speaking spectators, under the title of *Itsasoaren urdina* (Sea blue). In the course of our research on the television series *Le Bleu de l'Océan*, our attention was focused on its cultural referents, viewed as elements that reflect the characteristics of cultural identities. It is not our intention to compare the original with the dubbed version. Instead we will focus on an analysis of the images used in the series, since they constitute an important part of the text as a whole.

As members of a society, we make use of a language to express ourselves and to convey meaning. As Azurmendi reminds us, language is at the core of our identity, which in turn is a social and cultural construct: "Language is the house of Being. In its home, man dwells"[4] (Azurmendi, 2007: 214). The same idea is held in the Cultural Studies tradition: "Language is taken to be at the heart of culture for two central and related reasons: first, language is the privileged medium in which cultural meanings are formed and communicated. Second, language is the means and medium through which we form knowledge about ourselves and the social world". (Barker, 2002: 11). We agree with Barker that in any society language is an identifying symbol; we would add that this is especially true in the case of minority communities that possess their own language, as is the case for the Basques.[5] For this reason we are looking into the representation of what is such an important characteristic of the idiosyncrasies of being Basque, of Basque identity.

Our first hypothesis is that the images reveal stereotypes and archetypes of the *euskaldunak* (the Basque people), which contribute to reinforcing the idea of a certain aesthetic, a landscape, a world that no longer exists, dark and with no name or genuine identity. This leads us to formulate some questions: How is the Basque language depicted in the original series? What kind of cultural referents are shown in the images? Considering that language and culture are inherent elements of identities, what are the traits of Basque identity that this soap opera represents?

The Basque audience is watching a soap opera set "at home" dubbed into Basque but produced "abroad" and in non-Basque language, and so a peculiar situation arises for the viewers. The research also looked into this matter. The second hypothesis concerns the reception of the dubbed version: the acceptance (or not) of the regional variations of the series may vary according to the geographical distance of the viewer from the linguistic model used in the Basque production. The following research questions have been posed: although the series was dubbed into standard Basque, it contains traces of regional variations of the dialect spoken in the Northern Basque Country. Are the viewers aware of these variations? Do the viewers regard the language of the characters as natural and plausible for the series?

Methodological approach and cultural image analysis

As suggested above, one way of looking at identities in audiovisual texts is to study the cultural referents they contain as the inherent character-istics that distinguish one culture from another, and even as a means of describing "otherness". This research constitutes a preliminary attempt to deconstruct the images into signs of identity. A descriptive analysis of the images will help to shed light on the first hypothesis. We base our

Ecology: Geography, weather, biology and people.

Social Structure: work, social organisation, politics.

analysis on Santamaria (2001), and Newmark (1988). Although these classifications were established for the study of cultural referents in translation, we believe that the categories can also serve as a grounds for the analysis of images alone.

As compared to Newmark's taxonomy (Newmark, 1988: 95), Santamaria proposes a more complete set of categories (Santamaría, 2001: 288). As we set out to apply this author´s categorization to the analysis of *Le Bleu de l'Océan*, we soon realised that it showed significant shortcomings: there was no mention of categories such as economy, primary sector (such as fisheries), tourism, health services, photography, decoration, dance, mythology, sciences and, most importantly, there was none concerning language or linguistics. The purpose of our study has been to examine and list the images assigned by the audiovisual text to each cultural category. In doing so, we set ourselves the task of assessing the meaning conveyed by the images we receive and the reality created by those images, or, in other words, the representation con-

Culture, arts, religion, communication.

Social universe: Social conditions, geography, transport.

structed by those images. The photographs below show the insights into *Le Bleu de l'Océan* drawn from the six main categories in Santamaria`s classification of cultural referents.

Representation of basque and other languages

There are four languages spoken in the series: French, Basque, Japanese and Spanish. As French is the original language of the series, all utterances by protagonists in any of the other three languages are subtitled. Unsurprisingly, in most of the five hundred minute footage of the series the French language predominates. The Japanese characters speak their native language. They are the image of refinement and exclusivity, they belong to the upper class. They have worked their way into Parisian society and made a name for themselves. Interactions held in Japanese are subtitled in French.

Material culture: Food, clothes, appearance, objects, technology.

Spanish is the language spoken by the people living "beyond the border": criminals and, above all, the leaders of drug trafficking rings. The barman in Donostia's old town speaks Spanish and Delcourt follows suit when bidding him farewell. When the newspaper *El Diario Vasco* is shown, the viewer should understand that people living in the Northern Basque Country speak Spanish too. Utterances in Spanish are left alone, not subtitled; Spanish is a "familiar" language to many French people. Some events that happen "beyond the border" are located in the pubs in Donostia, which are decorated with bull-fighting symbols representative of Spanish culture. In contrast, genuine Basque symbols are nowhere to be found.

Although *Le Bleu de l'Océan* is set in the Basque Country, the Basque language is almost absent from the series, and on the few occasions when it is spoken, the lines are subtitled. There are no more than two or three instances in which anybody speaks Basque and those speakers correspond to very specific characters or, more accurately, to mere stereotypes. The peasant woman living in the woods speaks Basque on her first appearance. The hunter speaks Basque to his dog. When he is in the presence of the protagonist, he only goes as far as to mutter something, to show his astonishment at her. But that does not mean to say that these characters are monolingual Basque speakers; on the contrary, they communicate in French as well.

None of the inhabitants of the village in which the series is set speak Basque, whether they are old or young, or even children. It seems as though Delcourt (the lead male) might be of Basque origin, or at least that in the past he spoke the language, as he is able to understand the old lady living in the cottage. But he did not pass it on to his children; they are unable to speak Basque. Talia, the leading lady, utters only one sentence in Basque. Although she is Delcourt's daughter, she was raised by a friend of her mother (as her stepmother, in fact) and we are to think that she learnt Basque in her company. In the sequences set beyond the frontier, in the Spanish part of the Basque Country, nobody speaks Basque.

As a result, what the viewer learns is that Basque is only spoken by peasants and shepherds: people who never escaped their humble origins. Basque is used in secluded hamlets and also to communicate with

Je suis à la recherche de Raoul.

animals, and if we let ourselves go by its presence in the film, its scope is limited, poor, marginal, occasional, and pertains only to those living in isolation. It is regarded as socially worthless, not fit for interacting in the "civilized" world, nothing but an exotic trait of the past. Those who have done well in society use Basque to greet fellow townsmen; but they seem either to have forgotten where their origins lie, or they despise their childhood tongue. They have left their language behind and, with it, the corresponding culture and worldview. Or at least that is all one can venture to say, since no trace of their past heritage remains in their everyday activities or in their consciousness. It is also striking that they have neglected their duty to transmit their language to the younger generations, thereby breaking their children's link to the language.

Apart from the scant instances in which the characters speak Basque, the catalogue of Basque terms in the series is very limited. There are a few names of pets (*Baika*, *Lezo*, *Pintto*), which we learn through the voices of their masters. In the tracking shots along the streets, we catch sight of the following names: *La Casa Amaia*, *Hotel Elissaldia* (with a French-adapted spelling and the consequent melting of Basque into thin air), *Ugaina* (the name of a house located in front of Biarritz beach), *Herriko Etxea* (the town hall, beside a Gendarmerie station), *Fronton de Biarritz* (the Basque pelota court), and not much else. As shown, most of the names have adopted the French spelling, with the result that Basque is almost entirely eclipsed. Geographical names take their French

rendering, their Basque names are no more: Saint Jean-de-Luz instead of Donibane; Espagne instead of Hegoalde or Gipuzkoa. The only exception is Biarritz, as exhibited on the walls of the pelota court.

The surnames of characters are overwhelmingly French ones, except in the following instances: Bonnat (the name of the fish-factory and its owner) – we also find the Bonnat Museum in Baiona; Vargas (the surname of Talia's stepmother, a surname of Spanish origin); Bicent Etcheverry (the detective's name, a local man). The "wrongdoers" in the series are: Jose Ferreira (the pelota player), Marc Esteban, Fabio (whom Mr Delcourt calls "Carlitos"), Miguel, etc. All these names have an Iberian origin, with a manifest Spanish echo. The newspapers read by the main characters are published in French (*Le Basque Republicain* and *Sud-Ouest*; no one is reading *El Diario Vasco* except for the detective Etcheverry); and the hand-written memos and legal notifications are also written in French. There is an exception in the nameplate of a law firm that exhibits Basque names (Larralde, Fagoaga, Larregain).

Taking into account that the series is set close to the border, it would seem logical for the names and surnames of the local people to be of diverse origins. However, as we can see, Basque names have adopted a French spelling, whilst everything belonging "beyond the border" is in Spanish and of Spanish symbolism. There is almost no reference to Basque origins, only a handful of names as mentioned above.

To sum up, the representation of Euskera (the Basque language) is little more than a trace. If Euskera (Basque) does not exist, it follows that there is no such thing as the Basque Country (in the way the Basques mean when they call themselves Basque). It could be just a bucolic stretch of countryside in French territory, with its own special folklore. Instead, what the viewers see is that in this place there is a frontier dividing two countries (France and Spain), two realities, two languages (French and Spanish), two police forces (*gendarmes* and *ertzainak* respectively), and so on.

Le Bleu de l' océan vs. *Itsasoaren urdina*

What happened when the series was dubbed into Basque? What decisions were made regarding the dubbing? As usual, the images in the dubbed text (TT) and the original (ST) are exactly the same; only the linguistic code has been altered. Translator-adaptors (through negotiation

with the directors of the dubbing-firms) and senior officers of ETB's
Basque branch agreed on the criteria for dealing with individual characters and for the dubbing as a whole. According to their criteria, French
speech (ST) was dubbed into standardised Basque language (TT), as is
common practice for ETB1. It must, however, be mentioned that for the
first time, the main characters' speech has tinges of "Northern Basque
dialect": some words and syntactic structures from this region have been
adopted. In the original series, a few sentences are uttered in Basque by
peasants and hunters; this speech has been left as it is in the original.

What do basque speakers think?

The second objective of this research is related to the reception of the
series. The results are part of a larger research project looking at the linguistic models for drama chosen by Basque Television. In order to
examine the impact of the above images on Basque viewers, we set up
five focus groups. These groups were set up with the sociolinguistic
situation of the Basque language in mind, in terms of age and gender. 35
participants contributed to the research, 18 were female and 17 male; all
belonging to the 18-80 age bracket. All of the participants contributed
voluntarily. The focus groups were carried out in the spring of 2011.
Each group was shown 10 minutes of footage from the Basque version of
the series – *Itsasoaren urdina*. After the viewing, the facilitator posed
some open questions[6] and the group discussed the series. The objective
was to interfere in the conversation as little as possible.

Out of the 35 participants, six of them (17.1 %) said that they had not
realised that the Basque in the video contained regional varieties from
the Northern part of the Basque Country. These people belonged to the
eldest age group, and none of them were from Iparralde. The rest of the
participants did notice that even though the linguistic model was based
on standard Basque some syntactic constructions and lexical items
belonging to the regional variety were used. As participant GA1 stated:
"Those who are literate in Basque may understand it better".

The group from the Northern Basque Country considered the footage
to be unrealisitc, for two main reasons: firstly, the language used
sounded strange to them, and, secondly the French actors featured in the
series were much too familiar to them and it was hard for them to
identify what was being shown on screen with the actors playing those

roles. For them, the language used is not natural and the story lacks credibility although, as BA4 says, the translation is quite good and is easy to understand. The problem, as BA3 states, is that although the story is located in the Basque Country, the topic does not refer to Basque culture. Even if Basque is heard, the informant felt that the language did not belong in the location the series claimed to represent. In this case it could be argued that the members of this focus group are highly familiar with the locations the camera shows, and they are aware that the linguistic model portrayed on television does not match real language use in the area. A great deal of their frustration stems from comparing fiction with the reality they know so well.

In the other groups (all from the Southern Basque Country) four people expressed the same idea. All of these were from the groups in Gipuzkoa. In total, 31.43% of the participants clearly stated that the dubbed version was not plausible. The participants ZB1 and ZB2 agreed very much with the people from Iparralde, saying that "although the series is set in Saint Jean de Luz and so on, you don't relate it to Euskera and the Basques… It looks more like a little town near Paris". AA1 and AB3 stated that the artificiality of the Basque version (the lack of authenticity) was not due to the language spoken in the original series, but due to some matters related to the dubbing (and in this sense, this series is no different from other dubbed films): difficulties in adapting the voices to the lip movements, the Basque voices don´t match the physical appearance of the characters, the same voices are heard all the time. The rest of the participants made no great objection to the criteria used in the dubbing. ZB4 even considered it an interesting way to acquire knowledge of some of the Northern Basque dialect, mainly concerning accent and words.

The method of analysis used to assess the cultural referents in productions of audiovisual fiction which involve a translation process can also be valuable for the analysis of images. Eleven years have elapsed since Santamaria defended her thesis and we have found that it still needs further development, especially with regard to the inclusion of a category connected with language. Despite this, it continues to be an interesting starting point for examining the way in which cultural references are transmitted not only through linguistic codes but also through images.

The colourful images displayed in the footage are meant to imbue the fiction with an appearance of "reality", an attempt to give the series more credibility. But this is the Basque Country in the very images found on postcards, in glossy pictures, stereotypes, void of real characters, images that are exclusively used for the purpose of portraying stereotypes and archetypes. Such images strengthen the prejudices that French television series viewers already hold, helping to reinforce their preconceptions about what being Basque is like.

Focusing on Luku's work on the theatre ¬with an awareness of the distance between theatre and television or other audiovisual media –, we agree with his contention as follows:

> France, according to the view of the French, is Paris. To them it is the world capital town, and when they move elsewhere (get out), you come across a sand band, dressed in rags and ignorant, French *badgers*. (...) A genuine French person, attending the feasts in Baiona or just watching a television programme, for example, will soon find a sort of exoticism, and a great distance on comparing it with the *centre*. And finally, leaving Baiona behind, and getting deeper into the countryside, we will find a *Scéne de pays* structure. It's here that the Northern Basque Country is invoked. To the French people from the centre, it's the barbarian exaltation and the summit of ignorance (Luku, 2009: 20).

This is precisely the view conveyed by *Le Bleu de l'océan*. This series was produced in France, with a Parisian bias. It was set amongst the exotic scenery of the coastal Basque Country and it reflects the sea, refinement, elegance, artistic atmosphere, connections with Paris, perhaps the favourite holiday resort for wealthy Parisians. But, as we move inward, we meet people with little or no contact with "civilization" – living in isolation, secluded in their huts or cottages – ignorance, vulgarity, indolence, we come up against the lair of barbarianism. Dark forests are the custodians of the only remaining trace of the Basque language, no more than an echo of nothingness: the *triste-landa*[7] of a language devoid of its own territory and culture.

There is little interest in bringing to light the reality underlying the images and symbols displayed: the images are but a metaphor for a way of life. Showing the culture of the Basque Country would seem out of place; this Pays Basque is just a beautiful setting. It is the ideal and much-sought after holiday resort for many French viewers. In fact that is exactly how the series portrays it. People who have no knowledge of the

Pays Basque will develop a notion of a dream-like country. A place that it is no longer the country of the so-called Basque speakers, a country where "Basque" neither refers to an ancient language nor to the culture of the people living in the region.

From the analysis of this series it might seem as though products such as this one make no sense on Basque television. There is a possibility that an audiovisual product like this – with a Basque cultural background but produced elsewhere and later rendered into Basque – might be rebuffed by viewers on the grounds of lack of realism. We would extend this reflexion to other languages, mainly minority languages, as they are especially vulnerable to falling into stereotypes.

Regarding the reception of the series, 82.9 % of the viewers from our focus groups perceived that the linguistic model of the series was not the most commonly used by the Basque Television, and they were able to make explicit that it contained lexical and syntactic structures belonging to the Northern Basque Country. All members of the Northern Basque group, as expected, identified the linguistic variation in the text immediately. These people considered the fiction to be far from realistic and, were not convinced. As for the rest of the participants in the study, the more linguistic competence the viewers had in Euskera (literate in Euskera, not in Spanish), the more aware they were of the presence of linguistic variation in the Basque dubbed version. This explains why some people who had learnt Euskera at school rather than at home could still tell the difference. Likewise, the closer the people are to the linguistic variation present in the series – the closer their own linguistic variety is to the variety of the Northern Basque Country – the more easily they pick up on the words and syntax from the Northern Basque Country.

Notes

1 I am most grateful to MJ Garabieta who helped me so much with this article, in her *non-spare* time.
2 Limerick translated by the author.
3 ETB1 is the Basque speaking tv channel of the Basque Broadcasting Corporation (EITB).
4 From Heiddeger's *Unterwegas zur Sprache*.
5 The Basques call themselves *euskaldunak*: "the people who speaks *euskara*". *Euskara* is the vernacular name of Basque language.
6 Questions like: "How do you like this video? Did you follow it easily?"
7 A term coined by Luku (2009:21).

Works Cited

Azurmendi, Joxe. *Humboldt. Hizkuntza eta pentsamendua*. Bilbo: UEU, 2007.

Barker, Chris. *Television, Globalization and Cultural Identities*. 1999. Buckingham: Open University Press, 2002.

Le Bleu de l'Océan. Dir. Didier Albert. Perf. Claire Borotra, Bernard Verley, Philippe Caroit, Bruno Madinier, Alexandra Vandernoot, Natacha Amal, and Jean-Michel Tinivelli. L.C.J Editions & Productions, 2004. DVD.

Luku, Antton. *Euskal Kultura?*. Iruñea: Pamiela, 2009.

Newmark, Peter. *A Textbook of Translation*. Hempstead: Prentice-Hall International, 1988.

Nord, C. *Text Analysis in Translation. Theory, Methodology, and Didactic Application of a Model for Translaton-Oriented Text Analysis*. 2nd ed. Amsterdam-NewYork: Editions Rodopi B.V, 2005.

Santamaría, Laura. "Subtitulació i referents culturals. La traducció com a mitjà d'adquisició de representacions mentals". PhD thesis. Universitat Autònoma de Barcelona, Bellaterra, 2001.

Portuguese Modernism on stage: on the periphery of Modernist canon

Inês Alves-Mendes

This article focuses on one aspect of Modernity: Modernism. The need for an interdisciplinary analysis encompassing the social and cultural elements that contribute to the making of different modernities is one of the most contemporary scholarly topics. In fact, as has been repeatedly said, modernity is not a unified phenomenon (Gaonkar: 2001, Eisenstadt: 2002, Friedman: 2008). If there is no such thing as a unified modern world and if, as some have argued, certain modernities can only be conceived as polycentric to the Western narrative of modernity (Friedman, 2008: 19) subsequently, modernism as modernity's aesthetic counterpart, should also be reappraised according to a plural perspective. In this spirit, this paper sets out to analyse some of the visual aspects of Portuguese modernism on stage.

The peripheral reception that modernism on stage has received in the wider debate of Portuguese modernism is probably due to the politics of canon formation and canon reception. The conventional perception that great artists should commit to canonical genres and conventional mediums bears some responsibility for the lack of academic work on Portuguese Modernism on stage, which must also encompass the visual productions of a peripheral genre, *revista*, commonly regarded as recreational or a light genre. Nevertheless, it was thanks to *revista*'s "light" reputation that an alternative space for aesthetical and political intervention was created, escaping the censor's strictness, before and after the establishment of the New State (1933).

The first Portuguese modernism changed the way in which literature and the visual arts were received, considered and produced in Portugal. Its socio-cultural impact and its repercussions are still being catalogued and analysed up to this day. It is my contention that the examination of modernism's impact on Portuguese culture and society is not complete without an exhaustive assessment of the visual aspects of modernism on stage.

The efforts of the *Orpheu* generation, apart from that of Almada and Pacheco, are of a greater literary impact rather than a visual one, although many of them dreamed of a theatre that would involve all the arts or, as Almada expressed it more precisely, a theatre that would be "a showcase for all the arts".[1] This paper builds on an article I published in 2011 in *Portuguese Modernism: Multiple Perspectives on Literature and the Visual Arts* (Mendes, 2011: 310-30) where I analysed the plays and the theatrical productions of Mário de Sá-Carneiro, António Ponce de Leão, António Ferro, Pacheco, Almada Negreiros and Fernando Pessoa. The paper concluded that in order to examine the modernist manifestations on Portuguese stages one should go beyond the dramatic works of the *Orpheu* generation and revisit the legacies of numerous works left by set and wardrobe designers.

There was indeed a group of visual artists whose work for the stage, from the 20s throughout the 60s, present solid artistic characteristics grounded on modernist aesthetics. All these artists design costumes and sets by using idiosyncratic and highly individual aesthetic traits. Nevertheless, it is possible to highlight recurrent shared features and recurrent themes in their works, namely, 1. the praising of modern life and modern technology; 2. the use of national folklore and national themes as a defining element of a collective identity. I will opt for surveying the second element as it consistently illustrates my contention: the national aspects of modernism on Portuguese stages, from the 20s to the 60s, are highly political and there is no ground for a neutral approach to the subject of national identity on stage.

How it all started: Ballets Russes or a proto-history of Modernism on stage

As it is known, the Russian Ballets had an enormous influence over the genesis of modernity in Europe and also in Portugal. The first modernist manifestations on Portuguese stages occurred thanks to the tour of Ballets Russes in Lisbon, in between 13 to 27 December 1917 (in Coliseu dos Recreios) and a final performance on 2 and 3 January 1918 (in Teatro Nacional de São Carlos).

The balletomane Almada Negreiros was not only an enthusiastic ballet-goer but he also promoted amateur ballet since 1915. Diaghilev's Russian Ballets were first performed in Paris on 18 May 1909, and it is likely that Almada found out about them through the French illustrated magazines that were widely distributed in Portugal or through his friends, Amadeo de Sousa Cardoso and Santa-Rita Pintor, who lived in Paris. It is also plausible that Almada was aware of these balletic experiences through his friends Ruy Coelho and Rui Lino, enthusiastic spectators of these ballets in Paris.[2] Therefore, and even before the Russian Ballets came to Portugal, an opportunity soon arose for Almada to explore his interest in ballet and turn it into something real, thanks to Helena da Silveira de Vasconcelos, the daughter of the Earle of Castelo Melhor. Helena made her Palácio Rosa a centre of attraction for the worldly milieu of Lisbon and ballet became an integral part of social events and parties.[3] When the Russian Ballets were finally performed in Lisbon, the newspaper reviews of the ballets were far from enthusiastic and, apart from Almada, António Ferro and a circle of a few others, Diaghilev's ballets were scoffed at as a "fantasy straight out of a lunatic asylum" ("uma fantasia de manicómio"), as journalist Rodrigues Alves put it.[4]

When the Russian Ballets left Portugal, the São Carlos Theatre showed Portuguese ballets, an initiative promoted by Almada with the support of Helena Castelo Melhor. The performance consisted of two ballets: *Bailado do Encantamento* (IMAGE 1) with choreography by Almada, sets and costume design by Raul Lino and A Princesa dos *Sapatos de Ferro* (IMAGE 2) displaying costumes and choreography by Almada Almada and stage set by Pacheco. Albeit the fact that the ballets conceived by Almada and his aristocratic friends did not have a modernist character, as can be inferred from the photos displaying symbolist costumes and sets, these balletic experiences laid the foundations for the visual interest in the Russian Ballets and consist in the proto-history of Portuguese modernism on stage.

The impact of the Russian Ballets would inform the *Orpheu* generation and their avant-garde experiences. In the art magazine launched by Almada in 1917, *Portugal Futurista*, Almada's enthusiam with the Russian Ballets is expressively illustrated in "Os Bailados Russos em Lisboa". In this text Almada presents the Russian Ballets as a means to educate the Portuguese in the contemporary art scene: "This is exactly what you, Portuguese, will learn with the Russian Ballets: educate yourself." ["É justamente o que tu, Portuguez, vaes aprender nos Bailados Russos: educar-te a ti proprio."] (*Portugal Futurista* 1, p. 2). It was thanks to *Portugal Futurista*, that for the first time, there was a real fusion between literature, visual arts and modern graphics (Dix, 2011: 161).

Unfortunately, the Ballets Russes, which had been a revolution for Almada, did not alter the panorama of the Portuguese performative arts immediately. Seven years afterwards, in 1925, António Ferro still harshly criticised the tedious and non-challenging artistic panorama in the *Diário de Notícias*.[5] Apparently, António Ferro was not aware of the popular theatre scene, unlike the plastic artist Almada Negreiros, who presented the first modernist set design for the musical comedy revue called *Chic-chic*, presented earlier in 1925. Therefore, it was thanks to '*revista*' (the Portuguese genre of musical comedy revue) that Modernism entered the Portuguese stage productions for the first time in the twentieth-century.

The national and regional themes on stage before Ferro

Even though this performative genre is commonly regarded as recreational, it was also highly engaged with the socio-political aspects of its time – the first *revistas* in Portugal in the 19th century, following the example of its French "ancestors" – were humoristic reappraisals of the events occurring in one-year time. *Revista*'s immediacy is clearly demonstrated by the reception to *Orpheu*'s launching, in 1915: the performance *O Diabo a Quatro* mocked the young modernists by depicting them as mad futurists. By doing so, *revista* was mimicking precisely the reception of *Orpheu* by the Portuguese press of the time (Parreira da Silva, 2008: 566). There were to be many modernist set designers who worked for the Portuguese genre *revista* and also for theatre. The best-known modernist set designer is perhaps José Barbosa, who, starting in 1927 with *revista Água-Pé*, introduced modernism in a decisive manner into the panorama of Portuguese set and wardrobe design with the first of many productions in this genre. In the following photograph, we can see the visual impact of the Ballets Russes on José Barbosa's production, especially in the costumes of *Água-Pé* (1927), which recreated the

Russian folklore, as in some of Diaghilev's ballets (images 3 and 4).

But the presence of folk themes is not only drawn from foreigner traditions. This same *revista*, *Água-Pé* (1927), exhibited costumes inspired by national (regional) themes, as can be inferred by photographs of the performance (ImageS 5 and 6). As a matter of a fact, the occurrence of regional themes in theatre productions is a frequent element on the twenties. Namely, in *revista*, a scrutiny of the song's lyrics in the twenties allows us to state that the praise of rural life is a constant feature. Therefore, not only visually, but also the spoken word (or, to be more accurate, the vocalized word of the songs) displayed elements of nationalistic tunes. These facts support the following contention: even before António Ferro presided the Secretariat for National Propaganda (S.P.N.) in 1933, folkloric, regional and national themes were already pullulating and populating the national imaginary in the context of the performative arts.

A similar situation took place in the literary scene in the early twentieth-century. In the aftermath British Ultimatum of 1890, a revival of nationalistic inspired ideals bloomed as a means of coping with the humiliation imposed by the British conditions. Leaving aside the authors of "geração de 70" and the precursors of *Orpheu* who have received vast critical appraisal,[6] Portuguese modernists have recurred frequently to themes of patriotic and national inspiration. Pessoa's brief relationship with *Renascença Portuguesa*, as illustrated by his publishing "*A nova poesia portuguesa*" in *A Águia*, testifies to this urge, felt by intellectuals and artists, to recreate and revitalize a decadent Portugal, as the image of a Phoenix reviving from the flames perfectly encapsulates. Pessoa's *Mensagem* functions as yet another paradigmatic case. Pessoa's nationalism operates on a mythic, exoteric and symbolic level, and it should not be confused with an alignment with the New State ideals, which Pessoa repudiated.[7]

Also Almada Negreiros, whose literary output supersedes his visual productions in between 1915-1917 (Sapega, 2011: 57) repeatedly borrowed from national and patriotic themes. It is relevant that, arriving at Paris, Almada concluded: "Art does not live without the artist's fatherland" ("A arte não vive sem a pátria do artista)." (Negreiros, 1993: 61). Also, from Paris, he wrote *Histoire du Portugal par Coeur*, published in 1922 in *Contemporânea*, where a mythic homeland is constructed by resorting to a naïve and child-like fascination that the exile certainly promoted.

If the use of national themes was recurrent in the cultural panorama of the early twentieth-century, permeating literature and the visual arts, it follows that an examination of its nature will have to address its political implications – and all the more so in the context of performative arts, which offered a privileged platform to address the civil community. Therefore, a more contextualized approach to nationalisms on stage is needed, especially after the establishment of the military dictatorship, in 1926. Under this assumption, it should be mentioned that the popular and patriotic display of motifs on stage were not necessarily aligned with the emerging authoritarian nationalism. On the contrary, as early as 1929, the *revista Chá de Parreira*, exhibited a Santo António character who functioned as an ironic embodiment of an emerging political figure: an Economics Professor from Coimbra University, also named António (Image 7). The image on display presents the cover of the lyrics of a "marcha popular", a successful song performed at this *revista*. The song mocked Salazar (Santo António), as you can read from the lyrics on the left hand side.

Already after the establishment of the New State, the famous *revista Arre Burro!* (1936), presented an interesting pun in one of its songs by juxtaposing Salazar and Falar. In fact, by contrasting European conflicts with Portuguese domestic peace, the audience was satirically informed that: "In Portugal/ It is just small talk/ Talkazar, Talkazar".[8] As can be noted, the translation from the Portuguese original text merges the verb "to talk" with the name "Salazar". The English word "Talkazar" is an intent to translate into English the invented word "Falazar", which mimics the sound of Salazar, as in the excerpt: "Em Portugal/ É que é só conversar/ Falazar, Falazar").[9] There are numerous Santo Antónios evoking Salazar from the 30s to the 60s – some openly evoking the dictator, others more subtly suggesting a parallel reading. Nevertheless, *revista* offered an unrivalled platform for the voicing of an ironic and humoristic viewpoint on Salazar – which only a peripheral genre could afford. Only *revista*, as the court's jester, was allowed to mock authority – the price to pay for it was, of course, not to be taken seriously. However, what better device was there available other than the jester's puns?

Revista indeed enjoyed a freedom unparalleled by other performative genres. However, *revistas* weren't always sided with the opposition to the

New State. On the contrary, this genre sheds plural viewpoints on the
nation's state. If there is, for instance, the comment to the second World
War in a clear positioning on the side of the allies, in 1944, in the show
Baile de Máscaras, there is, on the contrary, the siding with Mocidade
Portuguesa, as early as 1937, in *Cartaz de Lisboa*. It is also noteworthy
that the topic of colonialism surfaces the stages on and off in the 30s and
the 60s – generally supporting a colonial Portuguese empire, as happens
in 1934, in *revista Nobre Povo*. Also, in 1964, the show *Lábios Pintados*,
scoffs at the United Nations for supporting the end of colonialisms in
Africa. As can be observed, *revista* offers an x-ray of the Portuguese
society under the constraints of New State, mapping the internal ideological dissensions and the internal debates of a divided country.

António Ferro and the "domestication of modernism": Verde Gaio on stage

The periodisation of modernism is a controversial aspect in Literary and
Visual Studies. José Augusto França considers that modernism is trace-
able in the visual arts until the 1940s, in a volume frequently quoted
(França: 1991, 99). The study of modernism on stage raises, however, a
new set of complex questions. In the fifties and still throughout the
sixties, different aesthetics coexisted on stage and modernist sets and
costumes still permeated national productions. As a matter of a fact, the
same artists who were responsible for the euphoric genesis of
modernism on stage kept on working for theatre, maintaining the
modernist traits of their earlier work. Almada, for instance, designed
exquisite sets and costumes for *Auto da Alma* de Gil Vicente in 1963, for
Companhia Rey Colaço-Robles Monteiro (image 8). These sets and
costumes dialogue with Almada's broader visual production and, even
though the play was performed in the 60s, modernist elements were
certainly present in this work.

The fraught relationship between the arts and the state under the dictatorship assured that modernism lingered on stage throughout the 60s.
The manipulation of the arts by António Ferro, in order to serve the
ideals of his "política do espírito", was carried out through state commis-
sions to modernists. Therefore, modernism became, under Ferro, the
official visual discourse of the state: Almada Negreiros, Jorge Barradas,
António Soares, Mily Possoz, Maria Adelaide de Lima Cruz, Maria Keil,

Pinto de Campos, José Barbosa, Stuart Carvalhais, Thomás de Mello (known as Tom), and many others, cooperated either with the architecture or the décor of public institutions or participated in artistic initiatives promoted by the New State, such as the ballets Verde Gaio.

Verde Gaio, created by Ferro still under the spell of the Russian Ballets in 1940, was shaped in close collaboration with the musician Frederico de Freitas and the ballet dancer Francis. Ultimately, Verde Gaio contributed to the stabilizing of a visual discourse that would change the perception of modernism on stage, by connecting it to set of ideological values promoted by the New State. As Isabel Gil contended:

> The creation of the first Portuguese national dance company under Ferro evokes Diaghilev's influence not so much in the blending of folklore with nationalism, but rather in the promotion of dance within the limits of power structures be they economic, as in Diaghilev's case, or political, as in Ferro's (Gil, 2010: 13).

The ballets were inspired by popular dances and staged swarthy dancing pairs. Often, the dancers embodied localities or regions of the country, as their costumes testify. They also often embodied peasants, rural workers or fishermen, as this image illustrates (IMAGE 9). Furthermore, scenes of history and national legends were a recurrent theme as the titles of the ballets suggest: *Inês de Castro*, 1940, *Nazaré*, 1948, *D. Sebastião*, 1943, *Imagens da terra e do mar*, 1943, etc.

Even though Verde Gaio's balletic performance was far from desirable for a professional ballet company, as ballet experts have argued (Sasportes, 1970: 72), its visual elements were solidly anchored in modernism and in the work of modernist artists who fashioned its costumes and sets (and I'm referring in particular to José Barbosa, Maria Keil, Bernardo Marques, Paulo Ferreira, Thomaz de Mello and Milly Possoz, who contributed to Verde Gaio). Consequently, and despite the fact that Verde Gaio functioned in the context of the New State's cultural propaganda, the ballets' visual aspects are in its own right modernist manifestations on stage, still lingering in the 50s and the 60s. In fact, when studying modernism on stage throughout the twentieth century, one must acknowledge, as historian Nuno Rosmaninho brilliantly put it, that the New State carried out a "domestication of modernism" (Rosmaninho, 2008: 296).

There is an urgent need for critical reappraisal of Portuguese

modernism as scholars are confronted with the call to integrate peripheral authors of modernism, such as female modernist authors, and
peripheral genres, such as *revista* and theatrical productions. Like
modernity, Portuguese modernism can be examined through polycentric spaces the more and more comprehensive in order to embrace
authors and genres that, so far, still remain outside the canonical
narrative of Portuguese modernism. If it is true that a very diverse social
milieu attended *revistas* – not only different social classes and both sexes
coexisted freely in the audience – it is also a fact that *revista* , as an entertainment genre, has been traditionally located on the periphery of
cultural discourses. As the relationships between periphery and centre
are dynamic, not only did the *geração de Orpheu*'s aesthetical legacy
influenced *revista* – through the dissemination of the Russian Ballets –
but also, *revista* carried on *Orpheu*'s adventure to the (next) stage by
visually materializing modernism.

Notes

1 Almada quoted by Pavão dos Santos in Vítor Pavão dos Santos. 1993. *O Escaparate
   de Todas as Artes; ou, Gil Vicente visto por Almada Negreiros* (Lisboa: Museu
   Nacional do Teatro), p. 66.

2 *Ibidem*, p. 10.

3 With the help of the architect José Pacheco, and the musician Ruy Coelho, Almada
   choreographed a ballet that was presented on 6 April 1915 in the home of Helena
   Vasconcelos. The following year, on 7 March 1916, a new ballet, *O Sonho da
   Princesa na Rosa*, in which the hostess, Helena Vasconcelos, made an appearance,
   was performed in the palace of the Count and Countess of Castelo Melhor. The
   periodic *Ilustração Portuguesa* gave an account of the event on 3 April 1916.

4 Quoted by Pavão dos Santos, *ibidem*, p. 19.

5 In his column in *Diário de Notícias*, Ferro criticised *Pic-Nic*, a musical comedy
   revue that was on at the Éden Theatre, and the play *Tangerinas Mágicas* at the
   Trindade Theatre. His last review, in which he states that the stage setting of
   Tangerinas was expressionless, mobilised every set designer in town to insult the
   young modernist artists, whom they confusedly called "Futurists". See Vítor Pavão
   dos Santos. 2000. *A Revista Modernista* (Lisboa: Instituto Português de Museus), p.
   5.

6 Recently Paula Mourão explored this topic. See Paula Mourão. 2011. "Portuguese
   Precursors of the First Modernist Generation", *Portuguese Modernisms: Multiple
   Perspectives on Literature and Visual Arts* (ed. J. Pizarro e S. Dix) (Oxford:
   Legenda), pp. 12-23.

7 The recently published paper by José Barreto (in online magazine *Pessoa Plural*)
   sheds light on a previously unknown publication by Pessoa for the Lisbon journal
   Sol (on November 1926). Pessoa forged an interview with the Italian author
   Angioletti as a means to accuse Mussolini of betraying his own country. Pessoa

went on to state Mussolini was mad (Barreto, 2012: 1). A few days after, the publication *Sol* closed its doors – undoubtly on the afermath of the censors' work. See José Barreto. 2012. "Mussolini é um louco: uma entrevista desconhecida de Fernando Pessoa com um antifascista italiano", 19 Jun. 2012. Web. 20 Jun 2012.

8 Translation by the author.

9 Lyrics of the song available in Vítor Pavão dos Santos. 1978. *A Revista à Portuguesa: Uma História Breve do Teatro de Revista* (Lisboa: O Jornal), p. 210.

Works Cited

Barreto, José. 2012. "Mussolini é um louco: uma entrevista desconhecida de Fernando Pessoa com um antifascista italiano", *Pessoa Plural*, 19 Jun. 2012. Web. 20 Jun 2012.

Eisenstadt, Shmuel N. (ed.), 2002. *Multiple Modernities* (New Brunswick: Transaction Publishers).

Friedman, Susan S. 2009. "One hand clapping: colonialism, post-colonialism, and the spatio/temporal boundaries of modernism", in *Translocal Modernisms: International Perspectives (Transatlantic Aesthetics and Culture)* (ed. Irene Ramalho Santos and António Sousa Ribeiro) (Bern: Peter Lang), pp. 11–40.

Gil, Isabel C. 2010. "Heaviness and the modernist aesthetics of movement", *VI Congresso Nacional Associação Portuguesa de Literatura Comparada / X Colóquio de Outono Comemorativo das Vanguardas – Universidade do Minho 2009/2010*, Web. 14 Jun 2012.

Goankar, Dilip P. (ed). 2001. *Alternative Modernities* (Durham NC: Duke University Press).

Mendes, Inês Alves. 2011. "Modernist theatre in the first two decades of the 20th century" in *Portuguese Modernisms: Multiple Perspectives on Literature and Visual Arts* (ed. J. Pizarro e S. Dix) (Oxford: Legenda), pp. 310-30.

Mourão, Paula. 2011. "Portuguese Precursors of the First Modernist Generation", *Portuguese Modernisms: Multiple Perspectives on Literature and Visual Arts* (ed. J. Pizarro e S. Dix) (Oxford: Legenda, 2011), pp. 12-13.

Negreiros, José de Almada, 1993. *Obras Completas, Textos de intervenção*, vol. VI (Lisboa: Imprensa Nacional-Casa da Moeda).

Rosmaninho, Nuno. 2008. "António Ferro e a propaganda nacional antimoderna", *Actas do Seminário Internacional Realizado em Coimbra no Arquivo da Universidade (nos dias 28, 29 e 30 de Novembro de 2008)* (ed. AA. VV.) (Coimbra: Imprensa da Universidade de Coimbra), pp. 289-99

Santos, Vítor Pavão dos. 1978. *A Revista à Portuguesa : Uma História Breve do Teatro de Revista* (Lisboa: O Jornal), p. 210.

– 1993. *O Escaparate de Todas as Artes; ou, Gil Vicente visto por Almada Negreiros* (Lisboa: Museu Nacional do Teatro).

– 2000. *A Revista Modernista* (Lisboa: Instituto Português de Museus).

Sapega, Ellen W. 2011. "Lisbon Stories : José de Almada Negreiros", in *Portuguese Modernisms: Multiple Perspectives on Literature and Visual Arts* (ed. S. Dix e J. Pizarro) (Oxford : Legenda) pp. 55-68

Sasportes, José. 1970. *História da Dança em Portugal* (Lisboa: Fundação Calouste Gulbenkian)

Silva, Manuela Parreira da. 2008 "Orpheu", in *Dicionário de Fernando Pessoa e do Modernismo Português,* (ed. Fernando C. Martins) (Lisboa: Caminho), pp. 564-68.

Notes on contributors

Inês Alves Mendes is lecturer of Portuguese at the Department of Modern Languages in the University of ITESM (Monterrey, Mexico). She holds a PhD in Medieval and Modern Languages from the University of Oxford (May, 2011). She is a member of the research center CECC (Centro de Estudos de Comuinicação e Cultura), from the Portuguese Catholic University, where she is developing collaborative work on modernity.

Ur Apalategi Idirin is the permanent lecturer in Basque Literature at the University of Pau (France). He has published several books, including *La Naissance de l'écrivain basque* published in 2000 by the Paris publishing house L'Harmattan.

Larraitz Ariznabarreta Garabieta has taught at the University of Deusto and the University of Mondragon and is currently working at the Boise State University (USA). Her research efforts have been devoted to charting a cultural cartography of Basque nationalist exile(s) (1936-1970) through the discursive analysis of synecdochic exiled authors

Bernardo Atxaga (pseudonym of Joseba Irazu Garmendia) is a Basque writer. A prizewinning novelist his work has been translated into more than 30 languages. His books include *Obabakoak* (1988, Euskadi Prize, Spanish National Award for Narrative, finalist for the IMPAC European Literary Award; English, *Obabakoak*, 1992), *Soinujolearen semea* (2003, Grinzane Cavour Award, Mondello Prize, Times Literary Supplement Translation Prize; English, *The Accordionist's Son*, 2007), and *Zazpi etxe Frantzian* (2009, longlisted for the Independent Foreign Fiction Prize; English, *Seven Houses in France*, 2011).

Lídia Carol Geronès is a member of the Department of Foreign Languages and Literatures at the University of Verona (Italy). She obtained her PhD in Human, Heritage and Cultural Sciences from the Universitat de Girona (Spain). Her research interests are 20th Century Spanish Literature, Catalan Literature and Film Studies.

Peter Castellani is a freelance translator for United Nations. He holds a MA in Language Interpretation and Translation at the University of Bath and BA in French and Spanish Language and Literature at the University of Oxford.

Maria Dasca is Teaching Assistant and Lecturer in Catalan Studies at Harvard University since 2015. She holds a PhD in Literature from the University of Barcelona (2008). Her teaching experiences involve Iberian Cultures and Literatures as well as Catalan and Spanish as a Foreign Language. Her research interests include Contemporary Novel, Translation Studies and Cultural Transfer.

Josep-Anton Fernàndez Montoli holds a PhD on Modern Languages by Cambridge University. Since 2007, he is professor of Catalan Studies at the UOC. In 2006, he founded the Centre for Catalan Studies at the Queen Mary, University of London. He is a specialist in Catalan literature and culture in the 20th Century and in gender and sexuality studies. He has published *El malestar en la cultura catalana: La cultura de la normalització 1976-1999* (2008) and *Another Country: Sexuality and National Identity in Catalan Gay Fiction* (2000).

Miren Gabantxo-Uriagereka has a doctorate in Audiovisual Communication and Publicity from the University of the Basque Country (Spain). As a lecturer, she has taught subjects related to audiovisual language and film analysis since 2001. Until recently, she was Associate Dean of Infrastructures at the Faculty of Social Sciences and Communication of the University of the Basque Country.

Margarita Ledo Andión is Chair of Visual Communication at the Universidade de Santiago de Compostela, USC. She coordinates the

Grupo de Estudos Audiovisuais and is the director of the research and development project *Cara ao espacio dixital europeo. O papel das pequeñas cinematografías en versión orixinal/Towards the European Digital Space.* The role of small cinemas in original versión (CSO2012-35784). Her research on the politics of representation in photographic and cinematographic documentary image is reflected in works such as *Cine de fotógrafos* (2005) Barcelona: Gustavo Gili, Premio "Fundació Espais d'Art Comtemporani". She is also a filmmaker and writer; her films include the documentaries *Santa Liberdade* (2004), *Liste, pronunciado Líster* (2007) and *Cienfuegos, 1913* (2008), and the fictional film *A cicatriz branca* (2012).

Asia Lindsay is a British researcher born in Hong Kong who started her career focused on languages and media. Afterwards she worked for TED, where she started the TED Coding Club. After attending the Flatiron School in NY, she is now working at the Europe Community Lead for Toptal, the largest fully distributed high-skilled workforce in the world. She is a digital nomad who has travelled and worked in 30 or more countries so far.

Mari Jose Olaziregi holds a PhD in Basque literature. She is an Associate Professor at the University of the Basque Country. Since 2003, she has been the editor of the Basque Literature in Translation Series at the Centre for Basque Studies (University of Nevada, Reno) and the director of the Basque literature website. Mari Jose Olaziregi was a member of IBBY's executive committee in 2004-2006 and the Director for the Promotion and Diffusion of the Basque Language at the Etxepare Basque Institute from 2010 to 2016.

Micaela Ramon holds a PhD in Literature Sciences, Area of Specialization in Portuguese Literature. She is currently an Assistant Professor at the Portuguese and Lusophone Studies Department of the Universidade do Minho. She is the Deputy Director of CEHUM (Centro de Estudios Humanísticos da Universidade do Minho) since 2016.

Silvia Roca Baamonde is a Galician journalist and researcher. She worked as writer for Galician television and as producer for films for television. In the field of research, she is working on her PhD thesis on the representation of Galician people in films.

Laura Saéz Fernández holds a MA in Translation and Paratranslation from the University of Vigo (Spain) and a MA in Publishing Studies from the University of Santiago de Compostela (Spain). Former Galician lectora at Oxford University and lecturer in the University of Vigo, she has translated into Galician important literary works in the fields of feminism and Children's literature.

José Manuel Sande is a cultural programmer and cinema writer. He worked at the CGAI, Centro Galego de Artes da Imaxe/Filmoteca de Galicia, belonging to the Galician government, since 2006. He holds a BA in Literature Theory and a MA in Cinema Studies. He works as counsellor for culture for the local government of A Coruña.

Josep Soler-Carbonell is a Catalan researcher. He holds a PhD in Linguistics and Communication. His main research interests are sociolinguistics, language ideologies, language policy and language planning, and intercultural communication from a discourse approach. He has taught courses in language and culture and intercultural communication at Barcelona, Oxford, Tallinn and Tartu universities.

Xabier Payá Ruiz holds a Master of Multimedia Communication from the University of the Basque Country (Spain), Master in European Modern Cultures from the University of Birmingham (UK), and Expertise in Transmission of the Basque Culture from the University of Mondragon (Spain). Former lecturer in the UK, France and Spain, he has translated literary works such as *A Streetcar Named Desire* and *Life is a Dream* and published *Anthology of Basque Oral Literature*.

Marta Pérez Pereiro is a Galician researcher who holds a PhD in Audiovisual Communication and Journalism from the University of Santiago de Compostela. She worked for the Consello da Cultura Galega and developed her research on Galician and Welsh identities at the University of South Wales

Daryl Perrins is a Senior Lecturer in Film Studies who teaches Silent Cinema, British Cinema, TV Genres, European Cinema (Central and Eastern) and Cult Cinema at the University of South Wales.

Beatriz Zabalondo obtained her PhD in Communication Studies in 2014 from the University of the Basque Country (UPV/EHU). Since 2011, she has lectured at the University of the Basque Country. Before that date, she lectured at the University of Mondragon for seven years and worked as an audiovisual translator for over 25 years.